THE ACCIDENTAL ADVENTURER

BEN FOGLE

BANTAM PRESS

LONDON • TORONTO • SYDNEY • AUCKLAND • JOHANNESBURG

TRANSWORLD PUBLISHERS
61–63 Uxbridge Road, London W5 5SA
A Random House Group Company
www.transworldbooks.co.uk

First published in Great Britain
in 2011 by Bantam Press
an imprint of Transworld Publishers

A CIP catalogue record for this book
is available from the British Library.

ISBNs 9780593068496 (cased)
9780593068502 (tpb)

This book is a work of non-fiction based on the life, experiences and recollections
of the author. In some limited cases names of people, places, dates, sequences or
the detail of events have been changed solely to protect the privacy of others. The
author has stated to the publishers that, except in such minor respects not affecting
the substantial accuracy of the work, the contents of this book are true.

The Random House Group Limited supports the Forest Stewardship Council (FSC®), the
leading international forest-certification organization. Our books carrying the FSC label are
printed on FSC®-certified paper. FSC is the only forest-certification scheme endorsed by the
leading environmental organizations, including Greenpeace. Our paper-procurement policy can
be found at www.randomhouse.co.uk/environment.

Typeset in 12/15pt Minion by Falcon Oast Graphic Art Ltd
Printed and bound by CPI Group (UK) Ltd, Croydon, CR0 4YY

2 4 6 8 10 9 7 5 3 1

To Ludo and Iona –
I hope you will be proud of what Daddy did

Contents

In the beginning there is a canvas, a brilliant white nothingness waiting to be transformed by the brushstrokes of life. Splashes of colour, unique and individual to each one of us merge, clash and change. As the years go by, it becomes a painting on a painting on a painting, each new stroke of the brush shaped by the last. We all have a canvas waiting to be hung and this is mine.

Peru, 2011

Prologue

Shadows danced across the canvas like fiendish ghouls. Their long, clawed fingers scratched menacingly against the fabric. I lay rigid as a gentle breeze snapped at the loose skirt of my tent. The gloom of the trees was punctured by the full moon that came and went as thin tentacles of cloud scudded past.

My arms were stretched down my sides, soldier-like, and I lay on my hands to stop them trembling. The dark shadows continued to tango around my tent, scratching, scraping and rubbing against the thin fabric.

'Don't make a noise, don't make a noise,' I repeated, mantra-like, in my head. I held my breath for fear of emitting a sound.

BUP, BUP, BUP, BUP.

What the hell was that deafening noise reverberating around the tent? I held my breath again, but the pounding continued. It was my heart racing with fear, each beat creating a thunderous din. Blood was pumping around my body, thudding as it flooded into my ears. I started to sweat and my hands began to tingle; my self-induced rigor mortis had given me pins and needles. I could feel my leg begin to cramp. My nose itched and I needed to cough.

'Don't make a noise, don't make a noise.' My head ached with the thunder of words tumbling around. I had an impulse to scream and shout and swear.

'Grrrrrrr.'

My heart beat faster.

'Grrrrrrrrrrrr.'

I felt faint. This was it. It knew I was there. The sleeping bag began to vibrate to the beat of my heart. I had never been so scared in my entire life. A warm rush enveloped me, anaesthetizing the lower part of my body. I had wet myself with fear.

The scratching continued. I had to make a run for it. My life depended on it. I needed to wait for the right moment and run as fast as I could. Very slowly I unzipped my urine-drenched sleeping bag, pulling the zip just a few teeth at a time for fear of making a noise. Quietly I eased my body from the bag. My heart began to race even faster. I gripped the zip of the door flap.

'This is it,' I thought again. Sometimes life deals you a rotten hand and this was mine. I'd taken risks, but it was never meant to end like this. Here. Now. I still had so much I wanted to achieve. I hadn't even had a chance to say goodbye.

I screwed my eyes closed, braced myself in the running position. One, two, three – I yanked at the zip and ran. As my life flashed before me adrenalin propelled my legs faster than they'd ever moved and I ran for my life away from the wild beast.

Breathless, I reached a door. I stabbed into the darkness for the handle and clutched it tightly, yanking it down. The door creaked open and I threw myself inside. I raced along the darkened hallway and up the flight of stairs. I needed to get to safety and there was only one place.

I burst through the door and, still urine-soaked, leapt into the bed, wriggling my way in between Mum and Dad. Safe at last.

Like most small children, my first night in a tent began in our garden and ended in Mum and Dad's bed. It's amazing, the power of the mind – how the branches of trees and the neighbour's cat become beasts and monsters in a child's imagination.

This certainly wouldn't be the only time I would flee a tent in terror, but in later years the fear and the beasts would be a little more real.

As a child I never achieved much. A hopeless academic, I failed most of my exams, including some of my A-levels, achieving a U in Economics and an inexplicable N in Geography. Sport was even less inspiring. I was positively allergic to it. I was the last to be picked for any team and never represented the school, my class or, come to think of it, even myself. I used to forge sick notes to avoid the humiliation of failure. At eighteen, buckling as usual under pressure, I took my driving test seven times.

So what happened and how did I get here? That's partly the question that drives this book: how and, probably more importantly, why did a geeky, spotty, bow-legged, cripplingly shy, perennially homesick boy who hated camping become a sort of sportsman – perhaps even an adventurer? Is it the pursuit of happiness that has made my life follow its strange course, or is it a demented competitiveness? I still don't quite know how it happened, but somewhere along the way I turned my life upside down and became something I wasn't. Or maybe I just became something that I really was but, like so many of us, I just needed to find a different path through life to realize it.

Probably part of the conundrum is that ever since I was a child I have been searching for the real Ben Fogle. As the son of a famous actress, I was always known as 'Julia Foster's son'; then I became '*Tatler*'s Ben' after a brief stint on the magazine; then '*Castaway*'s Ben', 'Reality TV Ben', 'Daytime TV Presenter Ben', 'Posh Ben' . . . None of these descriptions has ever felt right, but we live in a world of stereotyping. Once you have been pigeon-holed, can you ever break free?

The most common question I am asked about almost everything I do is *why*? Why do I do the things I do? A psychologist would probably say that I am trying to redress the balance and make up for my childhood shortcomings. I would say I still don't know who I really am, nor indeed who I will be.

We all have turning points: a single moment, encounter or decision that changes everything and alters the course of our lives for ever. Perhaps my first came when my parents sent me away to boarding school. Though desperately homesick for the first year, the experience brought me out of myself and my confidence grew. It was here too that I encountered one of the most colourful characters of my life.

One Sunday morning, a strange man with ruddy red cheeks and a slight paunch strode on to the stage of the school's theatre to take the morning assembly. There was nothing particularly unusual about this man except for the enormous snake coiled round his neck.

He was Colonel Blashford-Snell.

Colonel John Blashford-Snell, eccentric, dogged, septuagenarian explorer, is the founder and president of the Scientific Exploration Society. Beginning with leading the first descent of the Blue Nile in 1968, he has undertaken over one hundred expeditions, including quests to discover the yeti and the Indonesian hobbit. In 1992 he successfully identified a race of giant elephants in western Nepal, believed by local people to be close relations of the mammoth. Since my first encounter with him, his team has carried a baby grand piano across the Andes for the Wai Wai tribe of Guyana to use in their church. In 2009 he set out on an expedition to Bolivia to look for the lost tribe of Moxtos, thought to have been destroyed by a meteor landing thirty thousand years ago. He claims to have found the point of impact – a hole five miles across.

The colonel behaves staunchly as a British gentleman, regardless of the terrain. He wears Savile Row suits with detachable arms, and never fails to celebrate Burns Night while in the field.

'Blashers', as he is known, opened my mind to a whole new world. Until now, I had always had an image of explorers as ex-army types like Sir Ranulph Fiennes, but here was a rather rotund, rosy-cheeked man with a sense of humour. It was like switching on a light bulb. Exploration didn't have to be purely a geographical and physical pursuit. Here was a man who seemed to make it fun, a real-life Tintin. What Blashford-Snell exemplified was that you could make fact stranger than fiction. I promised myself that one day I would set off on my own adventure.

If he was my first turning point, there have been many more since. My life has been a series of extraordinary encounters with people and places. I spent a year marooned on an island in the Outer Hebrides, becoming part of television history by appearing in Britain's first reality TV show, transforming my career and losing my anonymity as a result. Since then I have run marathons with Hollywood A-listers and played for the Costa Rican national cricket team against the Nicaraguans. From the sublime to the ridiculous, I have taken on Richard Curtis in the World Crabbing Championships in Walberswick and Chris Packham in the World Stinging Nettle Eating Championships. I once completed the annual ice-skating marathon in Sweden and as a result of a drunken bet I ran 150 miles across the Sahara Desert in the Marathon des Sables, often billed as the toughest footrace on earth. Over the years I have tested myself and been tested. That's partly what this book is about: this ridiculous urge to prove myself. Who am I trying to beat? I'm not an athlete, yet I can't help taking on ridiculous challenges.

I have been stabbed in Costa Rica, lost on a three-thousand-mile boat trip along the Amazon, rescued from the tallest volcano in the world and survived a tropical illness that required two months of chemotherapy. I have encountered Second World War plane wrecks in deepest Papua New Guinea and have repatriated East Timorese refugees. From almost losing a team member to altitude sickness on an expedition in Chile, to nearly toppling off a mountain with a girl in Nepal, I have had some hair-raising experiences over the years.

Strangely, I am a Knight of the Principality of Sealand, president of the Hedgehog Preservation Society and have an honorary doctorate from the University of Portsmouth for services to adventure. I have accompanied Prince William on a royal tour to Botswana and Prince Harry to the North Pole. My life is as varied as it is weird.

On TV my life has had just as many contrasts. I have been shown one day grooming guinea pigs for *Animal Park*, then a day later eating them for *Extreme Dreams*. I have presented films on blossom tours and jam-making with the Women's Institute, and on flesh-eating diseases in Ethiopia.

My life is a never-ending puzzle to me.

So what does it all mean? I don't really know. But in writing it down I am sure I'll find out more – and I hope it will strike a chord in everyone else who puzzles about their life and about how to create a life lived differently. This is a book about defying expectations, conquering shyness, battling laziness and, just occasionally, winning.

Part One

1

Amazon Dreams

It all started with my obsession with Latin America. I'm not sure why, but I dreamed of visiting this mysterious continent from an early age. I suppose it was partly the appeal of the unknown. I had grown up with a steady stream of newspaper and television images from Africa and the Middle East, but South America was a mystery to me and I wanted to explore it myself. And then at school my passion grew even stronger.

Education wasn't a happy experience for me. I use the word 'education' instead of 'school' because there is a distinction. I loved school, but I hated education. It was probably exacerbated by the fact that, as I have already said, I was a hopeless academic. I simply couldn't tolerate pressure and would buckle at the slightest strain. It was as if I had a little devil on my shoulder who would ensure I forgot everything at the crucial moment. I hated exams and I loathed education for it.

But I loved school. My parents sent me to board at Bryanston in Dorset, largely because no other private school would have me.

My first year was dominated by debilitating homesickness, the kind of homesickness that makes you physically sick. I can remember crying into my pillow each night and down the payphone each morning. At the end of a weekend at home I would throw myself on the ground and plead with my parents not to send me back. I have always felt rather guilty about the emotional strain this must have put on my mother, but then again, someone once told me that homesickness is the symptom of a happy home life.

Once I'd overcome this, I settled into Dorset life. Bryanston is set among rolling hills and I loved the countryside. I spent many happy hours wandering through the local farms and along the river Stour. It was an extremely happy few years, during which time I made some very good friends who remain so today.

For several years I shared a dorm with my best friend Leonardo Anguiano, the son of a Mexican diplomat. He had lived all over the world, but it was his tales of Mexico that enthralled me the most. Another friend was Thor Halvorssen, whose father was a Venezuelan politician who had been forced into exile. Then there was Edmund Solis, whose parents owned a hotel called the Jaguar Inn at the ancient Mayan ruins of Tikal in Guatemala. While I headed back to London on the 12.15 train from Salisbury for the holidays, Leo, Thor and Edmund would all fly off to these exotic countries. They would return next term with tales of howler monkeys and jaguars, of drugs runners and tequila. It was a little window into an alternative world, one that seemed to be filled with colour and spice, and I wanted a little bit of it. And so, having taken my A-levels, I determined to explore it myself.

First of all, though, I set out on another adventure. That summer my best friend Leo, another friend called Cass Gilbert and I decided to cycle to Monte Carlo. I'm not really sure how we picked Monte Carlo or why we chose to cycle, given that none of us had ever cycled before, but we set our hearts on it and it seemed like an inexpensive way to go on holiday. We borrowed bikes, bought a cheap tent, a pile of maps and ferry tickets to Dieppe. And off we set into the wilds of France, released from the manacles of education and school. We were free to do what we wanted, when we wanted.

We cycled for nearly ten hours the first day. By the time we stopped we had covered over a hundred miles and were feeling pretty flush with ourselves. Everything was looking good, until it came time to erect the tent.

Now much has been made in film and literature of the difficulties of pitching tents, but until this point I had been sheltered from such a problem, on the basis that I had never ever put up a tent. And neither had Leo. And neither had Cass.

For more than an hour we struggled with the poles and the fabric. We swore and shouted as we fought with the thing. It probably doesn't say much about a private education. I could tell you all about American political theory, but I couldn't pitch a sodding tent.

With temperatures fraying and night encroaching, we took the only obvious step: we laid the fabric of the tent on the ground, then we all crawled inside and slept in it as if it were a giant sleeping bag, with our heads exposed to the elements.

It was fine until the heavens opened and we received a drenching that passed straight through the two layers of tent. No one got much sleep that night, nor the next ten for that matter. We were cycling every hour of daylight, and even darkness, and we were sleeping for just a few hours each night; but at least by then we had given up on the tent completely and resorted to Youth Hostels.

I have often looked back on that cycling trip. It was certainly a key turning point in my life. We travelled a thousand miles under our own steam and it illuminated for me the power of the human body. I wasn't the only one transformed. My friend Cass Gilbert never stopped cycling. Indeed, he is currently pedalling across

Russia, having already circumnavigated the world *twice* on a normal bicycle and once on a tandem. It makes me smile to think how that adventure changed our lives. I still hadn't learned how to put up a tent, though.

Back at home, I became an ice-cream-scooper in my bid to raise enough money to travel to Latin America. It can't have been easy for my parents to see their son working in an ice-cream shop in central London. I'm sure they had higher expectations for me, especially given how much they had spent on my education, but my parents have always been incredibly supportive. They have always trusted me and for that I will be for ever grateful.

For five long months I worked every hour of the day and did any overtime I could in order to raise enough money for my air-fare. In the meantime I had applied to an organization called GAP. It was the beginning of what has become known as the 'Gap Yah', or gap year, and this was one of the first organizations to offer voluntary work and families to stay with overseas.

I can remember the excitement of sitting down with the application form and its giddy list of destinations. I don't think there was much science in my choice, but my eye settled on Ecuador – a country I had never even heard of, but it was in South America and that was good enough for me.

'Do you speak Spanish?' asked the application form. I thought for a while. What should I answer here? I spoke French . . . ish. I didn't want to jeopardize my chances of a place. 'I don't,' I thought to myself, 'but I will.' I wondered if I could bluff my way through using ambiguous tenses, but the form required a tick: Yes or No. I debated the ethics of a temporary white lie. If I ticked 'Yes' it would only be a short-term lie, or poetic licence as I liked to call it, as I planned to take Spanish classes before I left, which would technically make ticking 'No' a lie. I ticked 'Yes' and forgot to learn Spanish. The story of my life . . .

My application was successful and I was given a place living with a family in the capital of Ecuador, Quito. I had earned enough money for my return flight and I was itching to get going, but my placement wasn't due to start for a further three months, so I decided to fly out early and get a head start on my language skills before my volunteering began. In a fantastic effort of misunderstanding I decided to buy a ticket to Rio de Janeiro for three months of Spanish in Brazil – where they speak Portuguese.

I will never forget the feeling of terror and excitement as I kissed my parents goodbye at the airport. I was finally flying the nest. I would be away for a year that would change my life for ever. It was another turning point. A world of possibilities and adventures lay ahead of me. It was the beginning after which nothing would be the same again. I was heading off for a year that would turn into two and a whole new life.

I touched down in Rio de Janeiro without a clue in the world. I will never forget the smell as I stepped down the steps on to the runway. The air was thick and damp. A huge thunderstorm had recently passed, leaving puddles that were almost evaporating before my eyes in the heat. I could smell the thick green vegetation. I had never experienced an odour like it, and for me that smell will always remind me of those early years of excitement and possibility. At that moment the world was my oyster. Anything was possible.

For several days I wandered up and down the beach, my limbs pale, marvelling at the toned bodies of the Brazilians, for whom fitness seems to be a national pastime. But this wasn't what I wanted. I was after more, so I headed south to an area known as the Pantanal.

The Pantanal is one of the world's largest wetlands, covering somewhere between 54,000 and 75,000 square miles, the majority of which fall within the borders of Brazil. During the rainy season 80 per cent of the land is submerged, which has led to the development of a unique range of flora and fauna. The region is home to 35,000 plant species, as well as over 100 species of bird, 300 species of mammal, 480 species of reptile and 9,000 species of invertebrate. It is a land of jumping wolves, giant rodents and big cats.

One of the most intriguing species found in the wetlands is the rare maned wolf, the tallest member of the dog family. It has a fox-like reddish coat and its long legs enable it to spring through and over the tall grasses in search of its prey. Its urine, which it uses to communicate with others of its kind, is said to smell like cannabis – a coincidence which reportedly once led to a mistaken police investigation at Rotterdam Zoo.

The maned wolf shares the wetlands with the shy tapir, a species thought to have changed little over millions of years, and with capybaras, the world's biggest rodents, which, at over four feet long, can weigh as much as an adult human. However, both tapir and capybara commonly fall prey to one of the Pantanal's most deadly predators – the jaguar. The largest of South America's big cats, its name comes from the Tupi word *yaguara* – he who kills with one stroke.

I spent a week exploring this incredible wilderness on horse-back. The horses would often wade up to their necks past jacare crocodiles and anacondas. My guide once even showed me a photograph of an anaconda that had swallowed a fisherman *whole*. Unsurprisingly, it didn't fill me with confidence when we abandoned the horses and took to our feet in the wilderness.

'You have to wade through the water,' explained Daniel, our guide. This would have been a perfectly natural thing to do if we were in England, but not after I had just been shown a picture of a man inside a snake. It took a rather attractive eighteen-year-old Argentinian girl who was there with her father to convince me to submerge myself in the swamp, if only to save losing face. There was something particularly unnerving about wading through the murky waters past sleeping crocodiles, but it was an incredible adventure.

The Pantanal was exciting, but I still hungered for the Amazon. This was the stuff of adventures. Piranha and crocodiles, lost tribes and giant catfish. And so I found myself at the mouth of the Amazon in Belém, hitching a lift on one of the many river boats that plied the waters of the mighty river.

The shore could only be described as chaos, as thousands of people scurried from boat to boat, loading and unloading every cargo imaginable. Long, thin planks of wood protruded from each boat like tongues, some stretching for hundreds of metres out on to the muddy shore. Dogs and chickens scavenged along the shoreline.

Clutching my phrase book, I wandered up and down the rickety planks, asking on boat after boat whether they had any spaces, until finally I found a bare boat. It was set back from the hustle and bustle of the others and was notable mainly because it was empty. I spoke with the captain, who assured me that he was heading all the way to Iquitos in Peru. The journey would take up to a month, as he would be stopping in ports along the way, but for a price I was welcome to string my hammock on the deck. It was perfect. I could finally begin the adventure of which I'd always dreamed.

A hammock takes a little time to master. It's important to pull it as tight as possible to minimize the curvature created by the weight of your body. It's also important to 'pitch' it relatively high, to ensure some elevation from the ground. Most people tend to lie in hammocks like a banana, but then the canvas envelops your body and pins you like a sleeping soldier with your arms by your side. The best way is to lie diagonally across it, which means that the sides can take some of the weight and it supports your back more. A perfectly pitched hammock should create a flat surface. Practice makes perfect and I had a month to get used to it.

Having rigged it up, I lay back to watch the scene of chaos beyond, feeling rather smug in my comparative luxury and tranquillity. A little later, I set off into the market to collect the provisions I would need for the following couple of weeks.

My boat remained moored for my first night. I wondered what cargo would be loaded the next day. My hammock looked rather lonely on the vast deck. I had bought a basic mosquito net and I lay under it listening to the non-stop noise of the port, but the boat's gentle rocking soon sent me to sleep.

A noisy cockerel woke me early. When I opened my eyes it took me a while to register where I was. My view of the harbour had been obstructed; in fact, my view of everything had been obstructed. I had been penned in by hammocks. They were above me and below me. Elbows and feet spilled into my hammock and the outline of two large buttocks formed in the canvas directly above my face. It was a total invasion of my personal space.

I edged my way out of the tangle to find that the entire boat had been filled. Hundreds of men, women and children were pitching their hammocks and loading their bags, while boxes of cargo were ferried up the thin walkway by an army of workers. It was chaos. In fact, it was more chaotic than the port. I had to navigate through a spider's web of ropes and cords and hammocks to get back to my own, cocooned in the middle of the mêlée.

'Where's my shirt?' I wondered as I rifled through my belongings, which had been overwhelmed by everything else. It had gone. Suddenly my month on board didn't seem quite such fun, especially when a 'market trader' tried to sell me my shirt back.

It was midday when we finally set off, with a cargo of tons and tons of biscuits and about two hundred passengers.

The Amazon really is a mighty river, but at the mouth it is

positively oceanic. It is impossible to see the other side and it takes on the appearance of a vast, muddy sea. Which makes river travel like travelling on a . . . vast, muddy sea.

What I soon discovered was that Amazon river travel is what we might call the 'Slow Travel Movement'. It can also be a rather boring experience, particularly when you don't speak the language and you don't have any books to read.

The first major port of call was Manaus, the Amazonian capital. In the late nineteenth century this small town briefly became a global cultural and commercial centre as entrepreneurs from around the world rushed in to make their fortune from the export of natural rubber. It became Brazil's first urbanized city, and the second place in South America to have electric lighting, years ahead of many European cities. The city was equipped with running water, sewers and the continent's first electric tram system. As the affluence of South America's new elite – the so-called rubber barons – grew, the city expanded to include beautiful parks, a racetrack, a bull ring, twenty-four bars, eleven high-end restaurants and seven bookshops.

The rubber barons competed in demonstrations of decadence, spending their wealth on enormous yachts, mansions and pet lions. Barons would reportedly light their cigars with high-denomination notes, send their laundry to Paris and let their horses drink only champagne. Indeed, one baron reportedly had a palace built to house his horses that pleased him so greatly that he moved into a wing of it himself. Foodstuffs were imported from across Europe, and the barons dined on *foie gras*, Irish butter, potatoes from Liverpool and fine French wines.

Yet the greatest symbol of extravagance in Manaus was the Teatro Amazonas, the Amazon Theatre, the giant opera house that featured in Werner Herzog's film *Fitzcarraldo*. Incorporating tiles from Alsace, marble and crystal chandeliers from Italy and steel from Britain, it was filled with classical sculptures and

Parisian furnishings in the style of Louis XV. The opera house, despite the financial and human cost (half a visiting theatre troop reportedly died of yellow fever), was part of the mayor of Manaus's mission to make the city not just 'the heart of the Amazon' but a centre of world civilization.

Inevitably, the Amazonian rubber boom went bust. The age of decadence ended when seventy thousand seeds of the rubber tree were smuggled out of the region by explorer Henry Wickham and given to Kew Gardens in London, where they were germinated, soon to be shipped to Asian plantations. In Ceylon (now Sri Lanka) the rubber trees could be grown more systematically using cheaper labour, undercutting the price of Amazonian rubber, and Manaus's monopoly was lost. The barons' lifestyles became unsustainable. The electricity generators were no longer affordable. The opera house deteriorated and Manaus exited the world stage.

Days turned to weeks as we chugged slowly against the current. The journey was broken slightly by the occasional port call and by the frequent rainstorms. I lay in my hammock and watched as the river danced to the falling drops. It was mesmerizing.

The further upstream we travelled, the closer we appeared to navigate to the land. The thick jungle was often just a few metres away; often the flora, and sometimes the fauna, would come aboard. We also became used to the thousands of insects that descended on the boat each night, attracted to the lights. They would be swept off the deck in vast piles every morning. It was during this period that I had my first experience with one of the more fearsome inhabitants of the jungle.

When there was a thunderstorm, huge plastic tarpaulins would be unfurled to protect the passengers and their luggage from the rainfall. There were always plenty of volunteers looking for anything to break up the monotony of the day, and I welcomed the opportunity to be useful. During one of these downpours I began to untie the tarpaulins, working my way along the deck, and as I reached the third and pulled the rope, I felt something fall on to my T-shirt. It was an odd sensation because it felt quite heavy; but it also seemed to be defying gravity as it appeared to be stuck to my shirt.

I looked down to see the biggest, the hairiest and the scariest-looking spider I had ever seen. It was like something from a horror film. I had only ever seen them behind glass at London Zoo, not stuck to my T-shirt.

'Oh . . . my . . . God!' I screamed. I hopped around, praying it would drop off, but its legs appeared to be anchored into the cotton of my shirt. I even debated leaping into the river, but the hidden nasties lurking in the water seemed an even worse option. Being eaten by piranha or crocodiles, or electrocuted by the powerful electric eel would be bad enough, but it was the candiru or 'willy fish' – a small catfish with a barbed body that strikes fear into the hearts of swimmers due to its tendency to swim up any flow of human urine and lodge itself in the genitalia – that scared me most of all.

Fortunately, the boat's chef saved me from any such horrors, and from a heart attack, by removing the spider from my shirt. I never did find out what happened to it, but I later discovered that they are a great delicacy.

In the evenings we dined off fish caught by the string-vest-wearing chef in a vast net pulled behind the boat. They would be thrown straight into the frying pan from the river, scales, heads, intestines and all. Often there were bugs for good measure.

During the day I would sit cross-legged on the roof of the boat, away from the mayhem of the hammock tangle below. I would stare, mesmerized by the giant otters and the river's famous pink dolphins. One day the engines of the boat simply failed and we drifted helplessly into a flooded swamp strewn with trees.

Monkeys leapt overhead and I watched as a sloth clambered down a tree trunk very, very slowly. It was one of the most magical sights I have ever seen and made the whole trip worthwhile.

As a child I had read dozens of books about journeys deep into the Amazon, including that of Colonel Percy Fawcett, who was reportedly eaten by cannibals.

Colonel Fawcett – who later became the inspiration for Indiana Jones – undertook the first of seven complete expeditions to South America in 1906, where he was tasked with mapping an area between western Brazil and Bolivia. During his travels he claimed to have witnessed a number of fantastic and unlikely creatures, including a black cat-like dog, a sixty-two-foot-long giant anaconda (which reportedly attacked him in his boat, until he successfully sliced it in two), a double-nosed tiger hound that fed upon jaguars, a bloodsucking cockroach, a twenty-foot-long yellow poisonous reptile he named the *Surucucu agapa fogo*, a giant poisonous spider and, perhaps most strikingly, the *Bufeo*, a humanoid mammal belonging to the manatee family, notable for its very prominent breasts.

His choice of travel companions was also remarkable. For his expedition to map part of the Rio Verde his entourage consisted of two native men, a waiter, a silversmith and a baker. Fawcett reportedly had great respect for the tribespeople he met in his travels. On one occasion a local tribe fired arrows at his team. Rather than return fire, one of Fawcett's companions played the accordion, calming the situation, and Fawcett addressed one of the armed men in his native tongue. The community were so impressed with this behaviour that they helped the team set up their camp for the night and sent good word ahead of them upriver.

What catapulted Fawcett from the status of eccentric explorer to a figure of legend was his infamous final expedition, from which he never returned. He had developed an obsession with the idea of an ancient lost city in the Mato Grosso of Brazil, which he believed was the source of all human civilization and was linked to the lost city of Atlantis. He also sought the existence of a mysterious tribe with pale skin, blue eyes and red hair, living somewhere deep in the Amazon. In 1925 he set out on an expedition to identify this city, which he cryptically referred to as 'Z', taking with him his eldest son and his son's closest friend. Before leaving Britain he refused to reveal full details of his destination, but gave instructions that no rescue teams should be sent to find him should he fail to return. Not long into the expedition Fawcett's messages back to England stopped. He and his companions were never seen again.

Despite Fawcett's instructions, more than a dozen expeditions have tried to find him, with reportedly more than one hundred lives lost in the process. There is no definite evidence to explain what became of him, but many ideas have been put forward. It has been suggested that he and his team died of illness and hunger, or that they were killed by a tribe, either due to a failure to respect protocol and bring gifts or because of his son's sexual indiscretions. More outlandish claims are that Fawcett remained living in the jungle as chief of a cannibalistic tribe, or that he never intended to return to England, nor to find the lost city of Z, his true plan being to establish a theosophical utopian commune in the middle of the jungle.

Six weeks after leaving Belém we arrived in Iquitos. I had done nothing but sleep and watch as the thousands of miles of river disappeared beneath our little biscuit boat, but I felt as though I'd crossed an ocean. I can still remember my pride when I stepped ashore. It had been an incredible journey – although I still didn't know any Spanish.

2

Finding Myself

Ecuador had been my goal. I would be living here, high in the Andes, for the following year. It was January 1993 and I had been allocated a family called the Salazars. Mauro, a widower, lived with his daughters Lucia and Paulina and his son Javier in the north of Quito. I was alone in a strange country, unable to speak the language, but the family really helped me settle in. It's amazing how easy it is to communicate with sign language and noises. I became very proficient at making chicken and cow noises at dinner time. I grew very close to the Salazars and to this day call them my Ecuadorian family (I drop in unannounced whenever I'm passing through and it's always like the old days). They were incredibly welcoming and it is due to their warmth and patience that I had such a marvellous year.

I had been assigned to help out in an orphanage and also with a small company, about which I knew very little. My lack of Spanish was about to face its first real test.

I turned up at the little office block where the company was based and introduced myself as best I could. I had no idea what they did. Only a series of framed photographs of potatoes gave any hint of their business. I was allocated a tiny sub-office in a converted shower room off the main work area. The walls were lined with books, while a simple desk with a telephone and a small cupboard were the only furnishings.

I had been there for a couple of weeks when the telephone started to ring for the first time. Up until this point I had passed the time shuffling books and papers around the shelves. I had become an expert time-waster, making the world's largest necklace out of paper clips and the biggest elastic-band ball I have seen to this day. But today the phone rang. The only way to describe my reaction is panic. I could barely say my name in Spanish let alone conduct a telephone conversation. I sat staring at the phone for what seemed like an eternity, then from the main office next door I heard the scraping of a chair on the floor and the mutterings of one of my mysterious co-workers as he headed towards my office and the unanswered phone.

More panic. What should I do? It would be too embarrassing if he came in to find me at a bare desk next to a ringing phone. It is always surprising what people do when they panic and I can only put my reaction down to pressure. I ran to the tiny cupboard, crawled inside on my hands and knees and hid beneath one of the shelves.

I had just managed to pull the cupboard shut when I heard my colleague enter the room and speak into the phone. I could tell from his tone that he was exasperated. I held my breath, hoping he'd leave, but then I was overwhelmed by the unstoppable urge to sneeze. I stifled the sound as best I could, but he must have heard it because he stepped over to the cupboard and opened the door to find me on my hands and knees inside.

'*Hola,*' I smiled. He looked at me with a blank face, closed the door and walked off.

I left the business that afternoon and to this day wonder what it was that they did and what the man thought of me in the cupboard.

I stepped up my volunteering in the orphanage and also began work at a primary school, where I helped teach English while at the same time learning Spanish from a group of five-year-olds. I learned surprisingly quickly. What I discovered is that there is no better way of mastering a language than total immersion.

The year passed by in a colourful blur. I grew my hair long and started wearing the local Andean clothing and big, baggy knitted jumpers that still smelled of wet sheep. I made a great many local friends and it didn't take long to feel a part of the country. I went to family occasions and even a wedding with the Salazars, and Mauro introduced me as his English son. I loved Ecuador and felt proud of my immersion in this Andean country.

Like so many Latin American republics, Ecuador has had a tumultuous history, with more than its fair share of coups. In fact, by 2010 the country had had eight leaders in thirteen years. Each Ecuadorian term in office should last four years, but the last president to achieve that was in 1992–96. In August 1997 Ecuador bore witness to three changes of government and four leaders in one week, while on 21 January 2000 there were two changes of government in a single day.

During my time there, Ecuador was at war with its neighbour, Peru. Occasionally I would return home to dinner to find Señor Salazar sitting in front of the nightly news, a worried look on his face as the latest skirmish signalled an escalation in the conflict.

Like so many disputes, this one was created by an international ruling imposed on the two countries and was the result of a mistake in mapping. The Cordillera del Condor borderlands between Ecuador and Peru were first violently contested in 1941 in a twenty-six-day conflict that resulted in the 1942 Rio de Janeiro Protocol. Ecuador subsequently argued that the boundaries drawn by the protocol were geographically incorrect because the thick jungle made demarcating the border very challenging and seventy-eight kilometres had been left unmarked. In 1960 the Ecuadorian government declared the protocol null.

In 1981 a second conflict began, known as the False Paquisha War, after Ecuadorian troops crossed the contested border area, occupied a Peruvian military outpost and named it Paquisha, after another Ecuadorian outpost and village. The Peruvian government denounced Ecuador's actions as illegitimate and proclaimed the occupied outpost a 'false Paquisha'. Quickly, and with few casualties, Peruvian forces won back the outpost.

The third and final border war, known as the Alto-Cenapa War, took place from 26 January until 28 February 1995. Official figures place the total number of dead at around eighty combatants, but some suggest the figure may have been higher. Following the ceasefire and peace treaty the border was finally officially demarcated in favour of Peru.

I had been in South America for about six months the first time I was arrested. It was a Friday night and I was out with some of my friends drinking in a popular bar when dozens of uniformed police arrived, accompanied by soldiers in full combat gear. We wondered whether it was a drugs raid until they started asking for everyone's identity papers. My heart sank at the realization that I had no form of ID on me. I had been warned to carry my passport at all times, but complacency had given way to stupidity and I was promptly arrested.

To my relief, I wasn't the only one rounded up and shepherded towards the police van. A dozen of us were herded inside and driven to the police station. It was difficult to gauge the severity of our situation. I knew my passport was back at my Ecuadorian family's home, but how was I going to get it? I wasn't sure whether to laugh or cry. This was either going to be a fantastic tale or part of a tragic obituary.

I had never been behind bars before. There were more than fifty of us in a tiny cell. There was no room to sit and we were forced to stand shoulder to shoulder. We were an international bunch: I heard English, German, Italian and Hebrew as well as Spanish. No one told us what was happening. There was an air of menace about the place, but strangely I didn't feel any fear; in fact, quite the opposite – I was excited.

The hours passed and there was still no information. A couple of the group began to panic, but we were largely resigned to the situation. We were in a foreign country and we'd broken their laws by going out without our paperwork. I had heard about the importance of carrying ID papers abroad all the time – it is often used as an example of why we shouldn't require them ourselves here in the UK. The problem here was that we had no idea what the long-term implications would be. Would we be detained for a day or a year?

Morning broke, and finally a guard appeared and read out our names. 'Ben Fogley,' he said. We were ushered into another room. Where were they taking us? For the first time I started to panic. What if we were being transferred from the city police station to some secret prison where we would languish forgotten for the rest of our lives? My heart began to race as my excitement turned to fear.

An officious-looking military man sat at a desk with an enormous ledger. He beckoned me forward. This is it, I thought. My judge and jury.

'That will be a hundred thousand sucres,' he said in near-perfect English. I paid my fine (£20) and was released.

Soon after my little run-in with the police, I found myself attacked by a feral dog while I was walking to the orphanage one day. A street dog ran up behind me and sank its teeth into my calf, biting through my jeans and turning them red. The bite didn't require stitches, but, worse than that, I needed the full course of rabies jabs.

I have endured pain on various levels over the years, but I can honestly say that those injections into my tender, weak stomach were some of the most unpleasant I have ever experienced. These days the treatment has, thankfully, moved on, but twenty years ago it was still deeply unpleasant. I hated that dog for it, but at least I never developed rabies.

Overlooking Quito is the towering, smoking stack of Cotopaxi, the tallest active volcano on earth. At almost 6,000 metres (19,000 feet) it is a formidable mountain, and with its ice-cream coating of snow it looks like an Andean version of Mount Fuji in Japan. I had been tantalized by its sporadic appearances through the cloud cover that seemed to cling to the city, and my friends Guy Hedgecoe and Guy Edmunds and I resolved to climb it before the year was out. It isn't a technical peak that requires years of climbing experience, but then none of us had ever climbed a peak before. We'd heard countless tales of disasters on the mountain, but rather than put us off, the stories simply fuelled our desire to attempt it.

We found a local guide and hired the crampons and boots we'd need to scale the summit. Most people begin their ascent at the mountain's refuge at 4,500 metres. A rough track up to the hut means many people actually drive up, but we had been warned about the importance of acclimatizing properly and decided that we would walk up from the roadside, through Cotopaxi National Park, to give ourselves time to get used to the change in altitude. We would have a week to get to the summit.

Having never done any form of mountaineering before, our first task was to pack. Without a nutritionist, we had to guess what food to take and in a fantastically miscalculated judgement ended up packing hundreds of peanut butter and jelly sandwiches, several clutches of bananas – and nothing else. For some reason that I will never fully understand, we decided that we wouldn't need a stove or any hot meals. Quite how we anticipated surviving on sandwiches and bananas for a week will remain a mystery, but then again so do the minds of nineteen-year-olds.

One of the secrets of the Andes, and probably one they want to remain a secret, is that it rains a lot. In fact, it would be more honest to say that occasionally it doesn't rain. For four days we lived off our soggy sandwiches and squashed bananas as we trekked through the soaking valleys, where freezing mist clung to the damp heather. It was cold and wet as we trekked towards the invisible mountain hidden behind the rain-swollen clouds.

It was a huge relief to reach the safety and relative dryness of the refuge, where dozens of other climbers were also waiting to attempt the summit. The sandwiches had played havoc with our guts and we longed for some warm food. A kindly group of Italians took pity on us and swapped some hot soup for a handful of sandwiches.

Our guide Antonio joined us at the refuge. We had met him only once before, but he suddenly seemed younger, smaller and less experienced than all the other guides. I looked around at the various groups having their safety meetings while Antonio sat in the corner smoking a cigarette.

It was just after midnight when we rose for the summit attempt. The idea was to get to the top in the early hours of the morning so that we could be off the snow before the heat of the sun began to make the surface unstable. It was imperative that we were back before lunch or we risked being caught in an avalanche.

We had chosen a full moon in order to benefit from the bright moonlight. Reflecting off the snow, it meant you could trek without a torch. So bright was its glow that we could see our moon shadows as we trudged up through the scree and on to the snow and ice.

Antonio had given us a rudimentary lesson in how to employ the crampons and the ice axe, which we were to use to arrest any falls off the mountain. We were roped up and Antonio led the way. For several hours we plodded along. The air was cold and thin, but the landscape was magical. It was otherworldly. I had never seen a place like this before and I was feeling alive again. This was what life was about. I was doing things and seeing things I had only ever read about.

It was about four o'clock in the morning when we passed the first group of climbers descending the mountain. Surprise that they had reached the summit so quickly soon turned to concern when we discovered they were all turning back early. The weather had begun to close in and, one by one, guides were ushering their groups off the mountain. I looked at Antonio up ahead, but he gave the thumbs-up so we continued to ascend.

Guy Edmunds was struggling with the altitude. He had been suffering since we arrived at the refuge, where his face had puffed out like a hamster with a mouth full of food. His skin had become pallid and he was bleeding from the nose and gums. He couldn't go on and another returning group agreed to lead him back to safety.

Antonio, Guy Hedgecoe and I carried on. To this day I don't know if it was us urging Antonio or vice versa; whatever the motivation, we were going against every other group's better judgement and before long we were the only people left on the mountain.

The altimeter read 5,700 metres. We had been ascending near-vertiginous slopes and the weather had by now closed in. Thick clouds obscured the summit and visibility had been reduced to just a couple of metres. The wind had also picked up, reducing the temperature to minus 20°C. The sun had risen and, even through the cloud, it dazzled in the thin air. I pulled my goggles to my face, but my perspiration froze to the lenses. It was almost impossible to use them. Onwards we crawled and clawed our way up the steep slopes. We were still tethered together.

I felt as if we'd been climbing for days. Visibility was worsening and I was about to suggest we return when I noticed Antonio leaping up and down. What was he doing? The wind made conversation almost impossible and I felt dizzy through lack of oxygen.

'*El cumbre, el cumbre!*' I caught before his words were snatched by the wind. We were on the summit! I lay on my belly next to Guy. I had never been so exhausted in my life, but somehow we had made it. If I'm honest, Antonio could have made it up – we could have been on any flat surface. Visibility was less than a metre and we could have been back in Quito – except for the altimeter reading six thousand metres.

It was a great feeling. We may not have had the views I had always dreamed of, but I was higher than I'd ever been in my life and higher even than many of my mountaineering friends who had summited Mont Blanc.

My head pounded with the altitude. My lips were cracked and I could taste blood in my mouth. I sat there sucking on a piece of frozen chocolate, preparing for the descent, when suddenly a white object appeared from the snow.

I watched in astonishment as a huge snowman emerged from the cloud. It must have been six feet tall, with a huge round body and head and a long carrot for a nose. Two small arms made from sticks sprouted from its side and it started to run towards me.

'Whoa!' I remember thinking as it hurtled towards me. 'I've seen everything now.' I braced myself for impact but, as quickly as it had appeared, it vanished in a puff of snow.

I looked round at Guy. 'Did you see that?' I asked.

'See what?' he answered above the din of the wind.

I was beginning to hallucinate and it was time to get off the mountain.

What goes up must come down and, as any mountaineer worth their salt will tell you, getting to the summit is less than half the adventure. The descent is where most accidents and tragedies occur. Often mountaineers are blinded by summit fever and become so obsessed with the ascent that they forget entirely about the return. Many pay the ultimate price.

Where Antonio had led from the front on the ascent, he would lead from the back for the descent. This left us with the un-enviable task of walking blind down the mountain. I was at the front with Guy behind me. It was difficult to gauge where to put each step, harder still to work out which way was down. Occasionally I would veer off to the left or right, unable to distinguish the direction.

For hours we beat into a heavy storm. My legs and brain had turned to jelly. It was already noon and we were still a long way from the refuge. Guy was also struggling, but most worrying of all was that Antonio was exhibiting the first signs of altitude sickness. I had read about the warning symptoms, which include lethargy and confusion, and he was showing both.

'Come in!' he kept shouting in English. 'Come in!' When we failed to acknowledge him he would get angry and confused. We found ourselves trapped by huge gullies and drops, and often had to ascend again in order to get round obstacles. The flags that usually marked the route had been lost to the storm.

My goggles had frozen solid so I abandoned them altogether, leaving my eyes to the mercy of the intense radiation. Even in the cloud, the sun burns retinas, and soon I lost the sight in one eye to snow blindness. My legs kept crumpling under me. I was exhausted. We had to stop. Antonio got angry, but Guy and I both needed to rest. We sat with our backs to the wind while the storm raged around us. The altimeter was still reading 5,500 metres.

For the first time in my life I felt genuine terror. It was the first time I had been without a safety margin. I had no buffer, nothing to fall back on, no one to ask for help. I wished I wasn't there. I berated myself for getting into this situation. Why had we been so stubborn? Everyone else had turned back – why had we carried on? I wanted to blame someone, but we had no one but ourselves. Tears welled in my eyes before being frozen by the wind. My heart raced as my mind suddenly took in the magnitude of our predicament. We were on our own and we would live or die by our next decision.

I couldn't go on. My legs simply wouldn't allow it. I began to dig a snow hole. We would have to sit it out and wait for rescue. By now we would have been recognized as missing and a search party would soon be dispatched. If we could simply sit it out, then we would certainly be found.

But then Antonio grabbed me by the scruff of my neck and thrust me forward. He knew the dangers of staying put in this storm – we had to keep descending. I forced my legs to move and, somehow, three hours later we arrived back at the refuge, just as a rescue team were setting out.

What had started as a *Boy's Own* adventure with our peanut-butter sandwiches had turned into a nightmare. It had been a steep learning curve about the dangers of nature; above all, it had been a mortality check. It wouldn't be the last.

While the mountain had been a sobering experience, it was a subterranean mountain visit that would affect me deeply. The two Guys and two British girls, Joanna and Tamsin, who had also become great friends after spending six months in Quito, had travelled down through Peru and across Lake Titicaca before heading up into landlocked Bolivia. There we travelled to the infamous town of Potosi.

In Potosi, at 4,090 metres (13,400 feet) one of the highest cities in the world, lies the Cerro Rico mine, once a great source of silver but now predominantly used for the mining of tin. It is reputed to be the most dangerous mine in the world with its lack of protective equipment, and the average miner rarely passes the age of forty.

Perhaps it was these perilous conditions that led miners to erect statues and pray for the assistance of 'El Tio', the spirit owner of the miner, thought by many to be a mixture of the Andean Spirit of the Hills and the Christian devil. The sculptures of El Tio – the Spanish word for 'uncle' – found deep within the mines commonly depict him with horns, a greedy wide-open mouth, outstretched voracious hand and erect phallus. As patron of the mine, his greed must be placated, otherwise it will be human lives that he takes. In order to gain his protection, miners present him with gifts of cigarettes, alcohol and llama's blood. One of the most common offering rituals is the *ch'alla*, in which worshippers share drinks, coca and cigarettes with El Tio, placing a lighted cigarette in the statue's mouth. At the beginning of the agricultural year a llama is sacrificed at the entrance of the mine and either a dried llama foetus or a llama heart is buried at the foot of the statue. The mine is then left empty so that El Tio can gorge himself in peace. This ritual is thought both to invoke the reciprocity between communities and deities under the Inca system and also to reflect the subjection of indigenous peoples under colonial order.

The hellish subterranean world of the mine is El Tio's domain, therefore speaking the name of God is forbidden there. During the twentieth century the worship of El Tio found new meanings. When the mine was under private ownership, teams of workers were paid piecemeal, therefore paying homage to El Tio was a means of guaranteeing greater bounties of silver and tin, as well as a safeguard against death. However, after the mines were nationalized and the workers received a flat wage, the devil-worship became a force for rebellion, which the Bolivian government attempted to suppress.

Some argue that the statues of El Tio are a means of literally demonizing the multinational and later governmental mine-owners who subject the miners to daily torment. Others argue that the imagery of devilry reflects the miners' own sense of their fall from grace, as through their employment in the mine they are physically isolated from their families and communities and estranged from traditional Andean agricultural ways of life.

High in the Andes, Potosi is a bleak, cold, windswept place, but it was what goes on below the mountain that really shocked me.

To visit the mine, you must take gifts for the miners. It was certainly a first for me to wander through the local market buying sticks of dynamite, coca leaves, homebrew and homemade cigarettes in which the tobacco was wrapped in newspaper. There was certainly no health warning and, unsurprisingly, no filter.

Early in the morning we walked into the mouth of the mine and were immediately confronted with a statue of El Tio, smoking cigarette protruding from his mouth. Here for the first time in my life I left an offering to the devil – one of my Imodium diarrhoea pills.

Slowly we slithered our way deep into the mine. As we descended the temperature began to soar. We pushed our way through narrow gaps, often crawling on hands and knees and even slithering on our bellies to get through the tiny spaces. It was a claustrophobe's nightmare.

For more than an hour we squeezed our way through the impossibly tight shafts, until we met our first miners. They weren't the ruddy, old Welsh kind I'd expected to find, but boys as young as eight, working in just their underpants.

If making an offering to the devil had been strange, then giving dynamite and cocaine (coca leaves) to an eight-year-old was surreal and more than a little unnerving.

'We are about to blast,' said one of the boys, thanking me for my presents. 'You might want to move away,' he warned in a fantastic understatement. We were ushered just a hundred metres along the shaft before he lit the fuse.

A huge boom resonated down the narrow shaft and a cloud of dust enveloped us. How the shaft didn't collapse I will never know, but given the number of people who have lost their lives there we were probably lucky.

For me it wasn't the dangers of the mine, but the shock of seeing such young boys sweating and toiling in the extreme conditions. I was beginning to discover how different life was in most of the world.

Since then I have taken hundreds, perhaps thousands of flights, but there is one that still haunts me from my time in South America. I was in La Paz in Bolivia and wanted to fly to the rainforest to experience jungle life. I went to a flight booking office and unbeknownst to me I booked myself onto a military flight.

My first inkling that this wasn't going to be an average flight came when I arrived at the military airfield high on the outskirts of La Paz. Young soldiers marched around in their oversized army camouflage uniforms while a number of ancient-looking aircraft sat on the runway, their engines purring.

At the time, the Bolivian Air Force was supplementing its budget by taking paying passengers on their cargo planes. About a hundred other passengers were waiting for the flight, mostly Bolivians, with an assortment of cargo, ranging from boxes to sacks full of clucking chickens, their feet tethered. I watched in astonishment as one woman walked three pigs into the belly of the plane.

The assortment of luggage (military and civilian) was anchored to the middle of the aircraft while we all sank into our seats, which were made of simple netting strung along the walls of the craft. There were no windows, just a red light casting a strange, otherworldly glow on the bizarre scene before me. As I sat in my rudimentary seat, I watched a large Bolivian woman, clutching two screaming babies, work her way around the mountain of baggage. Before I knew it, she had thrust one of the babies into my arms. One of the pigs had wriggled its way loose and was sniffing at my feet, and one of the men next to me was chain smoking. Not your average flight indeed and we hadn't even taken off.

At the high altitude of La Paz (nearly 3,500 metres), planes need a lot more space to take off and land because of the thin air, and we rumbled along the runway for what felt like an eternity before lurching into the sky. Half the passengers were still on their feet, falling on top of one another as we soared high into the Andes.

About an hour into the flight, there was a sudden jolt and the plane pitched to one side. '*Fuego, fuego!*' shouted one of the passengers. My heart beat furiously and my stomach sank. I felt physically sick as my nose picked up the first scent of burning. Not for the first time did I see my life flash before my eyes.

Without windows we had no idea where we were or what was happening. There was no air crew for reassurance and all I could do was scrunch my eyes closed and hope for the best, all the time clutching someone else's screaming, snotty baby. I looked around and was astonished to see that I seemed to be the only one who was panicking.

I could feel the plane descending and my ears popping as we made an emergency landing. I had no idea if we were landing in a field or a runway. I just crossed my fingers and hoped.

The plane touched down with a heavy jolt. It was the roughest landing I had ever experienced and we all flew across the plane. I gripped the baby tightly with one hand and the net seat with the other as the smell of burning became even more intense.

The back of the aircraft opened and an ancient-looking fire engine raced past. My legs carried me off the plane faster than I knew was possible. All the time I was bracing myself for an explosion. I raced down the back of the aircraft and on to the runway, still clutching the screaming child. I looked back to see smoke and flames streaming from one of the engines. I couldn't believe my eyes.

I was soon joined by the rest of the passengers, including the mother of the child, while half a dozen military green fire trucks sprayed the flames licking at the engine.

It was a close call but it didn't put me off flying, although I never made it to the jungle. Not that time anyway.

Towards the end of my year in Ecuador I found myself back in Peru, having followed a pretty waitress from Quito to the Peruvian town of Cusco. A day after I arrived in the Incan capital, however, the girl ran off with an Israeli and I decided to drown my sorrows by climbing another mountain.

I had recently read Joe Simpson's *Touching the Void* and, rather than be perturbed by his unbelievable tale, I had felt compelled to climb in the same range. So I found a small mountaineering firm offering ascents to a number of peaks in the area and signed up to climb Hyuna, 6,200 metres (20,300 feet) high.

Part of the joy of gap-year travel is the roulette wheel of who you'll find yourself travelling with; in this case I ended up with Dave, a Metropolitan policeman from London. Worryingly, I don't remember any of the others in our group, but we were certainly a rag-tag crowd, a smorgasbord of nationalities with varying degrees of experience. How I ended up partnered with Dave I'm not sure, but I suspect that, because he was a policeman, I assumed he would be a good mountaineer. Go figure.

For several days we ascended the steep valley, walking alongside irrigation canals and fields while the snowy summit loomed overhead. After six days we reached base camp. There were just eight hundred metres between us and the summit, and we pitched the tent for the final time. Or, should I say, I pitched the tent for the final time.

It was calm and sunny when I unravelled the tent from my rucksack. We had pitched it half a dozen times and I felt confident enough to erect it on my own while Dave brewed some tea. The problem was that the ground was frozen solid with a thick layer of permafrost just beneath the surface. However hard I tried, I couldn't get the metal pegs into the hardened ground. So I erected the tent and simply filled it with our kit as a form of ballast to hold it to the ground. It was a costly mistake I will never make again.

Excited about our summit push, we snatched a couple of hours' sleep and, just after midnight, we arose for the final assault.

The wind had picked up in the night and was snapping angrily at the tent. Dave was up before me and had dressed and already cleared out most of his kit. Wearing my thermals, I hauled myself from the tent so that I could dress standing up. I was just pulling on my second boot when a powerful gust of wind struck the campsite.

'Tent!' I heard Dave holler. I turned around to see our whole tent flying through the air. It landed on the hard surface and somersaulted down the side of the mountain into the gloom. There I was, 5,400 metres up a mountain in just my thermals and my boots.

OK, so it wasn't exactly a Joe Simpson moment, but it meant our attempt on the summit was over and we spent the rest of the day searching the mountain for the lost gear that had been shed from the shredded tent. I'd learned a hard lesson. Always anchor your tent.

3

Still Finding Myself

I returned to England a changed person. I had lived a lifetime of experiences in a year. My mind was full of possibilities and I wanted more. I wanted adventure, I wanted excitement and I wanted the freedom I'd gained from Latin America. My senses had been overloaded and I wanted to go back, which is exactly what I did.

I had found myself a place at the University of Central England, in Birmingham – the only university that would award me a place with the C, U and N that I got in my A-levels. No disrespect to Birmingham, but it was a bit of a let-down. I had failed to get into halls of residence and found myself in a little house below Spaghetti Junction along with four strangers who were into their techno and jungle music. I had been given a place on a politics degree, but within a week I knew it wasn't for me. I found a job in a bar and worked double shifts until I could afford the airfare to return to the part of the world that had stolen my heart.

I had visited the continent of my friend Thor, but I still wanted to explore the countries Edmund and Leonardo came from, so this time I travelled to Central America via Mexico. I spent a few weeks in Mexico City before heading south towards the Mosquito Coast, a place I had dreamed of visiting ever since reading the book of that name by Paul Theroux about a mad inventor who creates an ice machine for the locals. What I found was stranger than fiction.

I spent several weeks travelling down through the Zapatista stronghold of Chiapas, where I picked up some dolls of one of the rebels' charismatic, blue-eyed leaders, Subcomandante Marcos. It was 1994 and, at the time, the Zapatistas were hitting the headlines all around the world with their modern terrorism. I was fascinated by their 'middle-class', educated approach to terrorism. If it is possible, they seemed to be nice terrorists, the kind you might invite in for tea with your granny. Educated and savvy.

A number of factors set the Zapatistas aside from other guerrilla insurgents. Firstly, although they are an armed group, they largely denounce the use of violence and many of the weapons they carry are merely models. When dealing with the media or public encounters with the outside world, men, women and children from Zapatista communities wear balaclavas or ski masks. This is not only a measure to protect themselves from retributive violence on the part of paramilitaries, but the anonymity also signifies their unity with other movements with libertarian socialistic ideals. As a late twentieth/early twenty-first-century struggle which utilizes the global interconnectivity of the internet as a means of communicating ideas, and which consciously positions itself as part of the international alter-globalization movement, the balaclava signifies that not only can anyone be a Zapatista, but that we are all Zapatistas.

The Zapatista movement is not just an exercise in living beyond the control of the Mexican government, but is also an experiment in different ways of organizing democracy, agriculture, education and health. Great emphasis is placed on the empowerment of women in the community, and also on protecting the community from its own vices; for example, alcohol is banned in many Zapatista settlements. There is an attempt to organize the entire region through egalitarian methods and on the principles of consensus and mutual aid. Members of the community alternate their roles on committees focused on different aspects of community life, most posts being held for only two weeks.

The administrative bodies of Zapatista territory are referred to as *caracoles*, the Spanish word for snails, and the image of the balaclava-wearing snail is an icon of the Zapatista community. The *caracol* has multiple meanings. In contrast to the rapid pace of neo-liberal globalization, the Zapatistas' sworn foe, they wish to build towards community and autonomy with the calmness and patience of a snail. It is also a reference to their Mayan past, as the conch shell (a further meaning of *caracol*) was a traditional tool for bringing the community together and summoning them all to one place.

The Zapatistas sustain themselves as an autonomous region through a number of industries, including the sale of coffee. Coffee beans are exported from their territories to Europe, where they are ground and packaged by a German workers' cooperative, and the coffee is then sold across Europe in radical bookstores, health-food cooperatives and social centres.

While the Zapatistas have no official leaders, there are a number of 'subcomandantes' who have become figureheads of the movement, the most famous being Subcomandante Marcos. Unlike many Zapatistas, Marcos is of Hispanic rather than Mayan origin, although his precise identity is unknown. He is thought to be university-educated and to have a background in more conventional Marxist politics, and he has written a number of books and communiqués outlining the Zapatista message. He once travelled three thousand miles across Mexico on a motorbike in homage to Che Guevara, attempting to build connections between different indigenous communities.

This was my first experience of an idealogical movement and it was an eye-opener. I found myself living in the town of San Cristóbal de los Casas, in the heart of Chiapas, in a small house with a group of young student activists who described themselves as Zapatistas but were really just politically active students. The region had a very different feel from the rest of Mexico.

It was here that I visited one of the strangest church services of my life. I have attended ceremonies in most religions throughout the world, as I have always felt it is an important way of understanding a culture. I am not particularly religious myself. I grew up in an a-religious household, although my father's family from Canada were Jewish, while my mother's were Church of England. Personally, I have never felt the need to find a religious identity. For many people religion gives meaning to life, but I have always found meaning in life itself. Nevertheless, I take great pleasure in attending church services – but the Catholic ceremony I attended in Mexico was the most extraordinary I am ever likely to witness.

Deep in Chiapas, heart of Zapatista territory, a unique mix of Catholic worship, Mayan divinity and corporate buy-in is practised. The Church of San Juan in the small town of Chamula, near San Cristóbal, has a number of peculiarities. There are no pews and absolutely no photography is allowed (enforced by the threat of jail), due, according to some, to a belief in the harmful effects of cameras on the spirit. The walls are lined with the statues of numerous saints, who for many also embody Mayan gods. A number of statues have had their hands chopped off as a punishment, for these bad saints had failed to act to save a previous church from destruction. Until recently the bad saints received little worship and were faced towards the wall in castigation. There is no priest, and no mass is held, although priests do visit regularly to conduct baptisms. Instead there is an emphasis upon direct communion with God, and much worship is also conducted by shamans, who hold positions within the church on a revolving basis.

Yet the most striking aspect of Chamula's religious practice is burping. Glasses of fizzy liquid are drunk during prayers and chanting in order to facilitate burping, which is thought to ward off evil spirits and expel bad spirits from the body. While pox (a drink of distilled cane-sugar juice) is sometimes used, the most popular beverage for purification is Coca-Cola and during the service I witnessed churchgoers clutching bottles of Coke which they downed to create the most spectacular burps I have ever heard. I still smile whenever I think about it. Coke is sometimes also spat liberally upon the many candles, for some reason I never discovered, or on individuals in order to bestow protection. Chanting and burping are occasionally also combined with animal sacrifice, with chickens killed upon the church floor in healing rituals or to invoke the favour of the gods.

But what makes Coca-Cola the new holy water? The extent to which the Chamula worship is a direct result of an audacious marketing ploy is unclear. Rather than being a case of direct sponsorship, it seems more likely that the drink's presence in church derives from its omnipresence across Mexico. Adverts for Coke adorn walls everywhere. Today Mexico drinks more Coca-Cola per capita than anywhere in the world, and is second only to the US in overall consumption. It is cheaper than milk and even than tap water.

I had always dreamed of visiting Guatemala and the hotel at Tikal owned by the Edmunds family, so I left the political hotbed of Chiapas in Mexico and crossed Belize into Guatemala, where I finally reached Tikal.

Though it now stands in ruins, Tikal was once one of the biggest sites of pre Columban Mayan civilization. During the Mesopotamian Classical Period (AD 250–900) it was the biggest city in the Americas and capital of one of the most powerful Mayan kingdoms; at its height it controlled much of the surrounding region economically and militarily. The city covered an area of more than 6.2 square miles and contained around three thousand buildings. The name 'Tikal' is thought to mean 'Place of the Voices', a possible reference to the stone depressions found at the summits of the temples which serve to amplify sound, enabling speakers to project their voices from temple to temple. Tikal had been abandoned by the end of the tenth century AD, probably due to a crisis of overpopulation, and its ruins have since become Guatemala's first UNESCO World Heritage Site.

Although not as old as the Egyptian pyramids, the six Tikal temples are still monumental examples of ancient architecture. Some of them rise to over sixty metres and they are thought to have been positioned to align exactly to astrological events. The sight-line between Temples III and IV, for example, corresponds to the point of sunrise at the winter solstice, while the positioning of Temples I and III reflects the points of sunrise and sunset at the equinoxes. The temples are also thought to represent Mayan ideas of the structure of the universe. The Mayan cosmos was divided into three parts: the Upper World, or heavens; the earthly world inhabited by humans; and the Lower Level, or underworld. Temple I, or the Temple of the Great Jaguar (named after an image inside of a monarch upon a jaguar throne), contains the tomb of Mayan King Ah Cacao (or 'Lord Chocolate') and can be seen as a point of connection and mediation between the underworld and the earthly world, in that its form resembles the shape of the Sacred Mountain (emblem of the earthly world) and its nine stepped layers represent the nine levels of the underworld through which Ah Cacao must travel.

The Mayans were one of the most theoretically sophisticated nations in the world, with a mathematical concept of zero and a highly intricate use of calendars, but at the time of the building of Tikal they were yet to invent the wheel or the arch, making the construction of the pyramids all the more remarkable.

Tikal also featured a number of ball courts, where religiously significant sports involving rubber balls were played. The winner would be sacrificed to the gods, ensuring him a good afterlife.

The Tikal ruins must rate as one of the most impressive, magical sites of human habitation in the world. Huge pyramids soar from the jungle canopy. Near-vertical steps lead up to their summits, from where you look out on the forest as over an ocean of broccoli. It is humbling and deeply moving to think of the sophistication of the society that built this city.

From Tikal, I finally headed towards La Ceiba and the gateway to the mysterious Mosquito Coast. Throughout my travels I had passed dozens of people who couldn't understand why I would bypass the riches of Central America for a mosquito-infested swampland, but I had my heart set on the region and I was determined to get there by hook or by crook.

The Mosquito Coast – La Moskitia – which borders the Caribbean and today runs through Nicaragua and Honduras, was a British protectorate from 1740. There were friendly relations between the Miskito Indians (after whom the area is named) and the English from the seventeenth century onwards, and reportedly Miskito kings and princes even visited British monarchs. Due to the wreck of a slave ship in the seventeenth century the Mosquito Coast also boasted a large African population, known as the Zambos. The region was famous for its resistance to Spanish settlement and acted as a safe territory for anti-Spanish activists. In 1859 Britain attempted to delegate the protectorate to Honduras, but this angered the Miskitos, so it was instead placed under the protection of Nicaragua while retaining its autonomy in internal affairs. It was fully annexed by Nicaragua in 1894 and, except for a northerly portion which was passed to Honduras in 1960, remains part of that country to this day. Although it likes to regard itself as a separate region, it has no official autonomy, but its traditional spirit of independence means that the Nicaraguan government tends to leave it alone. In the 1980s, during the Nicaraguan Civil War, the Mosquito Coast became a home to many supporters of the Contra rebels.

Possibly as a result of its insistence upon autonomy and distinction from the rest of Nicaragua, the Mosquito Coast has been largely neglected by the national government and until recently the area was very poor. There is still poverty there today; however, it is now coupled with pockets of affluence. In the past few years mansion houses and pricey hotels have sprung up, and locals have begun watching satellite television and drinking expensive beer. The wealthy are former fishermen lucky enough to have caught the 'white lobster'. Also known as 'godsends' due to the riches and blessings they bring upon the community, these white lobsters are packages of cocaine tossed overboard by drug smugglers being pursued by border guards. Sometimes smugglers will also beach their boats and disappear into the jungle to evade capture by the authorities, their haul duly being collected from the boats by locals. The smugglers later return to the coast to buy back their misplaced goods at one seventh of their market price – an amount that is still a fortune for the residents of the coast.

The Mosquito Coast is an essential passage point for the global drugs trade, with shipments of cocaine heading north and boats filled with cannabis speeding south. Until a few years before my visit, the lives of the people of the Mosquito Coast were untouched by drugs. One of the first white lobsters was believed by the locals to be baking powder, leading to the deaths of fifteen people in the village of Karpwala. In many ways these packages have indeed been godsends, benefiting individuals, with the prescription in some villages that at least 10 per cent of wealth acquired in this way must go to neighbours and 10 per cent to the church. Some indigenous separatist movements are also considering funding themselves and their efforts through drug money. However, the community's narcotic loss of innocence has also had undesirable effects, with many teenagers now hooked on crack cocaine.

La Moskitia, by the very nature of its geographical location, is extraordinarily difficult to get to. When I tried to get there I found no airports, trains, roads or commercial boats into the region. Puerto Lempira in Honduras, the regional capital, was closed to outsiders at the time of my visit. Honduras and Nicaragua were officially at war, so technically I was heading into a war zone. I found a tiny cargo ship delivering some goods to a coastal village a day's sail into the region. I hitched a lift and got the tiny vessel to drop me on the beach, where I walked for two days until I reached the first small, unnamed community, located on a thin bar of sand between the ocean and a vast swamp.

I befriended the local schoolteacher, who let me live in his house for a small weekly payment. It was a little wooden house on stilts with the largest spiders I have ever seen in my life. They were fist-sized and the bane of my life. I'm embarrassed to admit it now, but I used to chase them out of the room by holding a lighter to my spray deodorant and creating a plume of flames that sometimes cooked them like chicken on a barbecue. If the locals were bemused by this young Englishman in their midst, they didn't show it. They made me very welcome and I used to go to a different house each day for meals, for which I also paid a small sum. The menu seemed to be rice and mango three times a day. An abiding memory is of hunger. Oh, and in a knee-jerk reaction against the shoulder-length hair of the year before, I shaved my head and grew a beard.

It was hot and sweaty, but I loved it. It was exactly how I had imagined it. There was a little bar full of washed-up soaks from all across the world who had somehow ended up in this steaming jungle.

One day, after I had been there for nearly three months, I heard the distant thud of a helicopter and soon two enormous choppers appeared on the horizon. They were bigger than any helicopter I had ever seen and they circled the little community several times.

The entire village turned out to watch as ropes tumbled from the bellies of the helicopters and dozens of men in full army camouflage rappelled down on to the sandy ground. One after another they landed with a thud, followed by enormous canvas bags of kit. I wasn't sure whether we were being invaded, or even whose army this was.

'Hi, I'm Trooper Ritchie,' smiled one of the soldiers, holding out his hand to me.

They were a US army corps from North Carolina who had come down on exercise. They would be here for a week, during which time they were going to build a school and a playground. What struck me as most extraordinary was the fact that most of the soldiers were still spotty, they were so young; more significantly, most of them had never left their home state, let alone the United States. For these soldiers, La Moskitia must have been like landing on Mars.

For me their arrival was heaven-sent. I had some English-speaking company and, more importantly, they shared their ration packs with me.

A week later, the choppers returned and the men departed again for the States, leaving a pretty little wooden school, complete with swings, as a legacy.

Not long after this, I was in the small bar, drinking rum, when a rather crazy-looking American came up to me. He had a wild look in his eyes and his hair was unkempt.

'Do you want to see something really cool?' he asked.

'Sure,' I shrugged.

. We left the bar and headed up the coast. I followed him as he left the small path and pushed into the undergrowth. We ducked under low branches as we clambered up a small hill overlooking the Caribbean sea. I'm not sure why I followed or even trusted this stranger, but I suppose I was still young, naive and curious.

We had been walking for nearly twenty minutes when we reached a secluded bay surrounded by dense jungle.

'You have to be totally silent,' he whispered. 'You can't even move.' My heart began to pound as he crawled on his belly along the sandy ground towards the bluff.

The emerald-green waters of the Caribbean stretched out before us, waves crashing on to the white sandy beach below. It was a beautiful landscape, but I wasn't sure what it was we were looking at.

The man kept glancing at his watch. It was 6.30 p.m. and the sun was already low in the sky as dusk began to fall, when a tiny speck of a boat appeared on the horizon. It grew larger and larger as it sped towards us, and before I could blink it was in the small private bay. It was an enormous Sunseeker yacht. It must have been thirty metres long, the sort of boat you see moored in St Tropez or Cannes, but not here in the jungle of Central America.

A small wooden boat was launched from the beach, laden with large blue bundles. We sat there for nearly an hour while the local boat ferried back and forth. Darkness had fallen by the time the yacht disappeared into the inky night.

'Drugs,' my companion whispered once the boat had vanished. He explained that they had come up overland from Colombia, through the Darien Gap, then up through Panama and into

Nicaragua and then Honduras. Their next stop would be the streets of New York.

It was a sobering encounter with a scourge that has now dominated this part of the world for decades.

Central America had more than its fair share of bloody tragedy, war and coups throughout the twentieth century, but one of the most bizarre conflicts erupted between Honduras and El Salvador in 1969. As the world waited for the first human being to land on the moon, war erupted between these two countries, seemingly over a game of football. 'The Football War', or '100-Hour War', certainly featured aggressive sporting rivalries and the FIFA 1970 qualifying matches did act as flashpoints in this much-overlooked conflict, yet the cause of the Football War was not the game itself. The origins can be found in the economic disparity between the neighbouring countries and increasing national hostility.

Honduras, a country five times the size of El Salvador but with only half the population, was home to hundreds of thousands of Salvadoran immigrants, many of whom lived as peasants or temporary labourers. The Honduran government attributed many of the country's economic problems to the presence of these immigrants, leading to harassment and vigilante attacks against the Salvadoran population across Honduras. With the introduction of a new law which forcibly passed land from immigrant farmers to native-born Hondurans, thousands of Salvadorans were displaced, many returning to their home country, which was already subject to severe land shortages.

By the time of the first World Cup qualifying match between Honduras and El Salvador on 8 June 1969, tensions between the two countries were already running high. The first match was held in Honduras and, on the night before, the visiting Salvadoran team was kept awake by the abuse of the rival team's supporters. Honduras won 1–0, a dishonour that was too great for eighteen-year-old Salvadoran Amelia Bolaños. At home in El Salvador, upon news of her team's defeat she took her father's hand-gun and shot herself in the chest. Immediately regarded as a martyr to Salvadoran nationalism, she was given a televised state funeral attended by key government officials.

The second qualifying round was held on 15 June, this time in El Salvador. Again the visiting team suffered pre-match abuse, but on an accelerated scale. Reports circulated of bottles and rotten rats being thrown through the window of the Honduran team's hotel and the players were escorted to the match in armoured vehicles. The game was won 3–0 by El Salvador, a Honduran flag was publicly burned and rioting erupted in the streets.

While the antagonism between the two countries was abundantly clear, World Cup entry was still undecided. On 26 June, the day of the third and final qualifying match, won 3–2 by El Salvador, the Salvadoran government broke off diplomatic relations with Honduras. On 14 July El Salvador dropped its first bomb on Honduras and her troops marched into the neighbouring country. A ceasefire was swiftly brokered by the Organization of American States through the threat of economic sanctions against El Salvador and the promise to protect Salvadorans still in Honduras, and after only four days conflict ceased. With the world's eyes fixed on Neil Armstrong, the 4,500 combatant and civilian deaths went largely unnoticed.

After six months in La Moskitia I was off again, this time heading into the heart of Nicaragua, a country still smarting from civil war.

I had decided to cross the border at a tiny river crossing deep inland. It involved stamping out of Honduras in Puerto Lempira, where I had crashed illegally in the home of a friend of the schoolteacher, before a rough journey by truck to the main river. Here I would find a small boat to cross into Nicaragua, where I would have to wait for an army truck to take me on my way to Managua, the capital city.

The country bore the scars and bruises of conflict. Buildings were pockmarked with bullet holes and burnt out, while large craters marked the resting place of mortars. Vehicles lay burnt and destroyed at the side of the road and there was very little infrastructure left.

It was in the truck that I joined a group of several dozen locals, most in tattered clothes, a couple in old military uniform of unidentifiable provenance. It was several hours into the journey when one of the women asked one of the men about his missing arm.

'That's nothing,' said another in Spanish, lifting his trouser leg to reveal a prosthetic leg.

'Look at this, though,' bellowed another, lifting his top to reveal ugly red scarring from burns across his chest.

It was like a cross between *Monty Python* and *Jaws* as the passengers compared war injuries. Soon attention turned to me, the only Westerner on the bus.

'What about you, Gringo?' asked the instigator of the conversation.

In a panic I lifted my top to reveal a small scar on my chest.

'What's that?' she asked.

'A popcorn scar,' I announced in Spanish.

There were confused looks between the passengers. 'What's that?' asked the woman, looking puzzled.

'I was making popcorn when a boiling kernel popped from the pan down my top,' I answered, trying to look serious.

They rolled around laughing. It was the best ice-breaker I have ever had and one of the most memorable journeys of my life.

*

The Sandinistas, a Marxist guerrilla group, came to power in Nicaragua in 1979 after the overthrow of the dictatorial Somoza dynasty in a brief civil war, which was itself ignited by the murder of Pedro Chamorro, a leading journalist and democracy activist. Those who resisted the Sandinistas became known as the Contras, *contra* being the Spanish word for 'against'; the name also acted as a shortening of *contrarevolucionarios*, or counter-revolutionaries. The Contras included a wide range of groups such as Nicaraguan landowners concerned by the redistribution of wealth, and inhabitants of the Mosquito Coast, who feared government interference in their region. However, the Contras were predominantly identified with violent right-wing militias, mostly based in neighbouring Honduras, who opposed the Sandinistas through a bloody campaign of murder and destruction.

The Sandinistas, named after General Sandino, a guerrilla fighter who in the late 1920s and early 1930s helped expel US marines from Nicaragua, formed a provisional junta in 1974 and were formally elected in 1984. They were perceived by the US administration as a dangerous communist threat to the economic stability of the region, and the US instituted economic embargos against the country. The Sandinistas instead turned to the USSR and Cuba for support. The American government, now perceiving Nicaragua as a Cold War battlefield, began supplying money and arms through the CIA to the Contras. US involvement peaked in 1986–87 with the Iran–Contra affair, in which the Reagan administration was found guilty of illegally selling arms to Iran, then at war with Iraq, and using the proceeds to support the Contras, despite the US's own embargo on doing so because of the Contras' record of human rights abuses. When the scandal came to light, the Nicaraguan government sued the US in the International Court of Justice and won. However, the Americans refused to pay compensation.

The conflict finally ended in 1988, and in 1990 the Sandinistas were defeated in election by the National Opposition Union, led by Violeta Chamorro, a former leader of the 1979–84 provisional junta and widow of murdered journalist Pedro Chamorro; she remained president of Nicaragua until 1997. The Sandinistas returned to power, again under the premiership of their last president, Daniel Ortega, in January 2007.

The story for me is symbolic of the fragility of Central America. I was horrified to walk through the war-ravaged streets of Managua, but Nicaragua was an extraordinary place. War-torn and battle-hardened, the people had a resourcefulness and resilience that I hadn't seen elsewhere. The former Soviet Union had a stronghold in the country, which was filled with big red Russian buses and trucks and old Trabants. The Russians had invested heavily in Nicaragua with their rudimentary resources and the supermarkets were stocked with Soviet-made foodstuffs.

There was very little infrastructure for tourism and I found myself hitchhiking in the few private vehicles that were still operating, or squeezing into one of the communist buses. Tractors pulled huge double sections that were crammed full of war-weary commuters. Managua itself was as basic a capital as I have ever seen. The shops were empty and there was just a handful of low-grade hotels. I spent some time in Bluefields on the coast which had a large community of Rastafarians and a real Caribbean feel, but Managua was the real Nicaragua.

During my six months on the Mosquito Coast I had managed to pick up infections in both my feet. They had become ulcerous and eventually turned into dreadful abscesses. They were unbearably painful. I turned up at a hospital in Managua where I was given a pair of crutches and sent home with a course of penicillin to be injected into my bum twice a day.

'How do I inject my own bottom?' I asked the doctor, a little confused.

'Just ask someone in your hotel,' he shrugged, handing me a pile of needles.

I was staying in a particularly decrepit hotel, even by Nicaraguan standards, and the thought of the large, sweaty owner injecting my bare bottom didn't really appeal to me, but desperate times call for desperate measures and the owner was surprisingly happy to help. I was feeling pretty low and vulnerable and began to dip into a small depression. I was no longer sure why I was there, or indeed what I was going to do with my life.

I had been told to soak my feet in a bowl of warm salt water each evening, and it was during one of these soaks that I had one of my many coincidental encounters, this one with an old friend.

Linford was a friend of the family as well as an old schoolmate of mine. The son of Christopher Cazenove and Angharad Rees, we were both the sons of actors and had appeared in many plays together at school. Linford wasn't even meant to be in Central America, let alone Nicaragua, but he and a friend had been in Cuba and had decided on a whim to come south.

On this evening I had been feeling particularly low, with my feet sore and painful. The 'excitement' of Nicaragua was beginning to wane, and I was lonely and in need of some company. I was sitting alone watching a Latin American telenovela on the box when I heard a distinctive English accent. I was surprised that another Westerner was in town, never mind an Englishman. I watched as two young men walked across the courtyard.

The one who had spoken had a wispy beard, but apart from that there was a familiarity about him. We stared at each other in shock.

'Ben!' he said.

'Linford?'

I couldn't believe it. Of all the people in all the places in all the world, we should bump into one another *here*, in a dodgy little hotel in a war-ravaged capital. It remains one of the biggest coincidences in my life, though I like to think it was destiny.

Now Linford really came to my rescue. He cheered me up no end, and it remains one of those encounters I'll never forget. It still makes me smile to think of him and of how those miserable days on crutches suddenly became enjoyable.

I am telling this tale because several years later Linford died tragically in a car accident. I don't think I ever got to tell him how much that chance encounter cheered me up, and I wish I had.

Once again I returned to England a changed person. I had experienced another world and I was determined to learn more. My Spanish had improved immeasurably – which wasn't hard given that it had started at nothing – and I was finally offered a place at Portsmouth University for a degree in Latin American Studies. I'd be lying if I said my main motivation for the degree wasn't that it included another year away in Latin America, at the University of Costa Rica, but it would turn out to be a very different experience from before.

I ended up living in San José, the capital of Costa Rica, with Tom Rollo, a student friend, and with a Canadian called Kurt, who had just bought a bar in the city.

Not long after arriving I was introduced to a British family who lived down in the south of the country, near Turrialba, and invited me to stay with them. They had a rambling old farmhouse in the middle of a jungle clearing, where they helped run a macadamia-processing plant. The house had seen better days and the jungle had begun to encroach on the garden and the swimming pool. I will never forget my first visit to their home, at which a handful of other Brits were also staying. One of them jumped into the pool, only to be chased out by a snake. As if that wasn't enough to put you off swimming, the following day he got in again. I was sitting at the edge of the pool about to dive in when he suddenly began to panic.

'I can't feel my legs,' he said through gritted teeth. 'I can't move my body.' His face was contorted in pain. I helped haul him from the pool and afterwards we discovered that one of the pool lights was sending a powerful electric current through the water.

For me, that summed up the house. It was rambling and ramshackle, but I loved it there and my hostess, Suzanna, soon became a firm friend. Her children were away at school in England and I used to sit for hours listening to her incredible stories. I have never met anyone with more extraordinary tales to tell. She would recount stories of tea with Colonel Gaddafi during which they were caught up in a coup attempt and had to escape through the air-conditioning pipes, and of plane crashes in the Malaysian jungle. She even told me about car shoot-outs on the Bayswater Road. Her tales were wild and fantastic and I sometimes wondered whether there was an element here of Walter Mitty.

Many years later, back in England, I bumped into a mutual friend and we spoke of Suzanna.

'Did you never guess?' he asked. I hadn't a clue what he was talking about.

'Did you never ask yourself what she was doing living in the middle of the jungle? Or why she had so many fantastic stories to tell?' he asked.

I did, but she always seemed to have a good reason. Either she was working for the Foreign Office, or for a development agency or an oil company.

'She was a spy,' he whispered.

I never did find out if that was true, but I have always loved the thought that I spent so much time with a real-life James Bond.

Halfway through my time in Costa Rica I got my first wake-up call to the dangers of complacency. I had always been very careful about safety, but six months is enough to instil a feeling of invincibility in anyone.

I was walking back from Kurt's bar early one morning when I stumbled through one of the more dangerous parts of the city. I should have known the risks, but alcohol had numbed my senses. I can remember suddenly being grabbed by several people who pinned me to a wall. A hand encircled my neck. I was confused at first – I couldn't work out what was going on. I began to struggle and then I felt a jarring in my ribs and a sharp pain as I continued to struggle; another sharp pain and then the noise of running shoes on the pavement and I was alone.

I was leaning against the wall, holding my side. I ran my hand over my ribs and as I pulled it away I saw that it was red with blood. It was everywhere. I looked at my T-shirt and that too was soaked. I had been stabbed.

I made my way out of the dark side street towards one of the city's main roads and hailed a taxi to hospital. It wasn't a huge wound, but big enough to warrant twenty stitches. My broken ribs would have to repair naturally. It was a very painful couple of months.

Not long after this I heard that one of the other students from our university spending the year in Costa Rica had got herself into trouble. A lot of trouble. Tom and I hadn't heard from her since we arrived in the country, but we had heard it said that she had ended up with the wrong people. Then we heard a worrying rumour that she had murdered someone. The story went that she had been attacked in the Caribbean resort of Limón, a passer-by had gone to her aid, but in her confusion she had grabbed the assailant's knife and stabbed her would-be rescuer – to death.

Tom and I were horrified. We didn't really know the girl, but she had disappeared, a warrant was out for her arrest and we felt that there would be a terrible miscarriage of justice if she was prosecuted. It was an accident, surely?

We hatched a plan to smuggle her out of Costa Rica and up to Mexico. We researched bus routes to the Guatemalan border and which river to cross in order to avoid immigration, but first we had to find the girl. We spent days trawling through the dangerous neighbourhoods of San José. I still bore the stitches and broken ribs from my mugging and I felt uneasy knowing that my attackers would still be about.

We never did find her, and I never found out the truth of what happened, but it was a sad ending to the year.

Tom Rollo never came back from Costa Rica. He opened a bar and still lives there fifteen years later.

4

Castaway in the Outer Hebrides

'Where shall we go on our honeymoon?' asked Marina, my fiancée.

Our courtship had been brief. Just ten months. I had proposed after rowing across the Atlantic, so she probably had a fair inkling that my idea of a honeymoon wouldn't be in a Thomas Cook brochure.

'I have a great idea,' I smiled. 'I was thinking of a place in Latin America. It has long, wild beaches and plenty of wildlife. It's steeped in history and incredibly romantic.'

Marina's eyes glowed with excitement. 'Brazil?'

'No – the Falklands.' I made a little magical flourish with my hands.

'The Falklands?' she repeated. 'The Falkland . . . Islands?' She was genuinely surprised. This was good, I thought.

'But won't it be winter in the southern hemisphere?' she asked. She had a point there.

'Yes, but think how romantic it will be,' I rationalized. 'And guess what?' I had saved the best for last. 'There's a small house on the market near Mount Tumbledown that we could have a look at.'

Marina stared at me.

'How about South Georgia?'

She continued her stare.

'Antarctica?'

We settled on the Outer Hebrides.

I have always loved Scotland. I like to think it's because my grandfather was from Scotland, which makes me a quarter Scottish, or maybe it's because I spent parts of my childhood on the shores of Loch Ness, searching for the monster with my Scottish nanny, Katrine. In reality it probably has more to do with the life-changing year I spent on the island of Taransay in the Outer Hebrides in 2000, participating in the *Castaway* television series. I had fallen in love with Scotland and it seemed that the Scots had a soft spot for me.

I have always liked the idea of a metaphorical 'journey' and I particularly liked the idea of my life coming full circle. Taransay was where the points had started and where they would be rejoined. The island was such a big part of my life and I wanted to share it with Marina. I wanted her to understand what a beautiful place it was and why it held such a special place in my heart. She had been living in Spain during my *Castaway* year and never saw any of the programmes at the time. To introduce her to Taransay was the final piece of the jigsaw puzzle and would be an important way to begin our married life together.

We packed up jackets, wellies, tents, dog beds and, of course, our dogs Maggi and Inca, then edged our way out of London, the new Mr and Mrs Fogle. I have never been so happy, surrounded by my favourite things, heading back to my favourite place in the world. On we rolled through the Midlands, round Birmingham and Manchester. England disappeared in a blur – or maybe I should say England disappeared in the bounce, jolt and hum of my old Land Rover. Soon we had passed Glasgow and were heading along the shores of Loch Lomond, one of the most beautiful roads in the British Isles.

Our first night was to be spent in the tiny community of Glenelg, famous these days for the annual Drams in the Field music festival, which was in full swing when we arrived. Besides music, the festival involves a great deal of drinking and revelry, and it was with aching heads that we departed the next day on the last stretch of our journey to the Hebrides.

The Outer Hebrides are often used as a metaphor for somewhere really far-flung, in much the same way as Timbuktu or Outer Mongolia. They might not be quite as remote, but it certainly requires a lot of effort to reach them. We continued north, past the Kyle of Lochalsh, over the Skye Bridge and across the isle of Skye to the Caledonian MacBrayne Ferry. The Cal Mac, as it is known, plies the choppy waters surrounding the Western Isles and provides a lifeline for islanders. We would be travelling across the Minch to Tarbert on the isle of Harris, from where we would go by boat to Taransay.

I can still say with my hand on my heart that my time as a castaway in the Hebrides was one of the best years of my life. I look back on it with enormously fond memories. I had returned to Taransay twice since leaving the island at the end of the series, but this time was different. I was returning with my wife. I had always longed to have a family of my own, a wife and children. I just never knew how it was going to happen. During that year I had spent so many long evenings walking the island with my dog Inca, wondering how my life was going to turn out, worrying about the future and what it might or might not hold. Never in my wildest dreams did I believe it would take the course described in this book.

It was *Castaway* that changed my life. Nothing would be the same again. But why did I ever apply to be a guinea pig marooned on a treeless, windswept island with a bunch of strangers?

Castaway was the biggest turning point of my life, but it was only luck that I applied in the first place. After university, I found myself a job as picture editor of the society magazine *Tatler* in London's Vogue House. Part of the Condé Nast publishing house, it was full of pretty girls and frocks, but offered little in the way of a future career. I worked as PA to A. A. Gill and alongside Giles Coren, but it seemed like a dead-end job. I wanted more. I wanted wide-open spaces and wilderness.

One day I chanced upon a copy of the *Guardian* in which there was an article about the BBC's plans to create a 'ground-breaking social experiment' to mark the Millennium. They were looking for thirty-six volunteers to be marooned for a year on an island. I must admit that my first thoughts were of tropical islands and bikini-clad girls, but even the revelation that they were actually looking for an island in the Outer Hebrides didn't put me off and I called the BBC to find out how to apply.

I was put on a waiting list and so began the lengthy application process, which lasted the best part of a year: interview after interview, followed by selection weeks and then weekends. They kept us all on tenterhooks as they narrowed down the thousands who had applied.

At the time, in 1999, there was no such thing as 'reality television'. We were entering a brave new world. 'Ob docs' existed, in which cameras followed people in their everyday lives, but this was a whole new ball game, taking ordinary people out of their normal environment and putting them in an alien one . . . for a year.

Though *Castaway* is usually described as 'reality television', in fact I beg to differ. I think it was a pioneering venture into the genre, but it was more than that – it was a social experiment in which the lifestyle came first and the cameras were secondary. No one applied in order to court fame or fortune; we all did it for very innocent reasons.

If you watch the show today, it was an incredibly simple, naive project. A little like me, I suppose. I was in the right place at the right time. There is no way I would have created the career I have had I appeared on *Big Brother* or *Survivor*. For me, *Castaway* was the gateway to a new way of thinking and, more significantly, a new way of life. It gave me the opportunity to find myself. It gave me twelve long months to decide what I wanted to do with my life and where I wanted to take it.

We were never meant to be marooned on Taransay. The BBC, in an unprecedented act of democracy, asked us, the participants, where we wanted to spend the year. They had assumed we would vote for Rona, a small, wooded island nearer to Glasgow, but we voted unanimously for the treeless Taransay. Owned then by the Mackay family, it has traditionally been used for sheep grazing, but for one unique year the island was turned on its head with the arrival of thirty-six strangers.

It was a bold experiment. The goal was to see if we could become a fully self-sufficient, thriving community within a year. We would be required to build our own accommodation, grow our own crops and educate the children, who would also be included in the experiment. There were no fixed cameras fitted across the island following our every move; in fact, there were rarely even any film crews as we filmed the majority of it ourselves. It was like making our own home movie . . . which was then broadcast to nine million people.

The production company responsible for making the series chose an eclectic group of people as castaways: a schoolteacher, a family of Seventh Day Adventists, a Devon doctor and his family, a gay psychotherapist, and a Liverpudlian driving instructor, to name just a few. There were eight children, ranging from two to eleven years old.

We were dropped on the island on 28 December 1999 and weren't due to leave until January 2001, a little over a year later, but just two days after we arrived nearly half the castaways were evacuated from the island for health-and-safety reasons. Taransay had been lashed by the worst storms in twenty years and the families with children were deeply unhappy with the lack of infrastructure.

This was the first sign of a rift that would eventually divide the community in two, creating a separation that remains to this day. We had all been promised different things by the production company. The families had been assured safety, infrastructure and security, while the younger volunteers (myself included) had been promised a real Robinson Crusoe experience. The two systems weren't compatible and the resulting rift affected the whole experiment.

A few turf-roofed 'pods' had been built for us to live in, and the old animal steading had been converted into a dining room and kitchen. We had long-drop loos and a little wind turbine to operate the small bank of cameras that we were all taught to operate. We built a little school to educate the children, and even a slaughterhouse that conformed with EU policy on butchering animals.

We grew vegetables and fruit in three polytunnels, and we reared pigs, cattle and sheep for meat and milk. We kept chickens for their eggs and used seaweed as a fertilizer and peat as fuel. We were an eco-community ahead of our time. We even had a small hydroelectric dam and collected our water from the island lochs.

Each of us gave our particular skills to benefit the community – farmers, doctors, teachers, butchers, plumbers and electricians all used their strengths. Quite what mine was still remains a mystery, though I like to think I brought enthusiasm and diplomacy.

Against the BBC's wishes, we decided from an early stage that we didn't want a leader. We would be a plutocracy. It seemed to work, although the meetings got longer and longer as the year went on. I remember one that lasted a staggering six hours. The problem was that the community was always divided by opinion and it was almost impossible to resolve anything. In retrospect, we probably should have had a leader, but we were hippies at heart.

We didn't have any specific work hours, but we all volunteered to work in different areas. I was on the milking team, which involved early-morning and evening milking in alternate weeks. I loved milking the cows. It still relaxes me, as does baking bread. I *love* baking bread.

Cooking was also a communal effort. The community was divided into cooking groups of four, with each group responsible for cooking lunch and dinner for the whole island. You were free to fend for yourself for breakfasts and at weekends. I dreaded weekends.

There was no TV, no radio, no computers. Mobile phones didn't work and, apart from a satellite phone for emergencies, we were shut off from the outside world . . . except that we weren't. We were only a short distance from the neighbouring island of Harris.

Instead of waiting till the end of the experiment, the BBC chose to start broadcasting the series shortly after we arrived on Taransay, which rather changed the whole dynamic. Suddenly there were more journalists than castaways on the island. Helicopters and boats arrived on a daily basis, ferrying Fleet Street to our shores. All at once we became aware of our own images, and individuals became conscious of their actions. If I could have changed one thing, it would have been not to broadcast anything until the year was over.

Instead, it meant we had visits from Page Three girls sent by the *Sun*. Radio 1 broadcast a live concert by the band Dodgy, who landed on Pig Beach, and whisky and champagne companies began dropping 'gifts' on to our beaches, bringing with them a moral dilemma that further divided our community.

Many people who watched the programmes remember us for our arguments, but that impression couldn't have been further from the reality. True, we were an opinionated bunch and there was obvious friction between the openly gay Ron Copsey and the Seventh Day Adventist Carey family, but on the whole we were a happy group for much of the time. The divisions came later.

We had some very happy times on that little island. Birthdays were celebrated with gifts made from the flotsam and jetsam we found on the beaches and toasted in homemade stinging-nettle wine, while entertainment consisted of singing and language classes. I am smiling as I write this. That's how much I loved it.

On 1 January 2001 we were helicoptered off that island and back into reality. It was a shock to the system, but, though it felt like the end, it was in fact only the beginning.

Shortly before we got married, I got hold of the entire set of *Castaway* films, all thirty of them. I wanted Marina to see it and understand how it is now a part of my DNA. Whatever I do, my year as a castaway will always be a profound presence. It was sad watching those films. Like watching family films of times lost. They didn't make me happy. They didn't even make me nostalgic. They just made me sad. Happy-sad and sad-sad. It is difficult to explain my sentiments. I suppose it is like thinking about someone who has passed away. You smile when you think of the happiness they brought, but then you also have that twang of pain from the separation. I'm not saying I still have that after eleven years, but the psychologist Cynthia McVey, who studied us, likened our departure to a bereavement and it certainly felt like that at the time. Watching the programmes was strange and I haven't seen them since. It is odd seeing your younger self – a reminder of the unstoppable march of time and age, and ultimately of your mortality. Those films are stored away in a drawer for my children, Ludo and Iona, to watch one day.

Now here we were on our honeymoon, rolling our way across the turbulent waters of the Minch, meandering our way back up to Taransay, the new Mrs Fogle following her crazy husband on his island pilgrimage. I love my wife for following my many follies, but I think we both regretted all the whisky the night before.

We rolled off the ferry and on to Tarbert in Harris. It was here that Fleet Street had decamped for the first chaotic months of the experiment.

The project hadn't got off to a good start. The helicopter had dropped four crates of possessions, scattering gay porn across the Presbyterian land. An outbreak of pneumonia had left half the castaways bedbound, while a further contingent had mutinied on the grounds that the island wasn't fit for human habitation.

Three quarters of the castaways and most of Fleet Street ended up sharing the tiny Harris Hotel in Tarbert – predators and prey living cheek by jowl under one roof, sharing the only payphone in the area. Perhaps it helps to date it by the fact that mobile phones still didn't work here in 2000.

The hotel still has a newspaper montage of those crazy months. 'Refuseniks' reads one; '4 Star Castaways' screams another. There are paparazzi photos of the doctor and his family, with his boys Oliver and Felix sticking their tongues out. It is strange how that hotel is almost as much a part of the *Castaway* heritage as the island itself.

'Look,' I marvelled at Marina. 'Look, look, look . . .' I was overcome with emotion. I don't know why it still affects me so profoundly, but I will never, ever forget the day I left that island.

The last few weeks had raced by in a blur of satellite trucks and outside-broadcast crews. The island had been taken over by the BBC for the live Christmas broadcasts. We, the castaways, had become quite territorial about having strangers on our island. Julia Bradbury had been helicoptered in to present the live broadcasts. I still feel sorry for her, landing in the midst of our island politics.

By the end of the year, the islanders were very much divided into two camps. A series of incidents and personalities had forced a wedge between the groups and you could slice the atmosphere with a knife. Somehow I had managed to remain on the fence. I could sympathize with both sides and I loved them all.

The morning of our departure had been planned with military precision. Julia would see us into the helicopter on the island with one crew while another awaited our arrival with a small group of locals and photographers at the other end.

I can still feel the emptiness as the helicopter took off. I can remember the stab to my heart as we soared above the island. I remember a herd of deer rushing across the machair (the unique grassy moorland typical of Scotland), the small loch with our blue water-piping, the raft on the beach, and then the turquoise-blue ocean. My heart ached as we soared across the open water. Tears streamed down my cheeks. I was heartbroken.

I can remember stepping from the chopper, then a flash of bulbs. For me the most moving part of the return were the small huddles of locals who had braved the January elements to stand at their farm gates and wave as the coach made its way back to the Harris Hotel. There had been much suspicion from the local people when we had first arrived, and this was the first time I had felt a warm bond with the community.

Here, journalists and castaways would be reunited one last time. It was where deals were hatched and exclusives sealed. I sold my soul to the *Daily Mail.* I still regret that. I was promised an incremental amount of money depending on how much I told them – I was even shown a 'shopping list', with sums of money for each subject: kissing, sex, blow jobs, orgies, etc. *Castaway* had suddenly lost its innocence. But I hadn't, and the *Mail* never ran my story and I never got paid. Easy come, easy go.

It was here that I had my 'Stephen Fry' moment. I'm not sure if you can really call it that, but I'm sure Stephen won't be offended. It was the moment it all became too much for me and I 'disappeared' with Inca. I woke in the middle of that first night in the hotel and panicked. I don't know what came over me, but I was overwhelmed with the urge to escape. A Land Rover had been loaned to me, so I woke Inca, packed my bags and left without saying goodbye. The next few days remain a blur. I must have worried everyone senseless, but I needed to be on my own. I was overwhelmed by the reality around me and wanted time to reflect.

I don't think anyone missed me too much until I failed to turn up for a live news broadcast, after which I made the news for all the wrong reasons. It was the *News of the World* who first tracked me down in a tiny bed-and-breakfast north of Glasgow. Eventually Paul, one of the producers of the show, came to find me somewhere in the Lake District. It was seeing him that brought me to my senses. He was, after all, almost one of us. He had shared the highs and the lows of that *Castaway* experience and I trusted him implicitly. I had had a few days on my own; now it was time to face the world and return to London. Now, when I think back to it, it seems like a dream. It is one of those periods in my life that feels as though it happened to someone else rather than me.

Marina pulled the overheated Land Rover into the tiny car park on Horgabost beach, where GMTV and breakfast television had based their trucks during the *Castaway* year. A large rusty JCB was at the water's edge and attached to the front was a long floating pontoon that had been hauled into the water by the digger. Angus was waiting in his familiar RIB (rigid inflatable boat).

Angus and his sheepdog had pretty much been our only connection to the outside world, and, in his collie's case, it had become a little too close. One of the castaways had caught him and Inca at it, and Inca was promptly picked up by a helicopter and flown to Stornoway for the morning-after injection. Dogs had been a contentious issue after one of the other bitches had turned out to be pregnant. The community was divided over the number of dogs on the island and a small minority were furious about this new canine invasion. In Inca's case, the producers weren't prepared to allow yet another litter of puppies to ruin a temporary lull in fighting.

Now Inca and Maggi hopped into the RIB, and we loaded our belongings. It was a typically overcast Hebridean summer's afternoon, with a thin drizzle creating a cloak between us and the island. My heart began to pound. What if Marina hated it? What would I do then?

We raced across the azure waters, the dogs tucked into our legs. I looked at Marina and was relieved to see a broad smile on her face. I felt another wave of emotion as the wind turbine came into view. For me the turbine had become a symbol of the year. It represented us and our values. It turned as we turned. It was the lung of our community, and even the whooshing sound of a wind turbine today brings memories flooding back. I always find it strange when people talk of the noise pollution made by wind turbines. For me, they are a catalyst for nostalgia.

Angus pulled the little rubber dinghy up on the rocks and we threw our gear, the dogs and then ourselves on to the slippery surface. With a wave and a 'see you in five days', Angus disappeared and we were on our own. I was back on Taransay.

They say you should never revisit your past; it will only ever lead to disappointment. In some ways, I agree. The geographical landmarks may still be there, but everything else that created that unique moment is lacking: the people, the time, the era, the experience, even your own emotional state of mind. I had been nervous about revisiting Taransay because I didn't want to ruin my memories.

The iconic pods in which we lived have all long gone, so I could only show Marina their footprint, and the remains of the infamous compost loos. But much of our infrastructure did still remain, although several years of winter storms had reduced most of it to skeletal bones. The polytunnels in which we had grown everything from peppers to strawberries had been ripped off their skirtings, leaving them bare and battered. The small bridge across the burn had long since collapsed, as had most of the miles of deer fencing we had installed to keep the hundred or so deer from our crops.

I was moved to see how Inca remembered her way around the island, under gates and over stone walls. She even remembered how to get into the old kitchen in the animal steading. Never let anyone tell you that dogs forget.

I can't explain the feeling of walking around that island. I swear I could hear the voices and laughter of the castaway children as we walked through the deserted remains of our once thriving community. During our year on Taransay there had been a number of supernatural happenings. I never saw anything myself, but the majority of the others, including the workmen, all had ghostly stories to tell. But now it seemed our own history had been added to the island's heritage. I like to think that in a hundred years someone might run into the ghost of a young man walking his black Labrador.

I took Marina to all my favourite places, to all the hidden spots where I would spend hours with Inca, daydreaming about what I wanted to do in life. If I had known then where things were leading,

I'm sure I'd have had an enormous smile on my face. They were happy days – me and my dog, dreaming of the future and only imagining the day I'd fall in love and get married. And here I was, with my new wife and Inca's new best friend.

'So,' I asked, 'what do you think of my island?'

Marina looked around, sighed and then smiled. 'I *love* it,' she beamed. 'I absolutely LOVE it.'

I knew I loved Marina, but in that moment I fell in love with her all over again.

'So when are we going to look at that house in the Falklands?' I asked.

Marina stared at me long and hard.

'Don't push it, Fogle.'

Part Two

5

Hello! East Timor

When I was young I longed to become a travel writer. I can remember reading Bruce Chatwin, Colin Thubron and Paul Theroux and dreaming of my own chances of becoming a writer like them. Little did I realize that my dream would come true, sort of, when I was made travel editor for that most august of literary publications – *Hello!* magazine. Well, you have to start somewhere, don't you?

I had loved my twelve months on Taransay, but staying put in one place for a whole year had only fuelled my appetite for exploring the world again. My itchy feet had returned and I longed to travel.

Shortly after returning home from the island I was invited to Los Angeles by BBC America. *Castaway* had been a hit in the States and half a dozen of us were flown out to Hollywood. We were met at the airport by enormous limousines that shuttled us to the luxury Ritz-Carlton Hotel, where, bizarrely, we were asked to make short TV trails for the series. A greater contrast between environments couldn't exist, but we were happy to play along. The BBC also held a press junket attended by more than two hundred journalists and for a couple of days we felt like Hollywood stars.

Soon after the LA trip, I got my first journalistic assignment when *Glamour* magazine asked me if I'd go to Japan for them, and so it was that I found myself in another busy city exploring capsule hotels and vending machines that, bizarrely, sold used schoolgirls' knickers.

I loved the chance to travel to a new country, but I wanted more. I wanted something to get my teeth into.

Then one day I had a call from my agent. '*Hello!* magazine would like to do an "at home" photo-shoot,' she explained. I'm not sure how I did it, but I managed to turn that offer of a celebrity photo-shoot into a series of adventures that would take me around the world, from the wilds of Zambia to the wretched refugee camps of East Timor.

Phil Hall, the former editor of the *News of the World*, had recently been appointed editor of *Hello!* He was looking to change its content and editorial and he suggested we meet.

'Why don't you become our travel editor-at-large?' he suggested. My face lit up. It was perfect. I was finally going to become a travel writer – of sorts.

I was teamed up with Ken Lennox, former picture editor of the *Sun*. Ken is practically royalty within the red-top photography world. A friendly Scotsman with a huge fund of stories, he became my companion for over a year as we travelled the world for *Hello!* We visited Sweden, Norway, the Falklands, Chile, Bali, Nepal and Zambia together, but the *Hello!* days were marked by one trip in particular – to East Timor.

One of my best friends at university was Jake Morland. We had finally met after being mistaken for one another by most of Portsmouth University, where we were both taking Latin

American Studies, but in different years. We not only looked and sounded similar, but there were also a frightening number of similarities in our lives. We had both spent much of our childhoods in Canada, we had both done our gap years in Latin America, we had both enrolled in the University Royal Naval Unit and we both aspired to work in international aid. The main difference was that Jake fulfilled that dream.

Shortly after graduation, Jake got a job with the United Nations High Commissioner for Refugees (UNHCR). Initially he was based in Geneva, but since then has been deployed all over the world. If there's a disaster, Jake will be there. If there's one person's job I am envious of, it is his. I envy him the fact that he has the ability to change lives; I envy him the fact that he can genuinely make a difference; and I envy him the fact that he gets to be part of history.

And so it was that I persuaded the editor of *Hello!* to send Ken and me to East Timor.

Extreme violence broke out in East Timor, in South-East Asia, in 1999, following a referendum on its future in which 78 per cent of the population voted for independence. East Timor had been under the occupation of Indonesia for the past twenty-five years, ever since it stopped being a Dutch colony. The Indonesian occupation had been brutal and repressive. Pro-integration paramilitary groups began a campaign of threats and violence in 1999 in the build-up to the referendum, and many suspect that they were trained or aided by the Indonesian government. Despite the intimidation, more than three-quarters of the people voted for independence. Immediately after the results were announced the paramilitary violence intensified, with hundreds of people massacred. The majority of the country's infrastructure was ruined, with three out of four buildings destroyed. Around 300,000 East Timorians fled from the violence of the cities to the mountains, while 260,000 were forced across the border into West Timor by the militias.

A number of aid efforts took place in East Timor, including a delegation of British reggae and drum 'n' bass DJs and performers who travelled there in August 2000 to try to entertain the conflict-ravaged population. Performances were held for the resistance leaders, and thousands gathered to see fire-walking, clowning, live music and stilt-walking.

In West Timor the militias' violence was directed against international humanitarian workers. On 6 September 2000, during the funeral procession of a militia leader, the offices of the UNHCR in Atambua were invaded and three UN aid workers were violently killed, their bodies set on fire. Following this came reports that militias were going from house to house, trying to flush out international aid workers, leading the UN to evacuate all its four hundred aid workers and to pull out of West Timor indefinitely, until the safety of its staff could be guaranteed by the Indonesian government. Jake Morland was the UNHCR spokesperson for West Timor, and was safely evacuated to Bali.

Meanwhile the 260,000 East Timorians exiled across the border were forced to live in squalid inadequate refugee camps without sufficient food or sanitation, still under the control of the pro-Indonesian militias.

Getting to East Timor is not easy. We flew to Singapore, then to Denpasar in Bali and finally to Dili, the capital of the war-torn country. In fact, East Timor didn't technically exist. When Ken and I touched down it was still under the control of the UN as the United Nations Transitory Authority of East Timor (UNTAET). The conflict had finished only a few months before our convoy of aid, driven overland from Portsmouth, rolled into town. It was still utter chaos in the city. Troops patrolled the dusty streets with their weapons and much of Dili's infrastructure had been destroyed by the Indonesians, who had 'scorched and burned' as they retreated back into West Timor. I was shocked to see the fresh bullet holes and mortar craters in the ground, but I was most taken aback by the shell-shocked people, still recovering from years of war.

Without any hotels, we were billeted on to a ship that travels the world from disaster to disaster to accommodate visiting press and dignitaries. Jake was living in a converted container within the UN compound. We spent a couple of days in Dili while he made the final plans for the repatriation of refugees from East Timor, which continued until after East Timor was formally declared independent in May 2002.

Jake was responsible for returning the 'forced' refugees who had fled to West Timor, where they had been staying in Indonesian-controlled refugee camps. The Indonesians were doing a great job at spreading propaganda about East Timor and UNTAET. Jake's job was to repatriate those 'exiles' back to their homes and families. I accompanied him on one of those missions. A fleet of Landcruisers headed up to the border with Indonesia, which was under the control of the Australian army. It was a rough area, with large refugee camps on either side and a processing area in the middle.

We would be accompanying several hundred people on the two-day journey back to their families in the highlands of rural East Timor. They were processed before boarding the vast army trucks for the long off-road journey ahead, then for two days we bounced along rutted tracks and roads, until at last we reached their home village. It was a deeply moving experience to witness the reunions between families who had thought they would never see one another again. I felt privileged to witness those emotional scenes and was incredibly proud of Jake for his work. I vowed to do the same as him one day, to help change other people's lives.

During my time with *Hello!* I travelled to Nepal to cover a rhino relocation project with the World Wide Fund for Nature, to the

Falkland Islands and to Bali. I visited the famous ice hotel in Kiruna in Sweden for *Hello!*, and stayed in the most expensive house in the world in Barbados for *Tatler* magazine with the famous travel writer Victoria Mather. The BBC sent me off to Fiji and Chile. It was an incredible year, allowing me to scratch the feet that had grown itchy during my year of isolation on Taransay.

I also visited Africa for the first time when I was sent by *Hello!* to Zambia on safari. It took only a single trip to make me lose my faithfulness to Latin America and find a new love in Africa. I was smitten.

6

How to Charm Worms and Get Ahead in Life

During my time with *Hello!* the BBC asked me if I wanted to have a go at presenting. The then controller of BBC1, Lorraine Heggessey, took me out for lunch and offered me a role as a presenter on the Sunday-morning show *Countryfile.*

If I'm honest, the thing that excited me most was the idea of working with the show's main presenter, John Craven, as in *John Craven's Newsround.* I was really rather star-struck. He had been a part of my childhood with his knitted jumpers and I had even had a signed photograph of him on my bedroom wall. Now I was getting to work with a true living legend. As if that wasn't enough, I would also be working with Michaela Strachan, one of my childhood crushes. Things couldn't get any better.

I reported on all sorts of stories for *Countryfile,* from islands to castles, rivers to national parks, but there was one strand that I enjoyed more than any other: eccentric British competitions.

*

Cheshire is often described as the home of footballers and their WAGs, but while it has an unusually high number of Porsche Cayennes and Bentleys, for me it will always be better known as the home of the World Worm Charming Championship – an event that brought me in front of a disciplinary committee and almost landed me in a BBC tribunal.

As a child I spent most of my summers with my grandparents in Canada at the cottage my grandfather had built on the shores of Lake Chemong, Ontario. I used to love fishing in the lake for fish with exotic-sounding names like pickerel, muskellunge and sunfish, but my grandfather's rules were simple: I had to catch my own bait and eat any fish I caught.

Simple, you might think. Except that I hated the taste of fish.

My grandfather refused to pay CD$1 for a punnet of worms from the petrol station when the garden was full of them for free. You just needed to know how to catch them.

He taught me a number of tricks, from pouring Colman's mustard water down their holes, which always struck me as rather mean (although it did pre-flavour the worm for the fish), to digging them up with a spade; but by far the best way of catching worms was by way of an elaborate hoax.

It began early in the day when we would go around the garden patting the ground with spades to simulate the vibrations of thunder through the soil. Then we would fix up the sprinklers all across the garden and water the lawn as if it were raining. We would wait until nightfall and the worms would appear in droves.

I'm not sure if there is such a thing as a worm psychologist, or whether anyone has ever studied the behaviour of worms, but rain seemed to bring them to the surface. I don't know if they came up for a shower, a drink or a wash, but it worked 100 per cent of the time, and the best thing with Grandpa's technique was that we didn't have to wait till it actually rained.

I can remember the anticipation before a great worm hunt. I

would tingle with excitement as the sun began to set over the lake. In some ways I enjoyed worm-hunting more than fishing, although that is probably because Grandpa didn't make me eat the worms.

As darkness set in and the mosquitoes came out, I would dress in my dark worm-hunting gear – long trousers and shirt to keep the mosquitoes at bay, but always bare feet for extra sensitivity. I would take a torch and fasten a piece of paper towel over the end with a rubber band to filter the light and make it look more like the moon. Then I would grab my worm-pot and head out into the wilderness like a professional hunter.

It was crucial to remain silent. If you had a worm-hunting partner it was vital that you talked in a hushed whisper or you risked scaring off your prey.

I would creep across the damp grass, feeling the thick green blades beneath my feet, holding the torch high above the ground until I caught sight of my quarry. The first sign was a weak reflection of light, a glimpse of a shiny brown back hidden within the grassy jungle. My heart would start pounding.

It was all about technique and style. You had to creep up on the worm and catch it unawares, or it would simply disappear back into the earth and the haven of its hole. So I would hold the torch away and silently crouch down close to the ground, my bucket behind me, the torch in my left hand and my right hand limbering up for the snatch. Timing . . . timing . . . timing . . .

Heart still racing, I would bring my right hand close to the soil a couple of inches above the worm's estimated location. Then slowly I would turn the torchlight back towards the ground. I didn't think worms had eyes, so I'm not sure why I was so worried about the light, but it was all part of the hunt.

There it was: a big, fat, juicy brown worm, hidden just below the grass with a good inch or two of body visible.

I would place my thumb and forefinger together like

chopsticks, practise opening and closing them a couple of times and . . . *snatch*! Like lightning my fingers would clamp around the slippery body before the worm had time to react.

And here's what separates the men from the boys. Pull too hard and the worm will snap. Squeeze too hard and the worm will snap. Loosen the squeeze too much and the worm will slip from your fingers back into the hole.

Believe it or not, worms kick up a pretty good fight and they are surprisingly strong. So once I had it between my fingers, the real struggle would begin. The worm would pull and I would hold my position. As soon as the worm stopped struggling, I would pull very, very gently until it began to struggle once again. It's a little like a tug-of-war. One side pulls and makes some distance, but then the other side pulls harder and they lose it again. This back-and-forth struggle could sometimes last a couple of minutes. Sometimes the worm would tire and give in; sometimes I would lose my grip and the worm would live to fight another day; and sometimes the worm broke in half, which was disappointing for both of us, although probably more so for the worm.

The pile of worms in my bucket would grow as I won fight after fight. Occasionally I would feel the slimy surface of a body underfoot as I inadvertently stepped on one. I can remember the excitement of catching a worm between my toes, much to Grandpa's delight. That almost made me a professional.

At the end of the night, with my bucket groaning under the weight of my haul, I would march into the cottage like a soldier returning from battle. Everyone would have to peer into my bucket and comment accordingly.

But best of all was the 'count'. No worm-hunting expedition was complete until every worm had been counted and the total compared to previous hauls. I would place some old newspaper on the floor in front of Grandma's rocking chair, where she

Top left: Standing in the autumn leaves with my younger sister Tamara in 1979. These London squares were my little windows to the natural world.

Top right: London, 1980. My first competitive race. I was seven years old and came second.

Left: Enjoying the sunshine with my father, Bruce, in his native Canada.

On an early family holiday in Florida with my ubiquitous fishing rod.

I loved fishing. Here I am on Lake Chemong in Canada, where I spent summers at my grandparents' wooden cottage.

An early attempt at rowing in an inflatable dinghy in Canada.

Emily, Tamara, me and my mother posing for one of many newspaper and magazine photographs. As a child it seemed quite natural to come home from school and take part in a photo shoot.

Aboard the biscuit boat on my 3,000-mile journey up the Amazon. This photo gives you a glimpse of hammock life on the cramped boat.

I could be anywhere in the world in this photograph, but in fact I was at the summit of Cotopaxi (6,000m), higher than I had ever been. It was a moment to treasure before we got into trouble on the descent.

Above: With Lonesome George, the famous tortoise, in the Galapagos Islands. My father came out to Ecuador and we explored the Galapagos together for two weeks. My hair got even longer as the year progressed.

Left: On the steps of Tikal in Guatemala. It must rate as one of the most impressive ancient sites in the world. I slept illegally atop one of the temples and it was magical to wake to the sound of monkeys and parrots.

Above: I'm so proud of this photograph of me in my uniform (back row, third from right) at Britannia Royal Naval College in Dartmouth, where I spent several summers training.

Below: Midshipman Fogle aboard HMS *Blazer* in the Norwegian Fjords. I was constantly being told to cut my hair but I valued my individuality. Perhaps it's one of the reasons why I never joined the Navy.

This was taken shortly after I proposed to Marina. We are on our first weekend away together in Holkham in Norfolk; it is an incredibly beautiful place.

Marina on the beach on Taransay with Inca and Maggi during our honeymoon. The Outer Hebrides, to me, are the most beautiful place on earth. The colours of the ocean are spectacular.

Above: I never knew how much I could love something until Ludo came along. We're like a little team and it's so much fun carrying him around in his backpack.

Below: The hills are alive with the sound of the Fogles. In Salzburg, Austria, where we spend our summers. Marina has the most incredible collection of dirndls and I am now the proud owner of a pair of lederhosen, as is Ludo.

would be knitting, and dump the writhing pile of slime on to the floor before picking each one up and counting them all.

One, two, three, four, five, five and a half (I used to count the halves, as two counted as a whole worm and increased my chances of a world record – or a Fogle record at least). My record was 277 worms.

Once counted, they would be decanted into smaller margarine containers with holes and earth. There were dozens of them stacked in the fridge. I pity anyone who didn't know us delving into our fridge for some margarine. They would have got quite a shock.

I can still recall the smell and feeling of those worm-hunting expeditions. They make me incredibly nostalgic. I miss my grandpa. He taught me a great deal during those long Canadian summers.

Which made me the perfect competitor for the Silver Jubilee World Worm Charming Championship. I wanted to make my grandfather proud.

The World Worm Charming Championships have been held annually near Willaston in Cheshire since July 1980 when a local farmer's son, Tom Shufflebotham, successfully charmed 511 worms out of the ground in thirty minutes. The championship's eighteen rules are strictly enforced by the International Federation of Charming Worms and Allied Pastimes (IFCWAP), a body that also regulates such sports as underwater Ludo and indoor hang-gliding. The World Worm Charming record was last broken in 2009 by ten-year-old Sophie Smith, whose team successfully charmed 567 worms to the surface, breaking Tom Shufflebotham's twenty-nine-year record.

There was one problem. The rules stipulated that worms had to be charmed without the aid of any products or of water. How could you get worms without water? What's more, you weren't allowed to pierce the ground. I fumed as I read the rules.

We were each given a square metre of ground that had been carefully marked out with ropes and we had an hour to charm as many worms as we could to the surface. The most popular technique was 'twanging', which involved planting a pitchfork into the soil and then rocking, hitting or twanging it. The movement sends reverberations down into the soil so that the worm thinks it's raining.

Raining! Grandpa was right. A huge smile drifted across my face, although I was still disappointed I couldn't use any water.

Other less orthodox approaches have also been adopted at the Worm Charming Championships, including playing rock guitar or the xylophone, or even tap-dancing to the *Star Wars* theme. Some competitors have employed more unscrupulous tactics, such as hiding worms up their trouser legs or chopping them in half to double their number – practices certainly in contravention of the IFCWAP's strict guidelines.

After seeking local advice I headed down into town to stock up on provisions. I bought my worm bucket, a small set of bells, a child's trumpet, a tambourine, a toy car, a tin whistle, a pitchfork and an alarm clock. I'm not sure why I chose these specific items, but I was sure as hell going to use them.

I returned to a carnival of worms. There were children dressed as worms, dads dressed in army camouflage, and worm-charming contraptions that would have made Caractacus Potts envious. There were bicycles mounted on blocks with the rear wheel removed and replaced by two sticks with boots on each end. As the bicycle was pedalled, the boots thumped alternately against the ground – 'Like thunder,' smiled the inventor. There were old lawnmowers that had been adapted, Heath Robinson-style, to 'twang' the soil with each movement; and my personal favourite was a stereo, its speakers facing the ground, playing various 'rain' songs.

I gathered my 'tools' and headed into the worming arena. This is it, I thought. My whole life of worming had been building up to this, the ultimate accolade, the World Championship. I had striven all my life to find something I was good at, something I could excel at, and this had to be it. If I couldn't win this, I couldn't win anything.

I stepped into the ring and sat cross-legged on my patch, planning my tactics. I eyed up the competition. There were nearly a hundred competitors.

'Focus, Ben.'

'. . . five, four, three, two, one.' Brrrrrrrrrrrrrrrrrrrrr! The claxon sounded.

I knelt on the dry grass, picked up the tambourine and started tapping it rhythmically against the ground. Nothing.

Next I took the tin whistle, placed the end to the soil and blew furiously. Nothing.

I jangled the bells and tooted on the plastic trumpet. Still nothing.

Every so often a cheer would go up as a worm was extracted from the ground. 'How on earth are they charming them?' I fumed.

I patted the ground with the tambourine and blew again on the tin whistle. As desperation set in, I resorted to a bizarre rain dance in the hope of natural precipitation that would return me to my familiar childhood worming environment.

The cheers picked up pace. I seemed to be the only one *not* catching worms.

'I thought you said you were good,' chuckled the director. If she wasn't careful I'd use her as bait.

'Think, Ben, think,' I berated myself. 'Get in the head of a worm.'

I lay flat on the ground and held my hands to my mouth. 'Worms!' I called. 'Here, worms. Worms!' Nothing.

Just as despair was beginning to set in, I caught a glimpse of something. A flicker of brown. It was the unmistakable body of a *worm*. I froze, my heart starting to pound. My childhood came flooding back. I could have sworn Grandpa appeared in the sky to guide me. Slowly, I lowered my hand. I practised the chopstick movement with my thumb and forefinger and ... *snatch*! I snapped at the ground. My fingers locked around its body, but it was thin, really thin. Too thin. Posh Spice dictated not just the waist size of Chester's WAGs but also of its worm population.

I had overestimated the power of my squeeze and the worm snapped in two, leaving me with a writhing half worm between my fingers.

'You killed it!' berated the director with a smile.

'It's not dead, it's doubled,' I corrected her before placing it in the bucket. At least I was off to a start. The problem was that there was only half an hour left and, by the sound of cheering and hollering, my fellow competitors had more than half a worm.

The clock ticked by and I tried some pitchfork twanging. Miraculously, worms began to appear. They were small and skinny, but they were worms none the less.

One, two, three, four, five – the pile began to mount until the claxon sounded once again, marking the end of the competition.

'Right, time to count the slippery little suckers,' I said to the camera before disappearing to the counting station where marshals were waiting to go through our hauls.

'Well done. You have seven worms,' announced my counter.

'It's more than that,' I corrected her.

'No, it isn't,' she said, holding out the bucket.

'What about that?' I asked, pointing to a worm in the corner.

'That's half a worm,' she said.

'So it's seven and a half worms,' I reasoned.

'No, it's seven. We don't count halves.'

'Why not?' I asked, genuinely miffed.

'Animal cruelty,' she said, without a hint of irony.

The weigh-in complete, it was time for the announcement. The tension in the field was palpable.

'The winner of the World Worm Charming Championship is Leon Holt, with two hundred and ninety-six worms.'

Two hundred and ninety-six! I nearly choked. Two hundred and ninety-six without water, in daylight. This ten-year-old had trounced my Canadian record. I couldn't even win at worming. My dream of world dominance had been shattered. My worming days were over.

And that was the end. Or so I thought, until the show went out a couple of weeks later.

'A complaint has been lodged with the BBC,' warned my agent. I was puzzled. 'Was it for animal cruelty?' I asked.

'It's for inappropriate language,' she explained.

'Inappropriate language' – what did that mean? I never swear. Apart from getting into trouble for saying I was 'knackered' during a coracle race shown on a Sunday morning, I was usually accused of being too prudish. It's a joke among friends that I never swear – and yet here I was with a formal complaint against me.

'The complainant,' began the report, 'alleged that during a *Countryfile* report on the Silver Jubilee World Worm Charming Championship, Ben Fogle said, "It's now time to count the slippery little fuckers."'

On a pre-recorded, Sunday-morning programme? But the complainant had it in for me, and although the BBC replied that I had in fact said 'slippery little suckers', the viewer was not satisfied and took the matter to the head of complaints. The head replied that 'throughout the worm charming the sound quality was less than perfect and there was a loss of sibilants; however, the phrase "slippery little suckers" had an alliteration which the alternative lacked'. The viewer was still not satisfied and took it to the governors' Complaints Committee.

And so it was that the board of BBC governors were forced to watch me taking part in the Silver Jubilee Worm Charming Championship and concluded that I had indeed said 'slippery little suckers'.

I may not have won the Worm Charming Championship, but I had made it to the BBC board of governors, and not many people can claim that. Success of a sort? At least I'd registered on the radar of those high above.

'I caught crabs in Walberswick', reads my favourite T-shirt. It dates from 2005, when I took part in the World Crabbing Championship in the Suffolk coastal town.

It was the first and last time Marina ever came with me on one of my filming assignments. We decided to make a weekend of it with the dogs. I thought it sounded rather romantic.

The last time I had been crabbing had been as a young boy with my maternal grandfather, Dick. He and my grandmother, Jean, lived just outside Brighton and we used to spend weekends fishing for crabs among the rock pools along the coast. I remember taking them back to my grandparents' cottage in a bucket of water. I was mesmerized by them. I would keep them for a day before my grandfather insisted we take them back to the rock pools. Both of my grandfathers always insisted on a healthy respect for nature.

Now, nearly twenty-five years later, I was crabbing again.

The Walberswick crabbing has become something of an institution, attracting thousands of spectators as well as hundreds of competitors. Crabbers have ninety minutes, armed with a single line and bait of their choice, and the person landing the heaviest crab wins. The bait is the key to success.

Marina, the dogs and I rolled up in my old Land Rover and set up our little crabbing spot on a steep bank next to the tidal estuary. It was one of our first dates together and I was determined to impress Marina with my crabbing prowess. I had to bag the trophy to bag the girl.

I had done a little research into bait and discovered that bacon and sausages were the most popular, while bread was the next favourite choice. My secret weapon was Marmite and cheesecake. All I had to do now to impress Marina was catch the biggest crab.

The starting gun fired and a thousand lines with their secret baits dipped into the murky waters. I smeared some Marmite on to the cheesecake, crossed my fingers and waited.

There was a flurry of excitement as each crab was plucked from a line and into a waiting bucket of water.

'Haven't you caught anything?' asked a small boy, peering into our empty bucket.

I shrugged and watched as he walked back to his father with his bucket full of crustaceans. I did a double-take as I realized his dad was the film director Richard Curtis. This could be even more humiliating than I originally thought.

For ninety long minutes I dangled my Marmite-smeared cheesecake in the murky water. The problem was that the saturated cheesecake kept disintegrating in the water, leaving only the tiniest morsel on the line.

All around me families and children were hauling in monster crabs while my bucket remained conspicuously empty. Marina wasn't looking impressed.

Finally, as the clock ticked down to the finishing time, I hauled a microscopic crab up from the depths and into my bucket. It was so small that the water in the bucket surrounded it like an ocean.

Perhaps unsurprisingly, my special bait failed to win the prize. I was beaten by just about everyone, including Richard Curtis. The shame.

The sky was a palette of greys that melted into the gunmetal ocean. The sun burst through a small gap in the clouds, momentarily illuminating the water. Seagulls circled overhead, their cawing drowned out by the cacophony of clinking halyards against yacht masts. A flag snapped in the brisk breeze. The cobblestones glistened from a recent downpour, sparkling against the grey-and-white world around.

A medieval castle loomed up from the waters, a reminder of more turbulent times, while a flotilla of dinghies and rowing boats, tethered to the harbour wall like loyal dogs, waited to ferry their owners to their boats and ships. A small fleet of fishing boats was unloading its catch.

It was early in the morning, but already the small castellated harbour was a hive of activity, as hundreds of people started to crowd against the harbour wall. Bright yellow sou'westers and red Gore-tex added a splash of colour to the dank scene.

Nervously, I made my way to the water's edge. The tide was low and the waves lapped against the concrete ramp. Gingerly I slid my feet along the slimy surface to avoid slipping on the coating of green algae. I used the super-glued barnacles as footholds as I made my way down, clenching my teeth tightly as my bare toes kissed the frigid waters. Clutching my paddle, I gently lowered myself into the small vessel and wedged myself in with my knees against the gunwales. My legs were shaking with the cold as I edged out into the chilly Irish Sea.

The crowd had grown, as thousands descended on the small harbour for this sporting spectacular. Here I was, just back from rowing across the Atlantic Ocean with James Cracknell, and by association I had become the hot favourite to win. I think they had mistaken me for a crack oarsman and I distinctly heard chants of 'Ben, Ben, Ben . . .' Gingerly I paddled my way to the start line. My heart was pounding. A news helicopter circled above, while film crews and photographers bobbed around in small boats. I spotted the familiar faces of Jeremy Clarkson and A. A. Gill in the crowd. Gill caught my eye and winked.

Several dozen competitors were lined up, muscles flexed in tight vests, steely determination glinting in eyes. Next to me a tall, lean man practised his stroke.

I was competing against some of the best. Many had spent years training and planning for this unique event. As always, I just seemed to have turned up at the last moment. I stared straight ahead.

The claxon sounded. The start of a race is like the opening salvo of battle. It is the moment friends become foes. All focus is on winning at all costs. The noise of clanking halyards and the roar of the crowd was drowned out by the silence of my focus; it is like being submerged under water: noises are muffled as the adrenalin floods through the body and fills the ears.

I speared my paddle into the grey surf, scooped at the water furiously. Left, right, left, right, left, right . . . I was mesmerized by the rhythm. The water turned white as dozens of paddles whipped it into a cappuccino froth of bubbles. I was neck and neck with the leader of the pack and making good headway, but then I seemed to start slowing down. Something was very wrong. With each scoop of the paddle, water rushed over the gunwales and into my vessel. I pulled more carefully at the paddle, but still great waves of water overwhelmed my craft and the bow was dangerously close to the waterline. I leaned back to counterbalance, but now the sea was pouring into the stern. Water lapped around my ankles, then my knees. I scooped it with my hands and tried to bail as fast as I could. It was no good. Before I knew it, I began to tumble backwards, my knees lost their grip against the side and my hands were thrown into the air as my vessel and I flipped upside down. I felt a rush of salty water up my nostrils as I tumbled into the icy Irish Sea. I could hear the crowd and their gales of laughter over the water as I clung desperately to my vessel to stop it sinking.

I was in the middle of Peel Harbour on the Isle of Man in the annual World Tin Bath Championship. I was racing against firemen and farmers, doctors and bankers, all competing in their 'pimped-up' tin baths. My 'pimping' had involved a lick of green paint, which was already beginning to chip and peel. My craft, like me, was starting to fall apart and somehow I'd managed to sink ten seconds into the race.

I hauled the bath to the harbour wall and clung on to the metal rung of a ladder. I emptied out the water and gently lowered myself back into the tiny vessel. I have a mental discipline at times like this which makes me talk to myself. 'Focus, Ben,' I berated myself as I tried to catch up. Left, right, left, right.

'Come on, Ben, you rowed the Atlantic!' hollered a local. But something was wrong. Once again I was scooping too much water into the bath, and before I knew it I was in the water again. There was another roar of laughter.

It is moments like this that plunge me helplessly back to my childhood and my constant failure to achieve anything. I hauled myself back to the harbour wall. I could hear the chanting of the crowd. My cheeks were flushed with embarrassment as once again I clambered aboard the tiny bath. If there's one thing I have learned over the years it is that stubbornness is a very powerful trait. It has served me well.

Once again I dipped my paddle into the water. Far ahead of me, most of the baths had finished. I was a child again, paddling alone. It was only a few hundred metres but it felt like an ocean. I limped home, the last over the line. Humiliated and defeated.

I dragged my tin bath up the slipway to more laughter from the crowd. A wave of nausea overwhelmed me as I staggered forwards. The world began to spin and my vision narrowed to a pinhole before I passed out.

'Ben? Ben?' It seemed as if people were still chanting my name, only this time it was two concerned-looking paramedics. I had come to in an ambulance, confused and disoriented. I was swaddled in a foil blanket and hooked up to a heart-rate monitor. I had collapsed from hypothermia. That could have been a perfect excuse for coming last in the race, except for the fact that it was the middle of summer, children were paddling in the same water and I was very publicly about to head to Antarctica to take part in the first race to the South Pole since Scott and Amundsen a hundred years before . . .

When *Countryfile* sent me to take part in the World Oyster Eating Championship in 2004 it wasn't my first foray into the world of competitive eating.

When I was at university I joined the Royal Naval Reserves and became an honorary officer on our ship, HMS *Blazer*, and all this before I could even tie a bowline. We would spend weekends and holidays aboard our little ship on deployments all around the British Isles and often beyond.

I was still in the Royal Navy when HMY *Britannia* was finally decommissioned and I was responsible for helping to escort her into Portsmouth for her final voyage. I have a photograph of *Blazer* on *Britannia*'s port bow, with thousands of wellwishers in the background. You can just make out my officer's cap on the flying bridge. I was so proud.

It was while I was an honorary midshipman officer for the Royal Navy that I found myself in Weymouth Harbour in Dorset during the annual World Oyster Eating Championship. I had always had a reasonable appetite, priding myself on being able to eat a whole loaf of sliced white bread for dinner and being able to finish a whole packet of chocolate HobNobs in one minute. How hard could oysters be?

I ended up eating sixty-seven oysters and winning the competition with its prize of a holiday for two to St Malo (where I tried to save a drowning man who turned out to be attempting suicide; he punched me while I tried to rescue him and we both ended up in the ambulance).

Now, as a *Countryfile* presenter, the opportunity arose to show the nation my prowess. Hillsborough in Northern Ireland was the location for that year's World Oyster Eating Championship and I was determined to win again and improve on my Weymouth score.

The rules of the competition were simple. No pre-picking of the oysters from the shells and no condiments (Tabasco, vinegar or lemon). You had to slurp each oyster off the shell as quickly as possible. The person to have consumed the most oysters in five minutes would be declared the winner.

My competition looked impressive. There was someone who resembled a Japanese sumo wrestler, a professional Mexican competitive eater, and some rather rotund Brits. We stepped on to the stage before an audience of thousands and enormous plates of oysters were placed in front of each of us.

When the claxon sounded I began sucking the slimy oysters off the shells, building up five or six at a time before swallowing. With each slurp I would take in bits of grit and shell which slowly began to accumulate at the back of my throat.

Twenty, twenty-one, twenty-two . . . On I slurped.

As I reached the fiftieth oyster I could feel bile rising in my throat. I began to sweat profusely. I looked out at the crowd and then at the film cameras all around. I couldn't vomit now. Not in front of all these people and certainly not on national television. I fought against the urge. My head was spinning, but I was determined to carry on.

Sixty-seven, sixty-eight, sixty-nine . . . I was already ahead of my Weymouth total. The clock was ticking, but I still had time.

Blood trickled from my mouth where the sharp shells had cut me in my haste. Thick tentacles of oyster goo dripped from my chin as I continued to slurp them down. One bad oyster here and it would be game over.

Eighty-five, eighty-six, eighty-seven, eighty-eight ...
Brrrrrrrrrrrrrrrrrrrrrrr!

The race was over. I dragged my arm across my mouth to wipe away the bloody slime. The crowd went crazy.

'Ladies and gentlemen,' announced the compère, 'we have a new world champion.'

I crossed my fingers and prayed for glory. This could be it. My chance to be a world champion.

'The winner ... eating two hundred and twenty-one oysters ... is Oki Wei from Japan!'

And with that my dreams of oyster-eating glory came crashing down. They disappeared down the toilet pan (literally).

Contrary to popular belief, I did not feel horny. Quite the opposite – I would argue the oysters acted as a contraceptive. It took me three years to eat another.

But that wasn't the end of my competitive eating. Oh no. I wasn't going to concede that easily, and so it was that a couple of months later I headed down to Marshwood in Dorset to the famous Bottle Inn for one of the most unusual spectacles in Britain – the World Stinging Nettle Eating Championship.

Stinging nettles have historically been used to relieve numerous ailments. In ancient Egypt nettle infusions were made to treat arthritis and lumbago, while the Romans, particularly the soldiers, advocated the practice of urtification (flogging oneself with fresh nettles) in order to stimulate circulation in tired legs. Some North American indigenous communities have tradition-ally encouraged pregnant women who are at term to chew nettles to stimulate birth, and also to chew the plant during labour itself to relax the joints; however, many medical authorities do not recommend the use of nettle medications by pregnant or nursing women.

Currently the nettle is commonly employed in a range of

herbal remedies. It is sold in Germany to combat prostate dis-
orders (including prostate enlargement) and as a diuretic. It can
also be used to relieve allergies, particularly hayfever, as it is
thought to reduce histamine production and have anti-
inflammatory properties. The nettle can also be made into a
poultice to stop bleeding, and can be used to deal with nose-
bleeds. Although stinging nettles tend to be known for causing
more harm than good, they can be made into a syrup and used to
treat nettle rash.

On Taransay, we created a mini distillery where we produced
stinging-nettle wine. It was pretty potent stuff – just a couple of
swigs were enough to leave you on all fours howling at the moon
like a dog.

For the World Championship in Marshwood, a huge medieval
banqueting table had been set out on the lawn of the pub along
which the thirty competitors would be seated for the competition. Stems of nettles had been harvested from the field and
vast piles had been placed next to each seat. The rules were
simple. You had an hour to eat as many nettles as possible. The
finally tally was done not in individual leaves but in yards of
nettles. Each stem had to be picked clean of even the smallest leaf
or it wouldn't count, and given that stems averaged about twenty
leaves each, that would be a lot of wasted eating.

The tactics were simple. You would grab the leaf with your bare
hands and fold it as quickly as possible into a neat little parcel
with the stinging hairs on the inside. This reduced the stinging,
which largely affected the fingers.

Drinking was encouraged.

Hundreds of spectators had descended on this remote corner
of Dorset as I pitted myself against the world's finest – and Chris
Packham, the TV wildlife presenter. I'm not really sure why
Chris was there, but then I'm sure he was asking the same about
me. Whatever his reasons, here was my chance to beat him.

A flag was raised to signal the start of the competition and I began neatly folding each leaf and carefully placing it on my tongue, then chewing on it as quickly as possible before swallowing. It was the same technique I use on Brussels sprouts at Christmas.

It wasn't long before my fingers were numb from stings, as were my lips from rogue stinging hairs that attacked me before I could eat them. My lips began to swell and, rather worryingly, my tongue went black, but onwards I munched, with one eye on Packham.

The bare, plucked stems began to pile up next to me as I munched my way through the nettles. It wasn't long before we were given a half-time warning.

A very large Dorset farmer next to me had been wolfing down an impressive number of leaves and his pile of stripped stems was positively towering, when I noticed him burp. His hand raced to his mouth, but it was too late and he vomited up the leaves – into an empty pint glass.

Everything stopped. It was like walking into a strange country pub where the music stops and everyone turns. There was silence. He looked slightly embarrassed through his green hue. He glanced around. Rules are rules. If you vomit up the leaves, then they don't count. So he drank his own vomit.

There was a loud cheer as everyone returned to the competition. I have to take my hat off to that man. He went on to win the competition, beating my twenty yards. But I beat Packham, which in some warped way was victory enough.

I felt rough for days.

Over the years on *Countryfile* I took part in the Burning Barrels festival in Ottery St Mary, in Up Helly Aa in Shetland, in Cornwall's famous Furry Dance, and in the World Conker Championship. I competed in the World Lawn Mower

Racing Championship, the World Coal Carrying Championship and the World Toe Wrestling Championship.

I loved these challenges. They stirred in me an inner competitiveness that had always remained dormant. I liked the humour and tradition, but secretly I enjoyed the thrill of the chase. I may have been hopeless at most of them, but they awakened something in me and I wanted more. I wanted to prove myself. If I couldn't win at worm charming or crabbing, perhaps there was something I *could* win. I just needed to find it.

7

Mad Dogs and Englishmen

Drunken bets are never a good idea. I have found myself in a number of pickled-induced pickles over the years, but this had to be the drunken brag to beat all drunken brags: 'I could easily run a hundred and fifty miles across the Sahara Desert,' I slurred. I was on my fifth pint of Greene King, which had obviously numbed my senses and memory enough for me to forget the fact that I had never run in my life. A bet is a bet, though, so, never one to break a promise, the next day I called the event organizers of the 2004 Marathon des Sables to book a place.

The MDS, as it is known, has grown into a mythical thing over the years. It has become a rite of passage for many and attracts masochists the world over. It is an event to make grown men weep and endurance runners shudder.

The 151-mile (243-kilometre) race across the Sahara Desert in southern Morocco is often described as the toughest footrace on earth – six marathons back to back across one of the driest, hottest, most inhospitable places on earth. Dehydration, sunstroke, scorpions, blisters, heat exhaustion, sandstorms, getting lost and poisonous spiders are just some of the hazards of the desert. The race is also entirely self-sufficient: runners have to carry their own food, sleeping bag, cooking utensils, clothing and emergency equipment in packs weighing up to twenty kilos.

The course is divided into six stages that include wadis, mountains and strength-sapping dunes – but, mostly, vast expanses of remorseless, scorched, blistering Saharan flatlands. The crippling terrain is worsened by the epic sandstorms that blow up out of nowhere. With a total absence of water in the air, sweat evaporates. Instantly. Perhaps unsurprisingly, only about half of those who enter finish the race. And I was just about to volunteer myself to run it. Oops . . .

'Hello, I'd like a place in next year's Marathon des Sables,' I announced with trepidation down the phone.

'I'm afraid we're fully booked. We could put you on the waiting list,' replied the organizer.

'How many are on the waiting list?' I asked.

'About a thousand,' she replied. Wow, there must have been a *lot* of drunk people out there, I thought to myself as I punched the air in victory.

'Oh, that's a shame,' I lamented and hung up. I'd kept my word, and saved my legs.

It's amazing how quickly six months can pass, particularly when it includes a birthday, Christmas and the New Year. As the days slipped by, so the inches grew on my waist. I've never been one to diet, and had always shied away from exercise, partly because the schedule and hours of my unconventional job rarely allowed for it (or so I reasoned).

I was working down at Longleat for the BBC series *Animal Park* when the call came through, and had my arm up a cow's bottom.

'Congratulations!' announced a female voice. Congratulations for what, I wondered – had I won the Lottery? Or maybe the BBC had given me a promotion to *Cash in the Attic* or *Escape to the Country*?

'A thousand people have dropped out and you have a place in this year's MDS,' she said.

'Wow!' I feigned delight. 'Why did so many people drop out?'

'Oh, mainly injury . . .' she replied.

I could tell she was smiling. *I* wasn't. I was standing in the middle of a Wiltshire field with an arm covered in dung and I'd just found out I had a place in the toughest footrace on earth.

Before I even had time to digest what she was saying, I was working out the maths. It's the end of January and the race is in April. That gives me less than twelve weeks to train. OMG.

I have never been a member of a gym. I have always found them smelly, guilty places. Guilty that you aren't training enough if you don't go and not training hard enough if you do. It has always seemed a win-win for the gym – they take your money to make you feel sweaty and bad, or guilty and bad. But now seemed as good a time as any to join, so I went along to my local centre and signed up for a three-month membership. Any longer seemed superfluous to needs. After all, I would probably be dead by then.

'How can I help you, mate?' smiled a fitness instructor as I stood in my brand-new trainers and running gear, feeling hopelessly out of my depth.

'I need to train for a race in twelve weeks' time,' I explained.

'No worries. Is it the Hyde Park ten-k?' he asked.

I shook my head.

'You're not going to try for a half marathon in just three months, are you?' He shook his head worryingly.

When I announced my plan he refused to train me on the grounds that when I died he would be held culpable.

It looked like I was on my own.

I've always enjoyed a challenge, but to date it had usually

involved something like moving to an island for a year, or to South America for a year. I've always needed a task, something to work towards and also, if I'm honest, to talk about. Something to give me a sense of purpose. But this time I was worried that I had bitten off more than I could physically chew.

'I'm going to run a hundred and fifty miles in six days,' I explained to my parents.

'But you can't run,' they replied, looking worried. They had me there.

'I'm going to run across the Sahara Desert,' I bragged to Kate Humble, my co-presenter on *Animal Park*.

'But you don't even run,' she said. 'I'm the one who gets up early and takes *your* dog for a run.' She too had a point.

Even my doctor looked worried when I went to him for the mandatory blood checks and ECG that the organizers required to ensure runners wouldn't be dropping dead along the course.

I had to start somewhere, so I ran around Lord Bath's safari park. It wasn't long before my breathing became slow and laboured. My legs felt heavy and my head light. Sweat was beading down my scarlet face as I puffed and panted. I looked at my watch. I'd been going for ten minutes! This wasn't going to be easy.

For twelve long weeks I rose early and ran loops around Hyde Park when I was in London and the safari park when I was at Longleat. The desert seemed so far from reality that at times it felt like some hideous dream.

The Marathon des Sables was started over twenty years ago by Patrick Bauer, a former concert promoter from Troyes in France, who created the race after he got lost and walked two hundred miles alone across the Algerian Sahara in 1984. He found the experience so harsh yet so uplifting that he decided to make it an annual event. The first MDS was run in 1986 and today the event attracts a thousand runners from all across the world, 250 of whom come from the UK.

I had first heard about the race when Chris Moon, the army disposal amputee, had run it in the mid-1990s. I had been fascinated by photographs of the runners, covered against the harsh desert sun, racing across dunes.

At this stage I should probably admit that I am naturally rather lazy. An extra hour in bed is a much more attractive option than an early run. It was a daily battle against my lazy demons to get as much training and running as I could under my belt before the race. But one-hour runs became two-hour runs, and before I knew it I was running for three or four hours at a time. I became obsessed; my life revolved around my training routine. My social life disappeared as my existence became one long run. I was the Forrest Gump of Wiltshire. Farmers would wave from their tractors as I jogged down muddy country lanes, through fields and past farms, but England was no substitute for the harsh realities of the Sahara.

Rumours circulated about other people's training regimes. I heard stories of eighty-mile runs and of competitors exercising on running machines in saunas. I heard of people wearing six layers of clothing to increase the heat as they ran, and even of some runners jetting off to Egypt at weekends for training camps. I had to make do with circuits around the lion enclosure.

I couldn't sleep the night before the race. What if I didn't finish it? Think of the humiliation! I had told just about everyone of my plans and there was no backing out now. I was to have the same feeling a couple of years later when I took part in the Atlantic Rowing Race. Both James Cracknell and I fell into a great depression shortly after setting out on the three-thousand-mile crossing. We were both terrified of the humiliation of failure. Just as I would experience then, the expectations were that I didn't stand a chance in the Marathon des Sables. It's an interesting dilemma for someone so fearful of failure, but as I have experienced time and time again, if you don't try, you'll never know.

All the British competitors were booked on a charter flight to Ouarzazate in the south of Morocco. The two hundred and fifty runners gathered at Gatwick airport, a mixture of army marines, endurance athletes, general hard-arse types and me, a daytime presenter with soft calves and a perma-tan. I felt hopelessly out of my depth.

'How much sugar you packin'?' asked a stranger. What did he mean? Was this some bizarre reference to drugs? Had I somehow got myself involved in some drug-smuggling crime syndicate under the guise of 'world's toughest race'? Maybe it got its name because we would all end up doing time in some stinking Moroccan jail?

I soon learned that he actually meant sugar. My nutritional packing had been minimal. As in a couple of packs of Rolos and some jammy dodgers – kind of basic.

'Sugar,' I worried. I needed more sugar. I spied a Starbucks and went over to the condiments counter. I don't know if taking all their sugar sachets technically counts as stealing, but I would like to clear my conscience now by apologizing.

Sugared up to the eyeballs, we landed in southern Morocco, where we would have several days to acclimatize.

I had been rather alarmed to discover that the race's insurance policy included a section on 'corpse repatriation', though to date there has been just one fatality – a twenty-year-old Frenchman who died of a massive heart attack in 1988. This is why the organizers now insist on thorough medical checks.

Rules of the race are simple but strict: compulsory kit included a set of emergency distress flares, and an anti-venom pump for scorpion and snake bites. This was an interesting challenge in itself.

'Where do I get an anti-venom pump?' I wondered. London Zoo?

'Boots,' the organizer replied.

Other rules insist on a full 2,500 calories of food per day, a medical kit including a survival mirror, blanket and salt tablets. Water is distributed at various checkpoints throughout the day. Runners wear a little card around their neck which is clipped each time they collect water or receive medication. There is a strict limit of two intravenous drips during the whole race to rehydrate your body and each competitor is given a modest nine litres of water per day – drink any more and you are eliminated.

And then there are the camels. Time limits each day are marked by two dromedaries that also complete the course. If you are unlucky enough to be overtaken by them, you are disqualified. Never has the sight of two camels caused such panic in the desert.

The exact course remains a secret until the day before the race, when runners are given a set of directions, complete with compass bearings and terrain description. I was reassured to learn that the organizers have lost only one competitor for more than a day. In 1994 a Sicilian policeman went astray in a sandstorm and wandered the desert for nine days, living off bats and his own urine before being found 125 miles away in Algeria, some forty pounds lighter. I just hoped I wouldn't enter race history by becoming the second.

At 6 a.m. a convoy of military trucks arrived at our remote desert hotel and we were shepherded into them for the journey across the Sahara to the even more remote starting point. For seven long hours we swayed in the heat, holding on to the overhead bar for stability as a thin layer of sand coated our faces with an orange hue. I was numb with nervousness.

The army trucks eventually dropped us at the temporary campsite that would be our migrating home for the next week.

Simple cargo nets had been placed over wooden struts to keep out the worst of the sun while still allowing a breeze, but that was it. Essentially we were sleeping out in the elements.

As a solo competitor, I needed to find a tent to share. I wandered up and down the rows looking for the least scary people.

'Mind if I join you?' I asked the friendliest-looking group I could find.

'Sure,' they smiled. I had joined an eclectic bunch. There were two middle-aged businessmen, who I decided were having mid-life crises; a husband and wife who were both doctors; and an internet journalist. We were a happy crowd.

The race itself is broken into six legs of varying length, and Day One was a 'mere seventeen miles' – already longer and harder than anything I had ever done in my life. I felt sick and vowed never to drink Greene King again for the trouble it had caused me.

'Where are your gaiters?' asked a Frenchmen in an all-in-one white paper suit. I felt too embarrassed to ask what gaiters were, let alone why he was dressed like a painter in the middle of the Sahara, but luckily he told me anyway by pulling up his trouser leg and revealing a silk sheath that stretched from just under his knee to his shoes.

It was a revelation. I looked around and noticed that everyone had them. They were every shape and colour imaginable, but one thing was glaringly obvious: they were all homemade. Every one of these competitors had laboured over these bizarre accessories, which could only mean one thing. They would keep the sand from getting into the shoes and socks and acting like sandpaper against the foot. They were really, really important.

I spent my final hours before the race begging and pleading anyone who might have some spare fabric so that I could make my own – something that didn't exactly enhance my 'racing credentials', more my 'cretin credentials'. A pretty young blonde army officer eventually took pity on me and produced some thin parachute silk and a needle and thread. I wasn't sure which I was happier to find, a pretty young thing or the silk.

I managed to create a Heath Robinson-style gaiter that would keep out the worst of the sand and allow me to blend in with the pack a little more.

The morning of the race arrived. Where most competitors had spent years planning and training for it, I had just twelve weeks of running behind me, and it showed. My rucksack was stuffed with an anti-venom pump, a bottle of sun cream, a pair of skiing goggles in case of a sandstorm, an emergency flare and about a hundred sachets of Starbucks sugar. Something told me my rival runners might have been slightly more scientific about their packing, but there was no turning back now.

A helicopter circled above, beaming images live to 120 million viewers worldwide. I felt sick with nerves.

I had received so much conflicting advice about how to tackle the challenge that it was difficult to know where to begin – 'Don't run too fast', 'Run the first day as fast as you can', 'Take shoes a size too big', 'Drink lots before each leg', 'Start off dehydrated to maximize your water' . . .

'Welcome to the nineteenth Marathon des Sables,' announced Patrick over the Tannoy system. 'You are about to join an exclusive club.' Looking around, it was as if I'd stepped into another world, with its own unique tribe. Everyone wore long Sahara hats and sunglasses. Faces had been coated with thick layers of sunscreen and zinc, giving competitors a white complexion. All the runners had their own running tops with nationalities and charities embroidered on the sleeves, and rucksacks with water packs. The water tubes hung from their shoulders like divers' breathing apparatus. And then there were the gaiters – every colour imaginable, some to the calf, others to the knee and a couple of extraordinary creations that went to the thigh. A couple of inventive runners had managed to strap umbrellas to the tops of their packs to give some shade.

Looking around only made me feel even less adequate, but this was it. I was running for my pride.

'*Dix, neuf, huit, sept* . . .' went the countdown '. . . *trois, deux, un* . . .' Brrrrrrrrrrrr.

We were off. The helicopter continued to circle overhead as the thousand runners streamed out across the desert.

I ran at a nice slow pace for the first hour, as runner after runner overtook me. At least there were no comedy costumes like in the London Marathon, where you're guaranteed to be over-taken by some bloke in a G-string or by Daffy Duck.

The sun beat down as I jogged on. It is a battle against the elements as the sun burns at exposed skin and the heat bleeds the body dry of liquid.

Four hours later and the finish line appeared. Today had been a mere tester, an appetizer for the main race. I hobbled into camp, deflated and demoralized by my first day, with a rather depressing set of blisters and an aching back. Blisters are a runner's biggest enemy and I knew that the key to success was minimizing them. I had already failed at my first task and I would need an appoint-ment with the infamous 'Doc Trotters', as the race's thirty French doctors are known.

A large military tent had been erected near to the camp where the doctors could work on the injured runners. As the week went by the tent would become busier, but today I had it largely to myself. Oh joy.

I lay on the floor with my blistered feet raised on a chair while a pretty French doctor examined them (every cloud has a silver lining, I thought).

'Ah, it is just a few small ones,' she said with a heavy French lilt. 'I take them off.'

Whoa there! Pretty doctor or no pretty doctor, what did she mean 'take them off'?

'It's simple,' she began to explain. 'The sand is very dirty, so to avoid infection we remove the blister.' She smiled.

'Aaaaaaaaaaaaaaaaahhhhhhhhhhhhhhhhhhhhhhhhhhhhhhhh!'

Before she had time to explain in more depth why she couldn't just pop and drain it like the doctors of most civilized nations would do, she revealed a scalpel and proceeded to cut around the outside of the blister, removing the skin entirely. As she poured neat iodine on the exposed skin, I understood why the Doc Trotters had such a fearsome reputation. And this was only Day One. I hobbled back to my tent, where I lay on my back and lifted my throbbing feet.

Later I lit my little stove and boiled some water to rehydrate my chilli-con-carne-in-a-bag.

'What am I doing here?' I asked myself. It wasn't the first time in this event that I had felt hopelessly out of my depth, and it wouldn't be the last.

Although each day's leg starts at 10 a.m., the tents are collected at 6 a.m. to ensure that they can be transported and erected at the next finish in time for the elite runners. The desert at 6 a.m. is freezing cold, just a couple of degrees above zero. For four hours the thousand runners sat shivering on the desert floor. I have never put freezing cold sun cream on my body before. A little later I would be dreaming of the coolness and shade of the morning.

As the sun appeared on the horizon, the temperature began to rise and by the time we were ready to go it was over 38°C.

Once again we gathered at the start line, faces still keen, eager and fresh. Day Two would be twenty-one miles on my 'blisterless' feet, which were now covered in equally painful red sores. This time I hobbled a little until my feet were numbed. In the heat, feet swell and I had taken the advice of buying shoes a size too large. I was already grateful for the extra bandage space, but I also worried that at this rate they would need to be two sizes too big.

Once again the race spread out across the desert and I could see a thin line of runners stretching for miles up to the horizon. A mirage cut through their legs, giving the impression of floating ghosts. For hour after hour I yomped across that lonely desert. For all the runners, I felt like the only person there, stuck in my private mental and physical anguish.

'Hi, Ben,' smiled another pretty young runner. 'I haven't seen you since school.'

I am terrible with names and even worse with faces. I couldn't quite place her.

'Hi,' I puffed. 'Great to see you.'

'You don't remember me, do you?' she said as we continued to run across the sandy valley. 'We were at school together. What are you doing here? I didn't think you ran.'

'I don't,' I panted.

'Well, it's great to catch up,' she smiled. 'See you later.' And she accelerated in a puff of sand.

'Well, that's just great,' I thought. 'I've just been overtaken by a girl famous at school for her massive tits.' Things were going from bad to worse. I had to pick up my game.

Once again I hobbled into camp and straight to Doc Misery, sorry, Doc Trotter. I lay on the ground as another pretty doctor examined my feet, tutted and reached for the scalpel.

'Aaaaaaaaaaaahhhhhhhhhhhhhhhhhhhhhhhhhh!' I could be heard back in England.

The sieve-like army tents gave little protection from the freezing night-time air. The Sahara has the greatest gap between nocturnal and diurnal temperatures of anywhere on earth. I shivered myself to sleep each night, with just a few hours' respite from the reality of the day ahead. I found myself dreaming of an English spring morning and a walk in the park with my dog. Bare feet on damp green grass.

Day Three's course was only twenty-three miles long. *Only* twenty-three miles! I never thought I'd say that, but of course there was a twist – twelve of those miles were across dunes. Until now we had been running largely on flat wasteland strewn with rocks and boulders and a sprinkling of sand. I had found that hard enough, but today was going to separate the men from the boys, and I was worried that I was about to be exposed as the fraud I was.

The sand splashed away like water. For every two steps forward, my feet would sink back one step, sapping energy and demanding twice as much effort. Have you ever tried walking along the beach in a pair of shoes on loose, dry sand? Well, make this into a hill and imagine running twelve miles across it. It was sheer hell. Worst of all, the sand leaked, or cascaded may be a better word, into my shoes. This turned my socks into sandpaper as the sand particles settled into the cotton. The last-minute gaiters had failed their first test.

The dunes reflected the heat like an oven, baking me like a bread roll. I could feel my feet swelling, and my sweat evaporated before I became aware of it. One by one, competitors began to fall by the wayside, overcome by the might of the Sahara. I saw several flares tearing through the clear blue sky, each one signalling another casualty of this epic race. I began to question my ability to carry on.

Midway through the dune section I was struggling. The clock was ticking away and I was in danger of missing the cut-off point and being disqualified.

'It's a killer, isn't it?' called a voice from the dunes.

Soon a large body joined the voice. 'Hi – Al,' he said, holding out his hand. It seemed terribly English to shake hands in the desert in the middle of a race.

'How are you doing?' I asked, relieved to have some company.

'I'm OK,' he said, 'but it's not the heat or the endurance that's getting me. I suffer severe agoraphobia.'

I was astonished as he went on to explain that just a few weeks before he had been unable to leave his house, let alone enter one of the biggest, widest, most open places in the world.

'I'm on medication,' he explained. 'Occasionally I feel myself panicking, but then I bring myself back.'

I had to take my hat off to Al. I was complaining about a couple of blisters. It put my suffering into perspective and I found an extra spring in my step as we traversed the open dunes together, me and Agoraphobic Al.

The sun was beginning to set as we descended the last dune for the final five hundred metres to the finish line. We made it with just an hour left on the clock.

For me, this was a turning point in the race, the moment I realized that the MDS was as much about human spirit and camaraderie as it was about physical endurance.

As the clock ticked down, runner after runner hobbled and limped towards the line. Bandaged feet and IV drips didn't stop those who had already completed the course from migrating to the finish, so a large crowd had gathered as the final runners emerged from the dunes, looking broken and worn. There was a roar of clapping and congratulations as a young woman collapsed over the line on her hands and knees.

There was a murmur as the clock neared the cut-off. Half a dozen competitors from the crowd marched out into the desert and a couple of minutes later appeared on the brow of a dune with a young runner. They held his arms aloft and there was a cheer of approval from all of us waiting at the line. One man took his rucksack from him while the others escorted him like a police convoy down the dunes. There was another roar from the crowd. I still get emotional just thinking about it. Cheering, clapping and hollering accompanied that young man as he hobbled the final distance to the finish and his waiting fans. This was *his* moment. I could see tears streaming down his face as he fell over the line. He wept into his hands, while dozens of wellwishers patted him on the back. For fifteen minutes he became the hero of the camp.

It was an unplanned act of selfless, compassionate humanity. Suddenly no one seemed quite so scary. It felt that we were all in this together. Marooned in the middle of the desert, we were all suffering to one degree or another. I didn't feel quite so lonely any more.

Not even another visit to Doc Trotters could dampen my spirits. I had a spring in my hobble. More than a dozen blisters had already been removed from my feet and the thick layer of bandages had become a second skin.

Day Four, however, was 'the big one'. In any other sense 'the big one' might sound exciting, but here it signified the terrifying prospect of forty-seven miles. Forty-seven miles? I don't think I had even walked that distance in my entire life and now here I was, feet bandaged like two mummies, about to attempt it in one fell swoop across the Sahara. If I didn't laugh I would certainly cry.

I hadn't had enough time to recover from the dunes and I had been beset by the desert Tourette's that seemed to have affected most of the runners. Various fruity words rang out. It was almost possible to navigate by following the swear words and curses that echoed across the desert. For someone who rarely uses bad language, I surprised myself with some of my outbursts.

The cumulative effects of three days under the scorching sun with limited food and water were beginning to set in and I was now relying on a heavy dose of painkillers to get me through.

We had twenty-four hours to complete the forty-seven miles. I'm often asked how I overcame the boredom. I'm not really sure how I did it. I have always been good at daydreaming and I sometimes disappear into another world. I often find myself in a different place and different time, but here in the desert I was very much in the here and the now.

Some describe the desert as a sort of cleansing experience. It certainly changed me. For the first time in years I had time to think about what I had done, what I was doing and where I was going.

I was at a transitional stage of my life. I had recently split from a long-term relationship, and I wasn't really sure where I was heading, metaphorically or physically. What was I doing with my life? Was there any structure and order? If so, what was it? If not, why not?

I thought back to my schooldays and my debilitating lack of confidence, and of those innocent early years in South America and all my dreams and aspirations. I remembered those long, windy walks with Inca across the machair of Taransay.

My life had taken so many twists and turns and somehow it had dumped me here, in the middle of the Sahara. Was it fate that brought me here, or do you create your own destiny? I had so many questions and so few answers. What I did know for certain was that I had forty-seven miles ahead of me and somehow I needed to get through what would be undoubtedly the toughest twenty-four hours of my life.

As day became night, I found myself hobbling over hidden shapes as I stumbled my way across the invisible sand. We were drawn like moths to a huge military laser that shot a thin beam of light miles into the sky to mark the finish line. As the sun dipped towards the sand, it was turned ruby red by the thin particles of sand in the atmosphere. It looked double the size of a normal sun as it disappeared and the temperature plummeted. Darkness fell on the desert and I still had more than twelve hours to go. I had entered the unknown, reached the edge of my knowledge. I had breached my known physical limits and was into the undiscovered.

I was also into the need for compass navigation, which again was the unknown. Until now I had been too embarrassed to admit that I didn't know how to use a compass. It had taken me long enough to learn to read a clock and I had always tried to avoid compasses. So now, just when I most needed to understand how to use one, I couldn't.

If in doubt, follow the person in front, I reasoned. That way we can all get lost together.

The sky glittered with more stars than I have ever seen. Shooting stars seemed to appear wherever I looked. My simple head-torch created a small pool of light in front of me, while I focused on the glowstick attached to the bag ahead. A line of tiny torches snaked across the blackness like some modern art installation. It would have been beautiful if it hadn't been so painful. Occasionally the sky was illuminated by the flash of an emergency flare as runners got into trouble or passed out, and I ran past a couple of people wrapped in their foil blankets, having given in to their demons.

It was nearly nine in the evening when I reached the checkpoint. I'd completed over twenty-seven miles, but there were still more than nineteen to go.

By now Doc Trotters' tent had been transformed into a scene from M*A*S*H. Three runners were hooked up to drips, while a team of doctors cut, drained and strapped various pairs of feet and administered painkillers. One man was in an oxygen mask, while another was being stretchered to a waiting helicopter. For the first time in days, I wasn't the star of the tent with my tennis-ball-sized blisters.

'*Spider!*' hollered an English runner, legging it from the tent holding his shorts like a skirt.

There was a moment of pandemonium as a very large camel spider wandered through the tent. Runners dashed outside, trailing bandages and IV drips behind them. It brought a rare flash of comedy to a scene that was far from funny. It's strange how black humour can get you through bleak moments.

Close to delirium, I collapsed on to a sand dune. Too exhausted to eat or drink, I manoeuvred my hurting feet on to my backpack and tried to rest. My feet throbbed with pain. They felt huge, like elephant feet. They groaned against my oversized shoes and I was forced to cut a small window of fabric from the front to allow my bandaged toes a little space. If I removed my shoes now, I knew I'd never get them back on. My socks were soaked with blood and pus that had spread up them like ink on blotting paper.

Camel spiders and scorpions were the last things on my mind as my body sank into the sand. The elevation gave my feet a temporary reprieve from the throbbing that seemed to reverberate in my head, compounding my headache. My bowels had been confused by the heat and the medication, and diarrhoea had left me further dehydrated.

Beeep-beeeep-beeep. My watch woke me at four in the morning. I hadn't even been aware of falling asleep. I edged my feet off my rucksack and the throbbing returned. When I stood up I immediately collapsed. The pain was unbearable. How was I going to do this? No one could get through this amount of pain. Every step felt like walking on shards of glass.

I downed a couple more painkillers and stuffed an energy bar into my mouth. I hated the energy bars. They tasted like cat sick, but I knew I needed them. I emptied a rehydration sachet into my water bottle and took a swig. The fact that I couldn't even taste the salt meant I was dehydrated. The coffee-coloured urine that I produced only verified it.

'At least you didn't piss blood like me,' reasoned a Scouser, who was also getting ready. Fair comment. It was the beginning of my life's lesson that no matter how bad you think things are for you, there will always be someone worse off.

'Ooh aah, ooh aah, ooh aah!' My mouth opened and closed like a fish with each step. The sun was still asleep as I marched, jogged, hobbled and shuffled my way across dunes and rocks. This was the hardest thing I had ever faced in my life, but at least it couldn't get any worse, I reasoned.

And for that arrogant sentiment the desert rewarded me with my first sandstorm. The wind whipped the sand into a stinging bite as it lashed at my bare arms, neck and face. I wrenched my goggles and a scarf from my rucksack and pulled them tight over my face. As the fine powder filled my lungs, it felt as if I were breathing underwater; my eyes watered behind the goggles. Visibility was reduced from twelve miles to just a few hundred feet as I navigated the final stretch to the finish line.

The route had taken us through the first civilization I had seen in more than a week. I ran through the narrow streets of a Berber settlement. The rough mud walls blended into the sandy landscape, creating a sort of mirage, broken by bright blue-and-yellow turbans. Alone, running through this otherworldly settlement, I felt as if I had awoken on another planet. To the locals, I must have looked like some sort of spaceman with my bottles strapped to my chest and my water pipe connected to my back. Then the village disappeared like a dream and I still wonder to this day whether it was real or a hallucination. My senses were numbed by painkillers. I had no sense of smell, just the agony of each step. Tears welled in my eyes. I longed for this to end.

Everyone was asleep when I arrived at the camp. There was no welcome party, no hero status. Just a sandy tent, a cat-sick energy bar and a short respite from running.

As the storm raged we were forced to spend the rest of the day zipped up in our sleeping bags while the sand buried the thin shelters. Tents toppled in the wind, and going out to pee brought to mind Captain Oates' last words, 'I am just going outside and may be some time.'

Tales of heroism and horror began to circulate around camp. One Italian, according to rumours, had lost his entire little toe, and an American had been evacuated to hospital unconscious. Sadly, Al had succumbed to his agoraphobia and had had to set off one of his rescue flares. But for the rest, broken bones, twisted ankles and knees weren't enough to stop us, as we hobbled around camp with the aid of walking sticks, backs bent double in pain. Between us, we had already consumed 4,300 painkillers (most of them taken by me) and used one and a half miles of plasters.

As the penultimate day dawned, I had to dig myself out of my sleeping bag, which had been buried under several inches of sand. Everything was encased in a grimy layer of sand. Sahara sand isn't like beach sand; it's more like dust. It gets everywhere. I wasn't sure if the colour in my face was from the sand or the sun. We hadn't washed or cleaned for nearly a week, but cleanliness was the last thing on our minds as we prepared for another day of hell.

The wind had died and the scorching sun had returned in time for today's twenty-six miles with a time limit of ten hours. In any other circumstance, ten hours for a marathon would be, quite literally, a walk in the park, but not today.

Lining up at the start line was like being in some hideous recurring nightmare. By now the pack had been significantly reduced, but somehow, miraculously, I was still in. Every part of my body was screaming at me to stop. My bowels had by now been thrown into complete turmoil by the concoction of antibiotics and anti-inflammatories. I was in excruciating pain from my feet and every step felt like walking on glass. I'd now also developed an unstoppable nosebleed from the dry dust. I longed to be anywhere but that terrible desert – but for some reason, for the first time since the race began, I had started to believe in myself. The impossible seemed possible.

I had an extra spring in my step. My stride was wider, my gait more confident. I had got this far and God help anyone who tried to stop me. The suffering had spread to most of the competitors by now so I had no excuse. What was a little pain in the grand scheme of things? In just a few days I would be home.

Day Five involved an enormous rubble-strewn plain of fist-sized rocks. They were perfect ankle-twisters and leg-breakers. Occasionally my foot would unintentionally land on a rock, bruising my sole, which added to my smorgasbord of foot pains, but even this didn't stop me.

I bounded across the desert like – well, like an Englishman who had just survived five days of desert hell. Six hours later, I hobbled into camp one final time. Suddenly the end was in sight. Just one night separated me from victory. Success. Achievement.

Hungry and smelly, we looked a ragged bunch on our sixth morning as we loaded our backpacks for the last time. There was an air of euphoria as we waited for the final gun to sound. Spirits were bursting with excitement. Just thirteen miles separated us from this desert hell and the nirvana of civilization across the finish line.

It was as though we had all been newly born and we raced as one. We worked together. This ragged group of desert runners had begun to morph with the environment. We had developed a synergy with the desert, and for the first time it didn't own us. We had adjusted to this new life.

We pounded across the desert. Feet hopped and skipped over boulders and rocks and glided through sand. We raced through the Bedouin village of Ait Isfou, women and children watching in disbelief as this grubby army of Western nomads huffed and puffed and cursed their way past, faces contorted in agony.

The pain had gone. My mind was focused on the end. I felt like a rock star at a concert. My smile stretched from ear to ear. Nothing I had achieved in life had ever felt this good. 'Look at me,' I wanted to shout, 'look at me!'

Before I knew it, my legs had carried me to the outskirts of Tagounite, the end of the race. Crowds of locals lined the streets. We had returned to civilization and the end was nigh.

I turned a corner and there it was: the finish line, like the gates of heaven. Was this just another mirage? Perhaps I was still dreaming. Time stood still and my mind swam as though I were drunk. I disappeared into a dreamlike landscape as the crowd roared their encouragement.

'Come on!' they hollered.

Time stood still. I looked at my legs and then at the finish line just ahead of me. Silence. Why was it so silent? I looked at my legs again. They were still moving.

I pulled my arms back and puffed out my chest. Head held high, I raced over the line. Suddenly the noise returned. There was a deafening roar as I collapsed on to the road, and suddenly it was all over. I'd done it. I'd finished.

Tears poured down my weatherbeaten, sun-scorched, sand-blasted face as Patrick Bauer placed my finisher's medal around my neck and kissed me on both cheeks. I was overcome with emotion. For the first time in my life I was lost for words.

I sat there on the road with my head in my hands as other runners fell over the line. I had never seen so many grown men weep. It was one of the most moving sights I have ever seen. It was a moment only those who had been through the same hardships could understand.

I sat there stunned. It was a moment of complete clarity, a turning point. I realized that I could achieve anything if I really put my mind to it. I had defied my critics and for once I had achieved something. I can honestly say that it was the first time in my life that I was proud of myself. My perpetual self-doubt had been replaced by assurance. The desert may have shredded my feet, but it had healed me and given me the confidence I had always lacked.

It was a very different Ben who returned from Morocco on crutches, with his medal around his neck, and it was a man who wanted to achieve *more*.

8

The Bear vs The Snake

'How would you like to take part in this year's charity boxing match for Sport Relief?' asked the BBC producer down the phone.

Boxing had never really appealed to me. It was an alien concept. I am the most un-pugilistic person I know and had never raised my fists in my life. I was about to explain this to him and politely decline his kind offer.

'You'll be boxing Aled Jones,' he added.

'I'll do it!' I shouted back, reneging on everything I'd just thought.

Aled Jones, I thought to myself. The young chorister with the voice of an angel? Aled Jones of *The Snowman*'s 'Walking In The Air'? He was about eleven, wasn't he?

It was 2004, the second year in which the BBC had asked celebrities to compete in a live televised boxing bout to help raise money for Sport Relief. The previous year had seen the rather unlikely duo of Ricky Gervais and Grant Bovey, Anthea

Turner's husband. Now they wanted to pit me against Aled Jones!

I had loved *The Snowman* as a child, and the song was a memorable part of my growing up. It's strange when your childhood joins your adult life. It has happened a number of times over the years. The first was when I filmed with Terry Nutkins, wacky presenter of *The Really Wild Show*, who used to travel the country with his pet sea lion; and of course my childhood really caught up with me when I joined *Countryfile* with John Craven. Now the past had come into focus again. Never could I ever have guessed as a child that I would one day step into the boxing ring with the voice of the Snowman – I almost thought of him as the Snowman – and try to punch his lights out. They're strange, the twists and turns of life.

I was teamed up with Frank Bruno as my mentor and Jim McDonnell as my trainer. Jim was one of the toughest people I had met. A one-time featherweight boxer himself, he had failed to make it in the boxing world but had found great success teaching others.

Fresh back from my Sahara triumph, I was still at the peak of my physical ability. Jim wanted to see what he'd got to work with, so we met at a boxing school called The Church on the Harrow Road in west London, which is in – an old church. It was strange seeing a boxing ring beneath a stained-glass window, but I was about to embark on a sport that is a religion of sorts to its followers.

Dressed in my new Lonsdale shorts I stepped into the ring, where Jim carefully strapped my hands with what looked like bandage before putting my gloves on. He then pulled a headguard over my head and put a mouthguard in my mouth.

Sunshine streamed through the window, casting a shaft of ethereal light into the ring. Jim stepped in with a pair of boxing pads and instructed me to hit them in rotation.

'Left one, right two, left one, right three, left three!' he screamed, as my gloved fist smacked into the pads. He bounced around lightly and within a couple of minutes I was gasping on my hands and knees. I had never been so drained in such a short time. It was incredible. I had only been in the ring for a couple of minutes and already I had a new-found respect for boxers.

'Looks like we have a lot of work,' smiled Jim before sending me off on an hour's run.

Before I could start sparring in the ring, I had to have a certificate from a BBC doctor. Hidden among the rabbit warren of corridors at TV Centre in White City is a little medical centre, the main job of which is to deal with vaccinations for foreign correspondents.

I waited outside reading an old copy of the *Radio Times*.

'Mr Fogle,' called the doctor.

I walked into the surgery and sat down.

'I just want to tell you how disappointed I am in you,' he said.

That came from left of field. I hadn't been expecting that. What did he mean? What had I done?

'I don't think you should be encouraging a contact sport like boxing,' he continued. 'As a presenter you have a responsibility,' he added. 'You are a role model and you should not be endorsing boxing. I don't mind telling you that I am disappointed in the BBC for broadcasting this.'

I had been surprised into silence.

'But it's for charity,' I reasoned weakly.

'It doesn't matter – you have a responsibility,' he replied.

'But I'll be fighting Aled Jones.' I didn't really say that, but I wanted to.

It is interesting how divisive boxing can be. My parents were horrified at the prospect. My father did his usual thing of reeling off the statistics on brain injury and death. He'd even got our dentist, who also happens to be a friend of the family, to call me and warn me about the dangers.

So why had I agreed? Why was I going against my parents' wishes? I have always believed in making my own educated judgement based on knowledge and experience. I had heard the medical opinions about boxing, but I wanted to experience it for myself before I made my own judgement. That may sound like drinking a bottle of poison to prove that it is poison, but this was just another challenge in a long line of risks I have taken and will continue to take. A calculated risk. I would wear head protection, we were using heavily padded gloves, and it was just one fight for goodness' sake – with a choirboy.

I returned to Jim with my medical certificate intact and my morals slightly damaged and immersed myself in the world of boxing.

A couple of weeks later I got a call from the BBC producer working on the *Sport Relief* programme.

'How's it going?' he asked.

'Great,' I said, confident that Aled wouldn't stand a chance.

'Ah,' he said, 'that's why I called. There's a bit of a problem.' He sounded worried. 'Aled can't do it.'

As the words sank in I could see the Snowman disappearing into the sky, dragging the little boy in the dressing gown. The little boy was looking down at me, giving me the finger. This was terrible news.

'But why?' I whimpered with disappointment.

'His mum won't let him.'

So if the Snowman's mum wouldn't let him, who would replace him? Maybe they'd get Charlotte Church instead.

'We've already found a replacement,' he continued. 'You'll be boxing Sid Owen, the actor from *EastEnders*.'

Hurrah. That would be 'Riiiiccckaaay', former amateur boxer from the East End of London who already had a broken nose. Brilliant, just brilliant, I thought.

I had gone from boxing a snowman to fighting a gangster.

Two days later and we met for the first time. The BBC had organized a press conference and weigh-in at the Sports Café in London. Various sports journalists and photographers had been invited, as had Frank Bruno, my mentor, and Barry McGuigan, who would be Sid's. I hailed a taxi dressed in my silk boxing shorts and dressing gown, bearing the embroidered name 'Ben "the Bear" Fogle', and crossed London.

The photographers wanted a picture of Sid and me staring menacingly at one another, the classic nose-to-nose pose. We stood there while they snapped away, but for some unfathomable reason Sid proceeded to chest-butt me. I'm sure it was only meant to be a bit of amateur-dramatics fun, but I wasn't ready for it and I went tumbling on to my back in front of the assembled paparazzi.

'Is This the Greatest Sporting Mismatch Ever?' screamed the headlines the next day. The die had been cast. I was the underdog and I *had* to beat Sid.

Shortly before the fight, I decided to invite my sister Tamara along to one of my sparring sessions. I wanted to show her the boxing world – but if I'm honest I also wanted to prepare her and desensitize her to the realities of the sport.

Jim was based in a tiny boxing academy in north-east London, where he had a boxing ring squeezed into a little wooden building next to a rugby field. He had organized for one of his heavier protégés to spar with me. My sister sat ringside with Frank Bruno, who had also come along to support me. I skipped across the ring, bouncing from boot to boot, holding my hands up close to my face.

A left jab spun past my head, followed by a right that caught me off guard. The glove smashed into my face and there was a small explosion of blood. It was the first time in my life that I genuinely saw cartoon stars and birds spinning around my head.

I wobbled and collapsed into the ring, blood pouring out of my nose.

Tamara was open-mouthed. She took one look at me and burst into tears. I looked at Frank, who let out one of his trademark deep, booming 'Know what I mean, 'Arry?' laughs. Now that was one of life's strange sights.

Fortunately my nose wasn't broken. That had already been done by a Royal Marine several years earlier while I was still at university and in the Royal Naval Unit. We had volunteered at a Royal Marine training week at Longmoor Camp, not far from Portsmouth, where we had to play the part of the population of a Northern Irish village, creating likely scenarios for the young soldiers about to be deployed there in the Troubles.

The exercise culminated in a full riot, during which we pelted them with potatoes while they charged us with riot shields. At the height of the final stampede, I collided with one sleep-deprived Marine, who first of all whacked me in the leg with his baton, then smashed his fist into my nose. I still love seeing the look on people's faces when I tell them I broke my nose in a riot.

Once broken, always broken.

The weeks flew by and, before I knew it, it was fight night. Television Centre had been converted into a boxing arena and a small dressing room became my changing room. Jim McDonnell turned up with a small posse of helpers. I'd never met any of them before, but they all seemed to have a role. There must have been six of us squeezed into that tiny room. A huge man started strapping my hands firmly.

The seven of us sat in silence while *Neighbours* played on the telly. I walked in small circles around the tiny room followed by my six disciples. There were still a couple of hours before the fight, so I wandered around Television Centre in a stream of nervous sweat accompanied by this posse.

'Float like a butterfly, sting like a bee,' whispered one of them as I walked down the corridor in my silk dressing gown. It was completely surreal.

I had thought long and hard about my walk-on music. Much longer than I usually spend thinking about songs. 'The music needs to say that you mean business,' Jim had explained, so I had spent weeks sifting through my music collection looking for something suitable, before settling for Run-DMC's 'It's Tricky'.

'Ladies and gentlemen, from *Animal Park*, it's Ben "the Bear" Foooooooooooooooooooooooooooogle!' announced the MC. There was wild applause as Run-DMC began to play. I couldn't help wishing he hadn't included the *Animal Park* bit. It rather took the edge off things. I might as well have called myself Ben 'the Rabbit' or Ben 'the Hamster' Fogle.

I marched into the studio accompanied by Jim, Frank and my posse, focusing on the ring as the crowd rose to their feet. Adrenalin pumped through my body. My nerves were on edge and I was trembling. I could feel the music reverberating around my head as sweat streamed down my brow.

I stepped into the ring and bounced my boots against the floor to get a feel for its spring. The lights were blinding.

'Ladies and gentlemen, from *EastEnders*, it's Sid "the Snake" Owwwwwwwwwwwwwen!'

Sid walked through the crowd. He suddenly looked bigger and fitter. He had a swagger and his 'crew' looked like they meant business. Frank Maloney, the East End boxing promoter, and Barry scurried behind him as he clambered through the ropes and into the ring.

Sid marched straight up to me in my corner and held his face close to mine. It was contorted with anger. I could feel his eyes boring into me. Frank leapt into the ring and threw himself between us. He enveloped me protectively with his great body, pushing Sid away with one hand.

I knew this was for charity, but I'd lost all sense of reality, and the lines between what was for show and what was real had become blurred. To me, Sid looked like he wanted to kill me.

Lulu had agreed to be the ring girl.

The referee beckoned us into the centre of the ring. 'Right, gentlemen, remember it's three rounds of three minutes. Keep it clean.' And with that we tapped gloves and returned to our corners.

I sat there while my team strapped on my headguard and handed me my mouthguard.

Ding-ding, the bell sounded. I rose to my feet and the crowd went crazy.

I disappeared into a world of my own. The roar of the crowd became inaudible and my heart raced faster than I knew was possible. Perspiration dripped from my face as I danced on my feet in my Lonsdale leather boxing boots.

'Float like a butterfly, *sting* like a bee,' I kept repeating in my head. It felt as though I had landed in someone else's life. I was in a dreamlike trance as I bounced around the ring, my ears buzzing as the blood thudded through my head. I could see the crowd but I couldn't hear them. Bouncing, bouncing, bouncing.

I held my hands aloft, protecting my face. Sid made a couple of jabs, but I had my guard and deflected each one with ease. I was still to make a strike. The clock was ticking down. *Bam.* I struck with my fist, but it hit his glove. *BAM.* Again I made contact with his glove.

We continued dancing around one another for what felt like eternity. Then in a split second I saw his arm lower and I threw a punch with my right hand, striking him on the face. I followed it with the left hand, also making contact. Sid stumbled and I threw my fist again. I was on a roll, but this time he had turned and I struck the back of his head.

Suddenly the roar of the crowd returned. It was like turning up the volume, but the roar had turned to a hissing 'Boooooo.' The ref gave me a warning and pulled us apart. There was a brief moment of humiliation and embarrassment before I disappeared back into my dreamlike world.

Sweat streamed down my face. Sid's supporters were so loud; it was as if the entire East End had turned out for the match. I caught a glimpse of Frank Bruno in the corner. I had spent so long training for this. I couldn't let it slip away.

I focused on Sid and let go a flurry of jabs. Left, right, left, right. Each one made contact before the bell signalled the end of Round One.

I slumped in the corner, adrenalin pumping through my body, able to hear the crowd again. Time slipped by and before I knew it we were back in the ring. I had just two more rounds to make my mark. The next three minutes disappeared in a haze of blows. We were both fighting for our pride. Sid struck me on the left cheek and then caught me with a right hook on the nose. There was no pain. I was numbed by the atmosphere.

Soon we were into the third round. I didn't have a clue about how the scoring was going. I was exhausted. It was like Day Three of the Marathon des Sables. I was fighting lethargy, my arms were leaden and it was hard to hold them up. I couldn't go on for much longer. It had already been the longest six minutes of my life, but I could tell that Sid had already passed his threshold. He was wilting and I could see him stumbling around the ring. It was now or never.

Left, right, left, right, left, right, left, right. My fists flew in a rage. Sid stumbled and I heard the referee shouting. Sid was on his feet but he'd been given a standing count. It was a blur. We stumbled and hugged and punched and fell into the ropes. The roar of the crowd rose and fell, and then it was all over. Ding-ding-ding!

The ref held us both by our gloves.

'The winner of the fight is . . .' The pause was agonizing and I prepared myself for the inevitable.

'. . . Ben "the Beeeaaaaaaaaaaaaar" Fogle!' He lifted my hand aloft and the crowd leapt to their feet.

Was this really happening, I wondered, or was it just another dream? I had won. WON! The words sounded strange. I wished my parents were there to see it, but I understood why they weren't.

I may have won on points, but we still had to wait for the public vote. They would decide on the worthy winner: the daytime animal presenter or the soap star. It was a nerve-racking few hours until the results came in. Somehow, incredibly, I managed to swing a 70 per cent majority. I still don't know how I did it, but I did and it remains one of my proudest achievements. I rarely talk about it any more, but it's always there at the back of my mind. The day I beat Sid.

Just as I was after the Marathon des Sables, I was flush with pride in what I had achieved. I may have sent Sid off in an oxygen mask, but that was the point, wasn't it? I had got into the spirit of boxing. I'd embraced it and it had enveloped me. People may disapprove of it, but I had discovered a sport with honour and discipline, a sport in which young people show respect for rules and for one another.

I had taken on the challenge to beat the Snowman, but had come away with a new respect for boxing as a sport. Above all, it had boosted my confidence.

9

Running with Lions

'Would you run the Lewa Half Marathon with the Battleback soldiers?' asked William.

The marathon was just a couple of weeks away, it was in Africa, across a wilderness brimming with lions, elephants and rhino, and I hadn't trained for months. In any other scenario I would have politely declined, but this request wasn't from some stranger, it was William Wales, Prince William, the future king of England.

The Battleback soldiers are a group of military personnel who have been injured during the course of their military careers, some in battle, while others have suffered injury away from the front line.

I first became involved with injured soldiers in 2009 when James Cracknell and I were asked if we would like to do a challenge for ITV's *Pride of Britain* awards, which celebrate the incredible achievements of Brits, both military and civilian. Phil Packer, the former soldier who had lost the use of his legs in a bomb blast in Afghanistan, was to receive an award and they wanted us to do something for the Soldiers', Sailors' and Airmen's Families Association (SSAFA) to honour him. We came up with the idea of the Ride of Britain, in which we would cycle a rickshaw from Edinburgh to London, arriving just in time to pick Phil up and deliver him live to the television studio for the award ceremony.

Phil had recently completed the London Marathon, despite being told he would never walk again. It took him ten days and was one of the most moving and inspiring things I have ever seen. The rickshaw ride was our way of showing our respect and raising money along the way.

On the first day of our ride, James and I arrived at 5 a.m. in a rainy, cold Edinburgh, where our chariot awaited us. A handful of wellwishers, including Miss Scotland, had turned out at the castle to send us off in our bright-yellow rickshaw. The idea was to take turns pedalling it, while the other recovered in the back. It was like rowing the Atlantic all over again, as we cycled two hours on, two hours off. We would be escorted by the film crew in one vehicle, while the support crew, including physios, medics and our rickshaw mechanic, followed in a camper van.

A piper marched in front of us as we juddered along the cobblestones and through the heart of Edinburgh. Soon we had left the city and were on to A-roads, a strong wind buffeting us as we headed south. The rickshaw was heavy to manoeuvre and we soon discovered that the extra weight in the back made it almost impossible to climb hills. Also, we could travel at only about ten miles an hour. We had more than four hundred miles to cover and just forty-eight hours to do it. There was no room for error. We couldn't stop.

As we cycled through Berwick-upon-Tweed a woman rushed up to me as I sat in the back and handed me two tweed blankets to keep us warm. Dozens of people swarmed around us, dropping money in the collecting bucket I had beside me. It was astonishing. Wherever we went, there were crowds of people to support us. Whatever the hour, families stood on the roadside and individuals stood on bridges to wave us on. It was heartening to see the level of support there is for our armed forces.

Most of my challenges and adventures had taken me to the furthest corners of the globe, where support usually consisted of the odd whale or penguin, but here on Britain's A-roads local news and radio had ensured a constant supply of wellwishers along the way. It's amazing how it lifts your spirits. I saw some of the best of humanity on that journey, during which children donated their entire piggy banks and the elderly their week's pension. The only problem was that it made the rickshaw even heavier.

It was late on Sunday, the second day, and James was on the pedals. I was humming along to the Kaiser Chiefs on my iPod with my tweed blanket over my knees for protection when I heard a siren. I looked behind us to see the blue flashing lights of a police car and a long line of traffic. We pulled on to the hard shoulder.

'Afternoon, gentlemen.' The police officer had a wry smile on his face.

'Hello, officer,' we chirped.

'Did you know that there is a twenty-mile tailback behind you?'

'That's the first time I've ever been stopped for going too slowly,' remarked James as we waited for the traffic to pass.

On Monday morning, as we approached the outskirts of London, we were joined by four police outriders as an escort through the city traffic. These officers usually worked with VIPs – prime ministers and royalty – not two smelly, sweaty blokes on a yellow rickshaw. Two of them stayed with us, while the other two bikes went on ahead to clear a trail. At traffic lights, one bike would ride through and hold up the traffic with an ear-splitting whistle, while the other ushered us through. It was seamless. We rarely had to brake, even in the heavy London congestion – the traffic parted before us like the Red Sea and we passed through unhindered. I'll never forget the faces of the London cabbies.

Before we knew it, we were cycling down Park Lane and through Hyde Park to the barracks of the Household Cavalry, where we were given a hero's welcome. We weren't, of course, heroes; but we had managed to raise the profile of SSAFA and delivered Phil Packer safely to the awards ceremony.

A couple of weeks later, SSAFA invited me to go to one of their homes, Defence Medical Rehabilitation Centre Headley Court, near Epsom in Surrey, to visit some of the injured soldiers. Of all the things I've done and people I've met over the years, nothing and no one can match the heroic bravery of those young men and women. Here were genuine heroes – not a word I use lightly. Quite simply, I was overwhelmed and inspired by their stoicism in the face of despair.

Headley Court is often the first port of call (after a stay at Selly Oak Hospital in Birmingham) for servicemen and women returning home after being badly wounded in Iraq or Afghanistan. Soldiers who may have lost limbs or suffered severe trauma spend months at the centre rebuilding their lives. But behind every casualty are the forgotten victims of war – the devastated families left to pick up the pieces, often as full-time carers; families who often struggle to cope with the terrible reality of looking after a loved one injured in war.

Like many, I have friends in the military and have been appalled and distressed by the number of deaths from fighting in battles as remote as they are incomprehensible. The almost daily obituary photographs of happy young soldiers in battle fatigues who have sacrificed their lives in the line of duty; the hearses creeping through the streets of Wootton Bassett draped in the Union Jack as another son, brother, daughter or father is laid to rest. I have been moved to tears by the loss of life and limb, as soldier after soldier has been repatriated in a body bag or on a stretcher.

I was also privileged to visit Norton House, near Headley Court, which has been turned by SSAFA into accommodation in which the families of injured soldiers can stay so that they can visit their loved one as he or she is recovering. Even better, once the soldiers are well enough they can, in turn, briefly visit their families and sometimes stay overnight before returning to Headley Court. It helps families and injured soldiers to come to terms with their traumatically changed circumstances – a vital part of the rehabilitation process. There is a similar place near Selly Oak hospital.

For the families of injured servicemen, Norton House has been invaluable. In those early, shocking weeks after hearing the news of an injury, many struggle to find accommodation near to the hospital or rehabilitation centre where their beloved is facing the battle of his life. It is also a retreat, somewhere for the injured and their relatives to spend time together, away from the hospital, to begin that long process of adaptation and recovery.

'Soldiers are often inherently quite uncommunicative,' explained Mike Turner, the house manager. 'Families come here to learn and understand.'

Many badly injured soldiers return from the front line in induced comas and lose a great deal of weight. Norton House is where they come to refuel and rebuild. These are men, remember, for whom fitness has always been paramount.

Mike, who served in Bosnia and the first Gulf War, says the nature of our wounded war heroes has changed. 'Trauma care is so sophisticated today that people are surviving with injuries that only a couple of years before would have certainly killed them.'

The home has had a number of triple-limb amputees and recently there has been a sharp rise in the number of women casualties, as the Taliban targets young female medics.

This is the reality of war in Iraq and Afghanistan: young soldiers – many still in their teens – whose lives are torn apart before they have time to begin them.

I spoke to one couple who had just arrived at Norton House. Their son had returned from Afghanistan where he'd been caught in a blast.

'We've just had some sad news,' whispered his mother. 'He's lost the sight in both of his eyes. He's only twenty-one. He'd get over the loss of an arm or a leg, but his sight? How's a young lad going to deal with that?'

As the number of Second World War veterans declines, SSAFA is working hard to ensure that they are able to meet the needs of a new generation of ex-servicemen and women.

On top of their physical injuries, the problems they face include homelessness, social exclusion, mental health problems, drug and alcohol abuse and debt.

As I left the house, a young lad rushed up to me. 'I'm back to Afghanistan next week,' he smiled. 'I'm off to Headley Court for another prosthetic and then I go back to war.' He lifted his trouser leg to reveal his artificial limb.

'You don't even have a limp,' I said, astonished.

'I hope to swim the Channel next year,' he added with a grin.

I was humbled. He and his comrades are real-life heroes.

It had been a privilege to spend time with these incredible people, so when I was asked to join a group of injured soldiers on the 2010 Safaricom Marathon at Lewa in Kenya, I once again leapt at the chance to help our brave servicemen and women. They hoped to overcome their own personal battles in coming to terms with their injuries while at the same time raising funds for Help for Heroes and TUSK, which raises money to combat a wide range of problems in Africa.

I met up with the Battleback soldiers in Wales a couple of weeks before the run. They came from a number of different regiments and had suffered a variety of injuries. One soldier stood out – Jen, who had been paralysed in a skiing accident. Although she had limited use of her lower body, she had decided to race in a wheelchair to maximize her chances of completion. She had been experimenting with a number of different chairs, from road-racers to all-terrain chairs that used a hand-crank, but no one was really sure what would work best because no one had ever done it in a wheelchair before.

I flew into the Lewa Wildlife Conservancy from Botswana, where I had accompanied Princes William and Harry on the first leg of their joint royal tour. I had managed a couple of training runs, but had been more concerned with training for a three-thousand-mile mountain-bike race from Canada to Mexico for which James and I had been preparing for months. We were due to depart in just a couple of weeks. So I had travelled around Botswana with the future king of England with a mountain bike under my arm. It wasn't the only time I had been accompanied around Africa by something strange. Shortly before James and I rowed the Atlantic, I travelled through Namibia and Botswana with a rowing machine in my luggage.

Running at Lewa was difficult. It is rocky and hilly, and the ground is covered in a thin layer of loose stones and gravel. At this altitude – three thousand metres – your lungs scream for oxygen. I joined the soldiers on a couple of training runs along the small airstrip. It was dry and dusty as we pounded up and down the little dirt track. In the end Jen had opted for a road-racing wheelchair with thin tyres. The inner tubes had been removed and replaced with foam to reduce the chance of a puncture, but it was still a risk.

As the race drew near, our enclosed camp began to fill as international runners assembled in this remote corner of Kenya. On the morning of the race we were up before the sun. There was excitement in camp as runners made last-minute preparations. I sat around the smouldering embers of the previous night's fire with the soldiers as we hydrated ourselves ready for the long race ahead.

Shortly before 8 a.m. the thousands of runners began to make their way to the start line. The bright-orange sun was rising above the African plains as we shivered in the early-morning chill.

Ian Craig, director of the Lewa Wildlife Conservancy, buzzed high above us in his tiny aeroplane, ensuring that the course was cleared of any animals that might want to eat us. Racing in a conservancy brimming with wildlife is certainly an incentive to run fast. No one wants to be at the back.

Jen had been given permission to leave fifteen minutes ahead of everyone else. There was a buzz of excitement as she wheeled herself over the start line. As the first person ever to attempt the race in a wheelchair, if she completed it she would set a course record. It was quite something to see her heading off alone into the African wilds. I was very moved.

Soon it was our turn. A torrent of runners was unleashed into the savannah, creating a small cloud of dust. Like sediment settling, the fastest raced to the front of the pack, while the slower settled to the back, and soon the long line was spread out across the conservancy.

The Battleback soldiers had also spread out across the field. Jen was coping impressively with the tough conditions and received cheers as runners caught up with her.

The first water break didn't come a moment too soon as the full glare of the African sun began to work on our already tired bodies. Sweat streamed from my face as I gulped down some water and soaked up some encouragement.

Soon it was back out into the wilderness. A herd of Grevy's

zebra looked rather puzzled as a long stream of runners in green zebra-striped Safaricom shirts ran past them. A couple of armed guards were the only indication that somewhere hidden in the bush were some of the park's carnivores, though I suspect we were all far too hot and sweaty for their liking anyway. A pair of springbok raced across the track in front of me and I watched as a warthog and its young disappeared into the undergrowth, their little tails sticking up like antennae.

There is something incredible about the interaction between man and nature. I couldn't help wonder what all the wild animals made of us. They could not, of course, know that all the sweat and tears was ultimately for them. The Safaricom Marathon raises more than half a million dollars a year for the Lewa conservancy. That money supports anti-poaching patrols, wardens, veterinary fees and maintenance costs.

I caught up with Jen as she was negotiating one of the many hills on the course. She had turned her wheelchair backwards and was hauling herself up the steep gradient. Despite the many offers of help, she insisted on doing it alone. This was her race and she wanted to complete it unaided. I loved her spirit.

Soon we reached another water stop and more supporters. The sun beat down from the clear blue sky, creating oven-like conditions for the runners. But soon we were descending a short hill and were on the home run. I passed the sign that divided the half-marathon from the full-marathon runners, relieved that I was running only the half.

It was a great feeling as I raced over the line, but even greater was watching the other runners completing the challenge. All the Battleback soldiers had finished – all except for Jen, who had been struggling with the many hills.

Then there was a roar. Not from a lion, but from the thousands of supporters crowding along the finish line. Jen had appeared on the home straight.

We all ran out to join her in a victory march to the finish. The crowd went wild as she hauled her dusty wheelchair over the line. Tears streamed down her face. She was overcome with emotion. She had not only proved to herself that injury is no barrier to physical achievement, but she had become the first person to complete the Lewa Marathon in a wheelchair. She touched many lives that day with her incredible achievement.

10

The Winner Takes It All

'I'm going to do the Viking Run in Sweden,' I announced rather casually to Marina over breakfast.

'What's the Viking Run?' she asked.

'A marathon.'

'But it's midwinter in Sweden,' she replied suspiciously.

'It's an ice-skating marathon.'

'But you can't ice skate!'

'Yes, I can.'

'When did you last skate?' she demanded.

'A couple of years ago.'

'When?' she pressed.

'When I was ten.'

'So, you're off to take part in an ice-skating marathon, and the last time you skated was nearly twenty-five years ago?'

'Yup,' I smiled.

'Then I'm coming too,' she stated.

I hadn't seen that one coming. Now this was going to be

difficult. It wasn't that I didn't want her there, but I didn't. That doesn't make sense, but that's probably because I wasn't sure why I had suddenly become so territorial.

For me, these challenges have become a way of defining who I am, marking me out and building my own confidence. Having Marina there competing alongside me would be great, but it would also change the whole dynamic and, in some bizarre way, the whole point of doing it.

Now don't get me wrong. I love doing things with my wife and our six years together have been marked by our overseas experiences. We have been lucky enough to travel the world together, but for some strange reason the Viking Run belonged to me.

'But you can't skate,' I reasoned.

'Neither can you,' she retorted.

She had me cornered on this one.

'Great!' I smiled through gritted teeth.

The race was a couple of weeks away, so the first thing we had to do was get fit. We had never been running together, which is a little strange, given that's almost how we met. I say 'almost' because it was while walking our two dogs, Inca and Maggi. I use the term 'walk' rather loosely. I would describe mine as more of an amble and Marina's a jog, verging on a run.

For six months I had spotted a beautiful blonde and a pair of red tracksuit bottoms running through London's Hyde Park with her sleek brown Labrador. Inca, my rotund black Labrador, and I would dawdle, amble and pootle along the path, coffee in one hand, poo bag in the other.

Occasionally the dogs would cross paths, but Marina was always too quick. She had that pretty-girl radar, to avoid all odd blokes wandering through the park clutching a bag of poo.

For six long months Inca would be dragged from path to path in the hope that we would cut this lovely girl off, but she always seemed to change her course at the last minute. I would spend the entire walk trying to work out how much time it would take her to complete a circuit and return through the middle of the park. I even contemplated hiding in a bush. With hindsight, it would have been easier for me simply to start jogging too. But I didn't.

Eventually we were introduced at a party. I completely failed to recognize her out of her running kit, but I was smitten. She was the most beautiful girl I had ever met. After that we began chatting when we saw each other in the park and eventually I plucked up the courage to invite her out for a drink . . . with the dogs, of course. I was terrified that the dogs wouldn't get on, but it was love at first sight for all of us.

In September 2008 we married in a romantic ceremony in Portugal. Two hundred friends and family descended on the medieval town of Monsaraz in the Alentejo, on the border with Spain. It was a little like marrying on the African plains – 49°C in the shade – but in typical mad-dogs-and-Englishmen fashion our guests baked under the sun in thick wool morning dress. We had the best week of our lives.

I didn't realize it at the time, but when I married Marina I also married Austria. It was a country that had never really appeared on my geographical map; I neither knew much about it nor had any great desire to visit it. A friend once joked that it was the destination for dyslexic travellers bound for Australia; I thought it was famous for long-dead composers, the former racing driver and airline boss Niki Lauda, and not much else.

But all that changed when I married Marina, who is half Austrian. Suddenly I became a fully paid-up lederhosen-wearing, yodelling honorary Austrian with a new – and genuine – affection for the country. Every summer we pack the car with dogs, bikes (and these days children) and wend our way under the Channel and across Europe for a summer of hiking, swimming and eating. My wife's family comes from Salzburg, the birthplace of Mozart and a breathtakingly beautiful city of UNESCO-listed spires, churches and cobbled streets. And of course *The Sound of Music*, which is all around you in Salzburg.

I grew up with two sisters, so was exposed to endless reruns of the von Trapp family singing about hills and flowers on our old Betamax video player. I can still remember every song and every word, and could probably give Connie Fisher a run for her money (Andrew Lloyd Webber, take note). But little did I realize when I fell in love with Marina that I would be marrying a real-life Julie Andrews and that we would become the von Fogles.

My mother-in-law, Monika, has a wardrobe of dirndls dating from the 1950s. The traditional dresses, historically worn by Alpine peasant farmers' wives, are now part of the national costume. Much to the delight of the men, every one of my mother-in-law's female visitors gets issued with a bodice, blouse, skirt and apron. Marina spends the summer in hers.

Those Austrian summers are idyllic – a far cry from the first holiday that Marina and I took together after we were married.

I organized the trip as a surprise for Marina. Subconsciously, it was a way of making up for our unseasonably wet and cold honeymoon, so quite how we ended up in western Sweden on a timber-rafting holiday still puzzles me.

'We would advise more than two people per raft,' said the woman when I booked the trip. I resisted the snotty impulse to tell her that I had rowed the Atlantic and so would have no trouble controlling a raft on a river.

'We'll be fine,' I said.

For three long days we drove up through France, Belgium and then through northern Germany until we descended into the depths of the Malmö tunnel and out into Sweden. We were driving because our two dogs, Maggi and Inca, are an important part of our lives and we wanted them on holiday with us. It was, after all, walking them that had brought us together, so not only had their icing-sugar figures adorned our wedding cake in place of the traditional bride and groom, but one of the reasons we had honeymooned in the Western Isles of Scotland was so that the dogs could join us.

We arrived in Värmland, a region close to one of Sweden's largest lakes, and were immediately introduced to the woodpile from which we would make our raft. A mountain of logs, each weighing up to fifty kilos, had to be lashed together to create a floating behemoth that would weigh upwards of three tons.

My wife is brilliant at just about everything. She is a successful businesswoman, an amazing cook, a brilliant mother. She is beautiful, funny and clever, but she isn't very strong. In fact, she has absolutely no upper-body strength at all.

A number of other groups and families had arrived at the same time, and the woodpiles had been set out along the river bank at equal intervals, giving the proceedings an air of competition. It was like *The Krypton Factor*. I knelt down and, with difficulty, lifted one end of a log on to my shoulders, before edging my way down to the middle of the timber and, with a jerk of my knees, hoicking it up. It's not easy walking down a sandy bank with a fifty-kilo tree trunk on your shoulders, but for six hours that is what I did, as we built layer upon layer of the raft, using ropes to lash the timbers together.

By early afternoon we were halfway through construction, while some of the other rafts were already setting sail. Next to us, a group of Germans had been working with ruthless Teutonic efficiency. One of their children watched me as I stood waist deep in river water, lashing two sections together.

'We've already finished,' he commented smugly.

'Have you?' I smiled back through gritted teeth.

'Yes, it took us just four hours,' he said. I could see his parents loading the raft, using a small ramp and a wheelbarrow.

'I hope it sinks,' I thought to myself.

Just before dusk, I tied the last timber in place and we loaded up the dog beds and the food box before casting ourselves adrift. We may have been the last raft to leave, but it felt good. My shoulder was bruised black and my hands were covered in splinters, but we'd got through the hard part, I thought, as we glided down the flat waters.

For the next seven days we would be at the mercy of the river; we would be mere passengers as we followed the current downstream. A large pole allowed us to punt to port or starboard, but we had no control over speed or direction.

As the sun set, it cast a beautiful golden glow across the river. Marina and I sat at the front of the raft and opened a bottle of wine to celebrate.

'How do we stop this thing?' asked Marina, while we sipped our river-cooled Chablis. It was a good point. We were moving at little more than walking pace, but how do you stop a three-ton raft?

While we were equipped to sleep and eat on the raft, as darkness fell it dawned on me that I needed to get ashore to let the dogs pee.

I stood at the front and pushed the pole into the darkening waters. They were too deep. I grabbed a paddle and attempted to steer us towards shallower waters. It had no impact whatsoever.

I thought for a moment. We had a long line. If I could get it around a tree, then it would act as a cantilever, slowing us down. I could then haul the raft ashore. But how could I get the rope around the tree? There was only one way.

As darkness descended, I stripped naked and jumped into the freezing river. The rope tugged from my hands as the coil began to unwind. I had to move quickly or the raft would simply pull me along with it. I swam towards the shore as fast as I could, but the noise and fun had excited the dogs, who both decided to join me in the river. Now the three of us were being swept un-controllably downstream while Marina looked on helplessly from the raft.

Soon I could feel stones beneath my feet. There wasn't much rope left in my hands.

'Maggi! Inca!' I hollered, as I wrapped the last remaining tether of rope around a thin tree. The tree creaked and yawed as it took the full weight, bending double as the river snatched at the raft. Finally, it groaned some more – and then the weight of the raft uprooted the small tree entirely, yanking it into the river, with me close behind. Maggi, Inca, the tree and I all started floating down-river after the raft, until it got caught on a tight bend and I was able to pull us all to the shore.

The raft began to take on a life of its own. It was like a living, breathing thing. We soon discovered that stopping it was next to impossible. To get the dogs ashore, we had to board them on to the small Canadian canoe that we had tethered to the raft. One of us paddled them ashore, lifted them out, let them do their business, then paddled hell for leather to catch up with the raft. The problem here was that Marina wasn't strong enough to lift the dogs in and out of the canoe without the risk of capsizing, and she didn't like being on the raft alone.

As if life on board an uncontrollable river raft wasn't hard enough already, our holiday coincided with the coldest, wettest summer on record. Marina sat in her bikini and raincoat, shivering in the 5°C chill. Even the dogs looked cold.

You wouldn't have thought things could get worse, but they did.

A small word, a simple word, but a horrible one: 'eddy'. I remembered the term vaguely from geography lessons but, given the mysterious N grade, it will come as no surprise that I had no idea what it was.

If you look 'eddy' up in a dictionary it will say something like:

'A current, as of water or air, moving contrary to the direction of the main current, especially in a circular motion. This phenomenon is most visible behind large emergent rocks in swift-flowing rivers.' None of which adequately describes the horrible predicament of being in one on a three-ton raft. It also doesn't explain that an eddy is often invisible to the human eye, with all its horrible power happening below the surface, nicely positioned to trap any unsuspecting amateur rafters with two dogs and no way of stopping their craft.

Until now the raft had followed the course of the river like a train on its track, but suddenly we appeared to be going in circles as the powerful current hauled us upriver. It seemed to defy science, and it looked as if we would be caught in the current indefinitely with no way forward and no way back.

Once again I grabbed the punting pole and went to the front. Fortunately, the water was shallow here and I wedged the pole into the stony bed. But I hadn't taken into account the momentum that drove the raft, and I found myself catapulted into the river. Marina must have known for sure at this point that she had married a complete imbecile.

I fished myself out of the water and sent Marina to the bow with a paddle, while I positioned myself directly behind her at the stern. I estimated where the current began to turn upstream and, just before we got caught in the eddy once again, we both paddled as furiously as we could . . . only to find ourselves sucked back into the eddy. Again and again and again. It took us four hours to escape.

Between the river and the rain, it wasn't long before everything we owned was a sodden mess, but things really started to go wrong when the lashings that bound the raft together began to come apart, leaving large gaping holes between the logs. The raft had taken on a list to starboard and it wasn't long before one corner was totally submerged.

'Only five more days,' I said, adopting my expedition mentality. Marina and the dogs were not amused.

We sheltered under a tarpaulin while we continued on our ceaseless river voyage. We hadn't passed any form of civilization since we set sail, and the thought of another night in a wet sleeping bag, on damp logs next to two soaking dogs, suddenly didn't seem such fun.

A large wooden barn appeared in the distance. If I could only stop this thing, then we might be able to find warmth and shelter for the night. I grabbed the line and dived into the river. Once again, I tried to swim faster than the raft so that I would have time to wrap the line around a large tree before the raft overtook me and took up all the slack.

I clambered on to the bank and found a solid-looking tree around which I flung the line, then anchored it to the ground with my entire body weight. The line stretched and strained and the raft began to turn in on itself before slowly, miraculously, drifting towards the shore and coming to a stop next to a sandy beach.

Marina leapt ashore and strode up to a small farmhouse. If you are a Swedish farmer, it's probably not every day that a beautiful bikini-clad girl knocks on your door in the pouring rain. It seemed to do the trick, however, and we were offered the sanctuary of a barn for the night.

A huge storm raged all night and continued the following day. At points it was hard to see where the river ended and the rain began. Should we carry on for the sake of it, or should we do what most sensible people would do and abandon the holiday?

My stubbornness, never far below the surface, reared its head. I didn't want to give up, not yet. Failure. The scourge of my child-hood had returned to haunt me even on a family holiday. The question of whether you can 'fail' a holiday may seem odd, but at that moment that's exactly what it seemed like and I wasn't about to give in to some stupid raft on a poxy Swedish river. After all, I'd rowed the Atlantic.

'Why don't I continue on the raft and you could follow alongside in the car with the dogs?' I suggested to Marina.

'That would be fun,' she replied.

The last I saw of our raft was through the rain-smeared window as the kind farmer drove us away in his Volvo.

That had been the last adventurous thing Marina and I had done together. Amazingly, she was now proposing to come to Sweden with me again, this time to do a marathon. It was a strange concept – even getting fit together seemed like an obstacle to me.

To be honest, I am quite a solitary runner. Social in every other aspect of my life, running for me has always been my 'me' time. I look forward to a run for the solitude as much as the endorphins. So it was strange getting changed into our running kit together. I felt like part of one of those smug couples you see in American movies where they exercise together.

'You're running too fast,' shouted Marina.

'Now you're deliberately going too slow,' she sighed.

I was doing that typical male thing. If you don't want to do something again, do it really, really badly – the washing-up, the cooking, the cleaning. We've all done it at some time in our lives to get out of a chore and it always seems to work. (I hope I haven't broken some 'male secret' by admitting to that.) I had a fear that running would suddenly become something I had to do 'together'. I would be forced to give up the one thing I relished doing on my own, so it was only reasonable that if I ran really badly with Marina then we wouldn't have to do it again.

It worked and we have never run together since.

We still had the small matter of ice skating to contend with. As a child I had gone to an ice rink hidden beneath Queensway in central London. I looked online and was astonished to find that it is still open. I called a friend who had appeared in ITV's *Dancing on Ice* to find out if they had a trainer to recommend, and before I knew it we had been booked in for a two-hour training session on a Monday morning.

Returning to that ice rink brought my childhood flooding back. I was overwhelmed by nostalgia as I sat on the wooden bench in the changing room, strapping the skates to my feet. As children, my sisters and I would spend hours going round and round in circles while eighties music pumped out of a dodgy Tannoy system. The rink had shrunk since then to make way for a bowling alley, but everything else remained much the same.

There has been a huge resurgence in ice skating since the ITV show, and even on a Monday morning I was surprised how many people were dancing across the ice. I walked along the plastic mat, teetering on my sharp blades, and tentatively stepped on to the ice. A smile broke across my face as I felt that familiar sensation of the blades cutting into the ice. I wobbled slightly and clutched on to the side for stability.

Next it was Marina's turn. I watched as she stepped carefully on to the rink. I could see her legs trembling as each skate was lowered on to the ice. There was a wobble and a sway as she fought against the slip of her blades. I could see the concentration in her eyes as she tried to stay upright. Her feet moved back and forth, gathering momentum with each movement. It looked as if she were running on the spot. Her arms flailed as she fought against gravity, before both her legs shot out in front of her and she landed on her bottom.

I had to hold in a guffaw of laughter as I raced to scoop her off the ice.

For two long hours we skated in circles like hamsters in a wheel. Our instructor taught us back posture and how to hold our legs. I surprised myself with my own ability as snippets from childhood came flooding back.

Marina, it is fair to say, wasn't coping quite so well. I can only describe her skating style as like a granny answering the call of nature in a wood.

It was funny, though.

With one lesson under our belts, Marina and I flew out to Stockholm to put our skills to the test in an 80-kilometre (48-mile) marathon from Uppsala to Stockholm.

I love Sweden, probably because of its similarity to Canada and the fact that my family have spent a great deal of time in the Scandinavian country. For nearly a decade my mother ran an antiques business in London, selling eighteenth-century Swedish furniture. She and my father would drive up to Sweden in a white hired van, travelling from remote farm to remote farm, where they would be invited into darkened barns brimming with beautiful furniture. They made many friends over the years, and although I had only visited the country a handful of times, I have always felt an affinity with the Swedes. I envy their lifestyle and their extreme seasons – freezing, snowy winters and boiling, mosquito-infested summers. None of this British ambiguity.

I particularly envy their outdoor lifestyle. I'm sure it's the reason they all have such great complexions. Fit and attractive, the Swedes have long valued and treasured their environment and I firmly believe that if we adopted more of their lifestyle principles the world would be a better place. Sure, they have twenty-four hours of darkness in winter, but skinny-dipping without inhibitions is also a national pastime.

In 1890 Pim Mulier, a Dutch sports journalist, undertook a much-fabled but never-before-attempted challenge. He skated along a series of frozen canals, rivers and lakes, passing eleven towns in Friesland, Holland, covering a distance of 125 miles in just under thirteen hours. To verify his achievement, he dropped in on houses en route, asking the people living there to sign and put the time in his notebook. With that, the *Elfstedentocht*, or Eleven City Tour, Holland's first ice-skating marathon, was born.

The first competition was held in 1909 with twenty-two competitors, most of them local farmers, one of whom reportedly completed the gruelling route while smoking his pipe. Since those humble beginnings, the race has grown enormously, with the most recent event in 1997 featuring more than sixteen thousand competitors. The build-up to the race is accompanied by intense excitement, or *Elfstedenkoorts*, Eleven City race fever.

The marathon begins in darkness, at 5 or 6 a.m., but the competitors' spirits can be warmed by the riverside stalls selling hot chocolate and traditional Dutch pea soup. Following on from Mulier's example, participants must get their cards time-stamped at each town they pass, and all competitors must finish by midnight. However, few complete the whole course. In the infamous race of 1963, less than 1 per cent reached the finishing line. The 1956 race has also been well remembered for its controversial conclusion, as the five strongest skaters linked arms and chose to cross the finishing line simultaneously. The medal was thereby presented to the sixth skater to finish and no winner was declared. The 1986 race even received royal patronage, as Crown Prince Willem Alexander competed under a loose pseudonym, with his mother, Queen Beatrix, awaiting him at the finishing line. The race has also faced some hostility, however, as in 1997 an anti-*Elfstedentocht* group tried to sabotage proceedings by pouring salt on the route.

However, the race can only be held weather permitting. The ice must be at least six inches thick. As a result, it has been held only fifteen times in the past century and there are fears that due to increasing global temperatures the event will become even rarer, perhaps occurring only four or five times a century.

Inspired by the *Elfstedentocht*, but concerned by the infrequency of the event, the winner of the 1991 Eleven City Tour and other key competitors travelled to Sweden to see if a similar event could be held there and in 1999 the *Vikingarännet*, or Viking Run, was born. It is named after the water transportation routes it follows, which are thought to have been first used by the Vikings. The event, like the *Elfstedentocht*, is still dependent upon weather conditions and thus only two weeks' notice is given before a run, leading to hectic preparations. The Viking Run normally has around eight thousand contestants, 90 per cent of whom are thought to be from tour-skating groups.

It was a Saturday morning in late January when we landed in a snowy Stockholm. It is a pretty cool city in every respect. It was minus 5°C and the waterways surrounding it were frozen, which boded well for our race. We had less than twenty-four hours until it began. We still needed to hire all the kit, enrol and practise on our new skates on a frozen lake.

Ice skating, tobogganing and cross-country skiing are to Swedes what hiking is to Brits. We found one of the city's many ice-skating parks.

'Hello, do you speak English?' I asked, exaggerating each word.

'Of course,' he shrugged, in better English than most English.

'We'd like to hire some skates for tomorrow's Viking Run,' I said.

'Sure,' he replied, producing the most ludicrous set of ice skates I had ever seen. The blade was twice the length of the boot. They looked more like miniature skis than blades.

'Ah,' I shook my head, 'could we just have normal skates?'

'These are normal skates,' he answered, looking slightly puzzled. 'This is what we skate on here in Sweden. You need the long blades for the different ice conditions. You'll also need some of these,' he announced, holding up what can only be described as two screwdrivers attached to each other with a cord.

'What are they?' I asked, puzzled.

'Spikes.'

'And what are the spikes for?' I asked suspiciously.

'For when you fall through the ice. You wear them round your neck and you use them to claw your way back on to the ice.'

'Of course,' I nodded with embarrassment.

'Have you ever done cross-country ice skating?' he asked.

'A little,' I lied, before scurrying off with my fourteen-inch blades and my spikes.

Marina and I booted up and carefully walked down to the frozen lake, using a temporary wooden balustrade. A circuit had been created that looked a little like a running track, only made of ice. It was about four hundred metres around and, the day being a Saturday, was crammed with the Swedish equivalent of park joggers.

My legs twitched and jerked to balance on the long thin blades. With no wall, this was going to be interesting.

I took a small step, then tried to kick off with my right boot, but the blade simply collapsed under my weight and I fell in a crumpled heap.

There was mild pandemonium as speeding Swedes in full Lycra struggled to avoid me. It was like stalling on the motorway as people swerved and leapt to avoid colliding with me.

It was Marina's turn to gloat as she glided effortlessly across the ice.

Have you ever tried to pick yourself up from the ice unassisted? If you haven't, you'll have to take my word that it is one of the most frustrating and humiliating things a human being can do. You must simply abandon all decorum as you struggle against gravity.

For five long minutes I fought against the ice before finally regaining my footing on the frozen lake. By now I had created a sort of negative force field – one which kept me away from everyone else rather than the opposite.

I gave my right boot another push and edged off on to the

race-track once again, just in time to meet Marina, who had already done two laps.

'Focus, Ben,' I thought, as I struggled to gain momentum.

The problem was the length of blade. My ankles simply couldn't, or wouldn't, counterbalance quickly enough and each time I found my boot collapsing on itself, sending my ankle on to the cold surface. I managed to stay upright, but I simply couldn't control the boot.

If Marina had resembled a peeing granny in London, I seemed more like a constipated Frankenstein's monster as I lumbered around the track with my buttocks clenched and my arms outstretched. I must have looked like the living dead as I made my way painfully slowly around the circuit.

Marina had lapped me four times before I completed my first circuit. My ankles were bruised and sore, but at least my feet seemed to be acclimatizing to their new world.

A couple more hours and we decided to call it quits. We wanted to be fit for the race the following day. As we hobbled off the ice and along the pontoon, an attractive Swedish couple walked towards us. They were both statuesque, blond, with flawless skin. Nothing remarkable, you might say, except that they were also stark naked. In their birthday suits, leaving nothing to the imagination.

While this might have been slightly surprising in summer, it was mystifying in the middle of winter, at minus 5°C, in the middle of a family park filled with children.

'Good morning,' they smiled as they walked past, oblivious.

We turned to follow them as they walked to the edge of the pontoon, where they stood overlooking the frozen lake before leaping into a hole cut into the ice. They didn't make a noise as their naked bodies were enveloped in the icy water.

We caught a bus back to the hotel.

*

The next morning it was cold and sunny as we rose early for the train to Uppsala, the starting point of the race. It was 8 a.m. when we arrived. Hundreds of men and women had been there since dawn. We queued up in the registration line, surrounded by Swedes.

'Hello, do you speak English?' I asked foolishly again.

'Of course,' came the ubiquitous reply. I'm not sure why I kept asking. I think it is my deep-rooted need to be polite, and the assumption that the people of a non-English-speaking country should speak English seems patently rude. But what I have discovered is that many people think that the assumption they don't speak English is ruder than the assumption that they do. I digress.

'Ah, you are the only foreign skaters,' smiled the woman.

'That means we're competing for England!' I marvelled to Marina as the magnitude began to sink in. We'd just signed up for the full eighty-kilometre race. That's a long way for professionals, let alone two English novices.

We had brought our little rucksack and stuffed it with granola bars, bananas and chocolate bars.

'Marina . . .' I wasn't sure how to broach the subject. 'About this race . . .' I stammered. 'I love you and I love doing things with you . . .' I could see her puzzling over where this was going. 'But this is a race and I think we should both race it,' I spluttered.

'What are you trying to say?' she asked.

'What I mean is that I don't think we should stick together for the sake of sticking together.'

Marina looked puzzled. How was I going to phrase this?

'Well, as this is a race, I think we should race it and . . .'

'And?'

'And I don't want you to hold me up.' There – I had said it. I didn't want her to slow me down. It was a race and I wanted to race it.

'So you think I'll slow you down?' She raised an eyebrow. I wasn't sure how to reply to this so I opted for a shoulder shrug.

'Let's see, Fogle,' she smiled as we walked towards the start line.

Five hundred Swedes were busy warming up. There was even more Spandex than blond hair as we waited to set off.

To be honest, I was still more worried about the spikes than the length of the race. Everyone wore them round their necks, as a sailor would wear a life jacket. They looked naturally at ease with them, as if they were some sort of Goth jewellery, but for me they felt dangerous and worrisome. They implied that we *would* fall through the ice. Given that we would be skating over lakes, rivers, canals and ponds, how were we to gauge its thickness? What if those in front weakened the ice with their weight?

I was suddenly overcome with worry. But before I had time to think it through, we were off.

It takes time to build up speed on skates. There was no marathon sprint, but a slow, laboured chug. We were more like tanker trucks than sports cars, slowly working our way up through the gears.

Given the number of expeditions I've done over the years, you would be forgiven for assuming that I am usually well prepared, so how I ended up at the start of an eighty-kilometre ice race across the wilds of Sweden in the middle of winter without a hat, jacket or gloves is as much a mystery to me as to you.

The course took us across a large lake marked with red flag posts, the fast sprinters at the front and the slow Brits at the back. For half an hour Marina and I skated together. I seemed to be getting the hang of the long blades and my ankles were holding out, but as time ticked by and my legs got tired, so did my ankles, with disastrous results.

Once off the lake, we crossed a shallow pond, navigating through the thick bulrushes and back out on to open water. By now Marina and I had been separated. I wasn't certain whether she was ahead or behind, but it was a fair bet she had fallen back slightly.

Two hours into the marathon and I came across my first obstacle. Open water. I had noticed a slight change underfoot. The ice was slightly submerged in water. A wooden plank with a rubber mat had been placed across a hole in the ice. Gingerly I stepped on to the temporary bridge, before edging my way across the opening and back on to relatively solid ice.

There is something entirely unsettling about finding cracks and holes in ice. No matter how much reassurance we had been given about its thickness, a hole is a hole. As a child I watched a horror film in which a man got trapped in a river under ice. Ever since, I have had a fear, bordering on the obsessive, about falling through ice. That film did for me what *Jaws* did for swimmers. I clutched at the spikes around my neck, ready to spear the ice with their sharp points.

Three hours into the race and my ankles were beginning to rebel. I would get into a nice comfortable routine when suddenly an ankle would collapse without warning. These failures became more and more frequent as the hours ticked by.

The course was spread out wide over the countryside and, apart from the lonely red flags fluttering in the wind, there was little to mark this out as a race; it was more like a battle for survival. The wind increased and the temperature plummeted. My hands and face were icy cold. My core temperature remained warm through exertion, but the cold air bit at my cheeks.

'F**k!' I hollered, uncharacteristically, as my ankle collapsed again and a sharp pain shot up my foot. I clutched at my boot and the pain soon disappeared. I always know when I am reaching my limits by the fact that I start swearing. The f-word is usually reserved for special occasions of pure frustration.

I struggled to get to my feet once again. My bottom was bruised from multiple tumbles and my ankle throbbed with pain.

I was in the middle of a vast lake, miles from anywhere. As with so many situations in my life, the only way out was to carry on. There wasn't the option of giving up.

Soon the lake began to narrow and I found myself skating past large summer houses on the water's edge and pretty little islands with wooden boathouses. Every now and again some cross-country skiers would swish passed with a cheery 'Hello.' I think my skating marked me out as English.

But where was everyone else? There was no sign of any of the other racers. I knew that the majority were ahead of me, but where were the rest? And what about Marina? I had been focusing so hard on my ankle that the Abominable Snowman could have skated past and I wouldn't have noticed.

'F**k, f**k, f**k!' I hollered. Things must have been getting bad if I was swearing in triplicate.

My ankle collapsed again. The shooting pain through my foot was unbearable. But onwards I skated. The sun was already beginning to dip, as the short Scandinavian winter day drew to a close. It was nearly 3 p.m. and there was still no sign of the finish line.

I followed the red marker flags across some more temporary bridges and even across a rocky peninsula, where I teetered on my blades like a Hollywood starlet in her Jimmy Choos. Eventually I was on the canal system, skating past buildings and under bridges. The end wasn't far now. Glory and victory – another sporting success story for my biography.

I would finish and wait to cheer Marina over the line. It would be so romantic, I thought. Why had I been so against her coming in the first place, I wondered, berating myself for my foolish insensitivity.

But where was the finish line? It had to be around here some-where. I had reached Stockholm. Where were the crowds? I skated towards a man clearing some bollards.

'Hello, do you speak English?' I asked. I should have predicted his answer. 'Do you know where the ice-skating marathon finish line is?'

'Yes,' he said, 'it was here.' He smiled, carrying on with his clearing.

'What do you mean "was"?' I asked, perplexed.

'Everyone has finished. We are dismantling it.'

'*Everyone*?' I asked.

'Everyone,' he reiterated.

'Except me,' I muttered, 'and Marina?' What about Marina? Where was my wife? She was behind me and therefore on her own. What if she had got lost? Or fallen through the ice? My mind began to race.

My heart pounded with fear as the reality sank in. I had told her I wasn't waiting for her and now if anything had happened to her it was my fault. All sorts of dark thoughts went through my head. Why had I set off without my mobile phone? Idiot.

'I'll have to skate back and find her,' I thought to myself.

Marina didn't have a mobile either. Maybe she would call the hotel, I reasoned, heading off to a payphone. I teetered into the phone booth on my battered blades and called directory enquiries, who put me through to our hotel.

'Hello. I think my wife is lost. I'm going to find her,' I announced, rather dramatically.

'One moment, Mr Fogle,' said the operator.

The line went quiet. What were they thinking of? This was a matter of life or death and they had put me on hold.

'Hello?' said a familiar voice.

'Marina!' I spluttered with astonishment.

'How you doing?' she asked nonchalantly.

'Where are you?' I blurted. 'I've been worried sick.'

'I'm in the bath.'

'What do you mean "in the bath"?'

This became an iconic image of the *Castaway* project mainly because it was used in so many publications. Inca was just a puppy at the time.

Left to right: Philiy Page, me, Toby Waterman, Tammy Huff and Padraig Nallen. Happy days on Taransay sitting atop 'Bomb Buoy', an enormous ship's fender that washed ashore.

Standing outside one of our pods in my infamous Guernsey jumper. It took us weeks to cover all the pods in turf.

Above: Racing in the World Tin Bath Championship for *Countryfile*. I sank and ended up in an ambulance with hypothermia.

Below: Dili, East Timor, at the UNHCR facility where I spent a week with my friend Jake Morland in 2001 on assignment for *Hello!* magazine. The East Timorese are a beautiful people and I was deeply moved by my experience of repatriating those caught up in the troubles with Indonesia.

The Marathon des Sables, the toughest race on earth. My green 'gaiters' were homemade in the desert using dental floss and some parachute silk borrowed from one of the runners. My feet quickly began to resemble those of a mummy and by the end they were entirely enveloped in bandages. The pain was unbearable – like walking on shards of glass. But nothing was going to stop me from finishing.

Above: Frank Maloney, Barry McGuigan, Sid Owen, me, Jim McDonnell and Frank Bruno at the launch of the Sport Relief charity boxing match in central London.

Left: A photo call before James and I took to the road in our rickshaw, cycling non-stop from Edinburgh to London in support of the SSAFA. Luckily we didn't cycle the whole route in our kilts.

Above: Early-morning training for our Atlantic row – in Namibia, where I was filming *Wild in Africa* with Kate Humble. I hated that machine for the hours it stole and it never prepared me for the reality of the Atlantic Ocean.

Below: Racing across Lewa Downs in northern Kenya for the Lewa Safaricom Marathon, which I ran with the Battleback soldiers. There is something incredibly beautiful and raw about running through the African bush.

Above: Marina on the Viking Run in Sweden, enjoying some mulled wine during one of the breaks and generally enjoying her surroundings. I am somewhere way, way behind.

Below: Our timber raft in Sweden, still under construction. It took us all day to build our little raft, which weighed more than a ton. This was the first and last we would see of the sun before the rain swept in.

'In the bath – like in a tub full of water with bubbles, where we clean ourselves,' she replied.

'Where?'

'You called me, so isn't that perfectly obvious?' I could hear the water in the background.

'Did you give up?' I puzzled.

'No, I finished, and . . .' she paused for effect, '. . . and you said it was a race and we shouldn't stick together,' she finished, with a proud flourish.

That'll teach me.

Part Three

11

The Cracknell Years

There is one person to whom I will for ever be inextricably linked. James Cracknell.

I often get introduced as James at events and have seen his name next to my picture in newspapers and magazines.

'You're the Olympic rower,' strangers shout. 'Show us your gold medals!' People stop me on the street and ask for rowing tips. It's all a far cry from the real me.

Mistaken identity has plagued me all my life. For years people used to think I was Chesney Hawkes, then I went through the Prince William years, which arguably still go on. Indeed I once arrived at Santiago airport to a bank of paparazzi who had heard I was Prince William. To say they were disappointed would be an understatement.

But ever since we met, we have become Ben and James, the less well-known Ant and Dec. To some people we may look similar, but we couldn't be more different in personality, which makes our friendship all the more remarkable.

I first met James at a Christmas party. I had decided to take part in the 2005–2006 Atlantic Rowing Race and, as if by luck, fate stepped in and placed a double Olympic rower in my sights.

Ever since my race across the Sahara Desert I had been looking for another challenge, something to get my teeth into that would stretch my own physical and mental abilities and also other people's perception of me. I had heard tales of people rowing across the Atlantic Ocean, and an internet search had revealed that not only did people cross oceans in small wooden rowing boats, but there was an actual race . . . against others in small wooden rowing boats. I loved the eccentricity of it. It was just the kind of challenge I was after.

Before I could stop myself I had signed up for this epic three-thousand-mile race. I even made a five-figure down payment for the race fee. It was only after signing up that I thought about little details like the fact that I had never rowed in my life. I didn't have a rowing partner, or a boat. But this was a challenge that could change my life and little details like those weren't going to put me off.

Now it might seem strange, but it never occurred to me that I might have bitten off more than I could chew. It never crossed my mind that it might be dangerous. All I could think about was who would do it with me.

When I met him, James was recently back from winning his second gold medal at the Athens Olympics and I needed a rowing partner. We'd never met before, but our lives were about to take a most unusual turn.

James and I are very different characters. He is a professional athlete who has made a career out of coming first and winning gold. He competed in the 1989 and 1990 Junior Rowing World Championships, winning gold in 1990. He first competed in the World Rowing Championships in 1997, as part of the men's coxless fours, winning in 1997, 1998 and 1999. James won his first

Olympic gold medal at the 2000 Sydney Olympic Games. He and Matthew Pinsent, competing in the coxless pairs, won the 2001 and 2002 World Championships, and in 2001 they also won the coxed pairs. James won his second Olympic gold medal in 2004 at the Athens Olympics, as part of the coxless fours, beating the Canadian world champions by 0.08 seconds. In 2004 he received an OBE for his services to sport.

James is focused, driven and extremely hard on himself. For him, anything other than gold would be considered failure. Indeed, at the time I met him, he was deciding whether to continue towards the Beijing Olympics. The problem with James's character was that a silver or bronze medal would simply negate, or cancel out, the two golds he had already won in Sydney and Athens. It was gold or nothing.

I would describe myself as driven, stubborn and determined too, but I don't think I'm motivated by competition or winning. True, I had flirted with competition over the years, but by teaming up with an Olympian I would be taking it to a whole new level, and one that had always scared me. Another hangover from my childhood lack of sporting prowess was to shy away from competition. It's probably one of the reasons I hate pressure.

James agreed to join me. To this day I'm not really sure why. I think it was partly on the basis that he still hadn't decided whether to compete at the next Olympics and wanted a year out of professional rowing to collect his thoughts.

We had a huge amount to do before the race. We had to become ocean yachtmasters, we learned to put stitches into one another and how to do fillings. We had to build our plywood boat from a flatpack and learn to use all the equipment on board. It was a full-time job, but we both had careers to keep up and we both struggled to multi-task. In the two months before the race, instead of training and planning together, I went off to Namibia for the BBC's *Wild In Africa* with Kate Humble. The only way I could train was with a rowing machine, which I would set up in the desert each morning before we began filming.

I spent several hours a day on that rowing machine, which I lugged around the world. It became my appendage, and all my travel plans revolved around the Concept2 ergometer. I hated that machine for the pain it inflicted and the hours it stole. I tried to row for two hours in the morning and two hours in the afternoon. If you have ever been on a rowing machine for more than about five minutes, you will know how boring it gets. Boooooring.

It wasn't the best way to plan for the biggest race of my life. By the time we reached the start line at La Gomera in the Canary Islands, James and I still hadn't been in a boat together – and our boat wasn't even finished.

In our haste to get everything ready, James and I never really got to know each other. We were still strangers from two very different worlds. I've often wondered why he agreed to join me, then just a daytime TV presenter. I think it gave him the excuse of an artificial handicap. There is a logical assumption that an Olympic gold medallist will always win – whatever the sport. By teaming up with a rowing novice – or virgin, as I liked to call myself – he had a built-in excuse. I could be the fall guy – a role I was happy to accept.

We made an unlikely duo to row across the Atlantic, the professional and the amateur. What we discovered was that we had very different motivations. James was there to compete, while I was there to complete the race. The 'l' makes a huge difference during months at sea.

I will never forget our first week on that boat. It must rate as one of the most miserable, bleak, depressing periods I have ever experienced. It was one of the first times in my life that I regretted something. I wished I wasn't there. We both did. We each disappeared into quite a dark place – not that we realized it at the time, as we didn't really communicate with one another. Conversation largely consisted of a few grunts and nods of the head. In retrospect, the only thing that kept us both on that little boat was the fear of failure. We simply weren't prepared to cave in to the assumptions that we wouldn't make it. Although James was an Olympic rower, we were both out of our depth. This was a whole new kind of rowing for James. We couldn't bear the humiliation of quitting. It was pure stubbornness that kept us rowing. I'm not sure what James was thinking – whether he regretted teaming up with a novice?

We had decided to row together for the first six hours of the race, after which we would break into a routine of two hours on, two hours off. One of us would always be rowing, while the other ate or slept. It sounded like a workable routine. I remember coming off the oars after those first six hours. I counted twenty blisters on my hands. I had a boil on my bottom. I was hungry, dehydrated and sunburned. I was homesick, and above all I was terrified of James. I suddenly realized I was aboard our little boat with a total stranger. We had nothing in common. No mutual friends, no shared experiences.

One day James asked me what I thought about during my two hours on the oars. I have always been a good daydreamer (at school I was sent to an ear expert because my teachers thought I was deaf in class – but I had just disappeared into a daydream). I told him how I took myself back to Latin America or my year on Taransay. I would imagine climbing in the mountains or sailing through the Galapagos.

'What do you think about?' I asked.

He told me how he spent the entire two hours working out how to get a better glide on the seat and a more efficient scoop with the oar. For his whole life, James had lived, breathed and eaten for rowing. It was all he knew and all he ever did.

About a week into the race, we finally decided to call home. We had a satellite phone but had determined not to use it until we had settled into life at sea. We still had no idea of how we were doing in the race. It had taken just a couple of hours to lose sight of the other boats in the mountainous seas. In fact, the only people who knew how we were doing were our families at home. Each boat was fitted with a tracking beacon which sent a message to a tracking station which would plot our progress on a map. Our friends and families could follow our progress and, more importantly, see how we were doing.

We had been divided over whether or not we should find out our position in the race, but James's curiosity got the better of him and his wife Bev told him we were in seventh place. James was knocked by the disappointment, while I celebrated the fact that we were doing so well. It was another clarification of our different characters, personalities and motivations. We were getting to know each other, but we were learning how different we were rather than how similar.

We became like an old married couple, bickering and fighting our way across the Atlantic. It took a capsize to make us re-evaluate our relationship. We were a thousand miles from land when our boat was pitch-poled by an enormous wave. We had become complacent with life on the high seas. We felt invincible. We were the masters of our environment and nothing was going to touch us. We had given up wearing safety harnesses or life jackets and had left all our equipment strewn on the small deck.

We lost everything in the capsize, very nearly including our lives. It was the closest I have come to meeting my maker. I really thought it was curtains. I remember coming up from the depths of the Atlantic to see our tiny boat upturned and no sign of James. I was racked with guilt. I remember berating myself for getting into such a stupid situation in the first place. We had been flipped by a wave, but I wondered whether I could have done something to control the boat. What if I had held off the crest of the wave? I had flashes back to that mountain in Ecuador when we had been stuck in a storm.

For someone who has found himself in a number of tight squeezes, I am not actually naturally attracted to danger, and to be honest I had never really thought about the perils of rowing across a three-thousand-mile ocean in a boat made of plywood and glue. We should have got the hint from the safety officer who very nearly pulled us from the race before we had even begun due to our lack of preparations. When we arrived at the start of the race we met some teams who had spent four years planning the trip. We had spent less than a year. Where everyone else had spent months doing sea trials, and in some cases even rowing other oceans, we hadn't even been in our boat together. In fact, the only time we had been on the water together was in Henley when James took me out in a scull in front of his former coach. 'What do you think of Ben?' he later told me he had asked his coach. 'Your friend is going to have a very sore back,' had been the response.

We were so absorbed in the rush to get to the start line that we never had time to contemplate the dangers. They just sort of crept up on us.

I will never forget my fear when I came out of the tiny cabin to be confronted by the most enormous waves I had ever seen. The whole ocean had changed from flat calm to raging surf in just an hour and it was terrifying, but we just had to get on with it. To start with James was on the oars whooping with delight, but now, several weeks later, we had capsized and I was in the Atlantic Ocean, a thousand miles from land.

I was able to get back to the boat and somehow managed to help right it. James had been asleep in the cabin when we capsized and he emerged slightly battered and bruised, but we were both alive. We had lost our electrics, our water desalinator (for converting salt water into fresh drinking water), our GPS, the sea anchor that stopped us being blown backwards, and our satellite phone. In fact, we had lost just about everything that was important to us.

I can still remember reaching for the EPIRB – the emergency beacon each boat carried to call for rescue. I was about to push the button when James announced that we had to carry on rowing. We still had our oars and a stash of emergency drinking water in the ballast of the boat, he reasoned. Rescue could take anywhere up to a week, by which time we would almost be in Antigua. We had to keep rowing.

It was the best decision we ever made. It was a watershed in our adventure, the moment that two strangers finally became lifelong friends. We at last had a shared experience to draw on; but, above all, it was the moment when our goals collided. We both wanted to get to Antigua as quickly as possible. We became more efficient, covered more miles each day and, dare I say it, we almost started to enjoy the experience.

Ten days later, after forty-nine days at sea, we were the first two-man boat to row into Antigua, although we were placed second in the pairs race because we incurred a penalty for using some of our ballast water after the capsize.

My whole life changed as we stepped ashore. I had placed another bung in my leaky childhood complexes. This achievement was on a whole new scale from anything before it. I remember receiving a letter from the adventurer David Hempleman-Adams commending me on our achievement. I still treasure that letter. To receive an endorsement from one of your own heroes is an incredible feeling. So much had been riding on the row. Not only had we financed most of it ourselves, but I wanted to prove to the world that you could do anything if you really set your heart on it. Here I was, a non-rower who had managed to cross an ocean in a tiny rowing boat. This time I had managed to change public perception. I had proved that I was more than just a posh daytime presenter from a reality show. Suddenly I became Ben the Atlantic Rower. It was a huge turning point in my life and one that I still look back on with great pride. I had to fight deeper than I had ever done before and it was the first time I had drawn on all my past experiences: the boredom of Taransay, the trepidation of the boxing match, the pain of the Marathon des Sables and the insecurities of my childhood.

A little bit of James's Olympic dust seemed to have rubbed off on me. After our rowing achievement, my career went off at a different tangent as the BBC commissioned a brand-new series called *Extreme Dreams*, to which I will return later. But perhaps more significantly, I proposed to Marina. I knew that I wanted to ask her to marry me from the day we set off in our tiny little boat. It was one of the things that kept me going. I even made her engagement ring out of a little piece of rope from the boat. The journey across the Atlantic gave me time to think about life, where I had been and, more importantly, where I was going. I think I knew Marina and I would be together for ever from the first time I saw her in the park (or at least I hoped we would), but here, after forty-nine days at sea, I felt sure it was right. Just thinking about her makes me smile. She had packed me off with a pile of envelopes each marked with a mileage and I was to open them one by one when we'd completed those distances. Each envelope contained a photograph with a message from our year together. I loved looking at those photographs. I would stare at them for hours on end. They would make me laugh and cry in equal measure. When I told my parents, my father sighed with relief and told me that he would have sent me back home in the rowing boat if I hadn't proposed. They had loved Marina from the first minute they met her and it was obvious to them too that we were perfect for one another. Marina accepted and we married just eight months later. James was my best man, although he missed his flight and missed the wedding.

My friendship with James flourished as his wife Beverley and Marina also became great friends, but it was two years later that he and I got itchy feet once again and decided we needed another challenge. We had both heard about a planned centenary race to the South Pole. It was billed as the first race across Antarctica since the great race to the Pole between Captain Robert Falcon Scott and the Norwegian Roald Amundsen in 1910–12.

We had wanted a challenge that would test us both, in which we could be equals, and given that neither of us had much cross-country skiing experience and that we both hated the cold, it seemed the perfect event. Up until now our friendship had always been based on inequality. James had always been the stronger, the fitter, the faster, while I had struggled to keep up not just with him but also with his high expectations.

We signed up for the race and then started our search for a third teammate. First of all we approached the actor Jonny Lee Miller. We had seen him at a number of marathons and knew that he had trained for the Marathon des Sables. We liked the fact that he could multi-task. I got his email address from a friend and we sent him a message inviting him to join us. 'This is the best offer I have ever received,' came his reply. Given that he had once been married to Angelina Jolie, we took that as high praise indeed and so he joined our team. We spent several months commuting back and forth across the Atlantic and training with the Royal Marines in Norway, until Jonny had to pull out due to work commitments.

Just six months before the race and we were back to square one, so we decided to advertise for a third teammate. We received thousands of applications, many from Polar experts, but we eventually chose Dr Ed Coats, a young doctor from Bristol. We chose Ed for a number of reasons. He was fit, active, passionate and he could multi-task. Above all, he was also a great bloke. After the girls met him they pointed out that he could have been our brother. Until then I had honestly never seen the resemblance, but I can now. We all have good chins.

The race to the South Pole was a huge challenge for us all. We spent many months training and getting fit, but then I managed to contract leishmaniasis, a flesh-eating bug caused by the bite of a sand fly, just a couple of months before we were due to depart.

I had heard tales of leishmaniasis over the years, but a little like the much-feared candiru, the small Amazonian fish that swims up your willy, I had always assumed it was something that just didn't happen. Until I contracted it myself.

I had spent seven weeks out in South America filming a third series of *Extreme Dreams* for the BBC and I had returned to London lethargic and nauseous. I had self-diagnosed malaria, but several blood tests at the London School of Hygiene and Tropical Medicine had all come back negative. It was the appearance of a large open sore on my arm that finally gave the game away.

I was being treated by Chris Van Tulleken, who had been the on-screen doctor in the BBC series *Blizzard* in which Bruce Parry had led a team against Polar explorer Inge Solheim (who would be racing against us to the South Pole) in a re-creation of the famous race between Scott and Amundsen in original kit. Chris was a cold-weather expert. 'Make sure this doesn't happen to you,' he smiled as I walked into his surgery for the first time. On his screen was a photograph of the frostbitten willy of a competitor in the North Pole Race several years before. The poor man had thought he had zipped up his trousers after peeing, but he had left his flies open and his willy exposed to minus 30°C.

For a month I travelled in and out of hospital while I received my infusion of antimony – a poisonous cocktail that was enough to kill the parasites but not me. For a time my chances of getting to Antarctica hung in the balance, but somehow I managed to get through and, more importantly, convince the doctors that I was fit to race.

In December 2008 we flew from Cape Town down to the Russian base of Novo, where we spent several weeks on an acclimatization trek. Antarctica is the driest, windiest, coldest place on earth, with the world's highest average altitude – 3,600 metres (12,000 feet). We would be racing against seven other teams in a thousand-kilometre footrace to the South Pole, hauling our own sledge, which weighed upwards of a hundred kilos. We had spent months training up and down the beaches of north Devon.

Indeed it was during one of these training sessions, at Croyde, that I found myself branded for life with a constant reminder of our South Pole adventure. It was 3 November, my birthday, and we went to the famous Thatch pub to celebrate. It was mid-week, early winter, and just a handful of hardy Devonians had ventured out. One of them happened to be the local tattooist, with his kit. The evening got a little more drunken than anticipated. Ed ended up vomiting across the bar, James passed out in the loo and I finished by getting a tattoo of a compass.

Or so I thought. A couple of years afterwards I was invited to appear on the BBC's *Would I Lie to You?* with Rob Brydon. Each panellist has to nominate a 'surprise guest' with a story so wild that everyone will think they are lying. I asked the researcher to look for the mystery tattooist, and so it was that two years later I finally met my marker – sober at least – only to have him reveal that it wasn't a compass at all, but a nautical star. He also told me that we had planned to do a huge penguin but had changed the design at the last minute. I'm glad someone remembers the evening.

The Race to the Pole had been beset by bad weather, so it was 1 January 2009 before we finally set off. From the start we had somehow managed to get ourselves into the lead, while the two Norwegians, Rune Malterud and Stian Aker, chased us down. Their small figures were always on the horizon as we headed south for upwards of eighteen hours a day.

All expectations had been for me to fail. I had only just finished my course of treatment at University College Hospital and my body still hadn't had time to recover properly. The doctors had given their consent to my participation, but I was still worried about how I'd cope. Surprisingly, it was neither myself nor Ed who struggled, but James. He took the race too hard. He tried carrying too much weight and his boots caused debilitating blisters which collectively wore him down; the weather induced asthma and he contracted pneumonia in one of his lungs from pushing himself too hard. As with the rowing, James had started the race as if it were a twenty-minute sprint down a river, not a thousand-kilometre slog across snow and ice. The effect was devastating and he fell apart before our eyes.

James can do many things, but self-preservation has never been one of his fortes. I had seen it on the Atlantic and during our training for the South Pole, and now, on the ice, he was driving himself into the ground. It was like a form of self-flagellation. I sometimes wonder whether he actually enjoys pain.

By the halfway mark it was looking unlikely that James would be able to continue, but a combination of stubbornness and a cocktail of medication improved his asthma and the pneumonia that had caused debilitating coughing fits.

Antarctica is a hauntingly beautiful place that can be deceptive in its bite. There are many hidden dangers here and it had begun to wear us all down. We were skiing for eighteen hours each day, giving us just a few hours of sleep after we had melted snow and made a meal. Everything takes ten times longer in the wind and cold. I have never liked the cold and found it hard to control my body temperature.

It was too cold for iPods, which would have their battery power drained by the extreme temperatures, and so I would spend hours on end with my head to the ground, trudging along through the arctic tundra. The sledges weighed about eighty kilos, which was fine on the flat snow, but they became dead weights whenever we reached the sastrugi, which are essentially ice waves, carved by the wind.

We took it in turns leading, as the leader had to cut the tracks into the snow and ice, which took extra effort, as well as navigating. I hated being in the lead and counted down the two hours until I could follow from behind again.

My pretty good system of taking myself out of any environment by daydreaming worked a treat. As we trudged along I had imaginary conversations with people and took myself on imaginary dates with my wife. I could practically taste the food.

Antarctica does all sorts of things to you, but it is particularly famous for bringing out emotions. We all found ourselves breaking into uncontrollable tears for no apparent reason. I still don't know why. I think it was a mixture of sleep deprivation and exhaustion, combined with the isolation. James continued to struggle, but we worked as a team and somehow we muddled through.

We arrived at the South Pole after eighteen days to find the Norwegian flag fluttering from the mast. We had been beaten by the Norwegians by just four hours. We may have failed to rewrite history, but we had certainly narrowed the gap from the four weeks between Amundsen and Scott. We had given everything to that race and reaching the end was surprisingly emotional for all of us.

Once again I returned home with a beard and a spring in my step. My confidence had been firmly bolstered by the expedition. My nose may have been damaged by frostbite, but nothing was going to dampen my spirits.

The BBC series about the race, *On Thin Ice*, was a surprise hit, but viewers didn't warm to James's competitive streak. I was surprised by some of the barbed attacks he had to field over the coming months and often felt hurt on his behalf. Many viewers found it difficult to understand the drive and character necessary to win an Olympic gold medal. Having met a handful of Olympians over the years, I have come to realize that they're a unique breed. To win gold takes a certain character.

Television is a very sweeping medium and the editing can be quite harsh. I have seen its power many times over the years. Characters often need to be stereotyped and the way a film is edited will frequently accentuate certain traits, with the result that other small nuances of personality or behaviour are lost. This can make all the difference to the public's perception of and reaction to someone. I first experienced it on Taransay, where each person in *Castaway* was given a persona. It's all finc and well if you are Mr Nice, but James found himself fielding the flak. He didn't like what he saw, and it must have hurt him.

'Now you're not a very nice man, are you?' people would stop in the street to say. 'I wouldn't like to be in your team.'

'Isn't he mean?' they'd say to me, pointing at James. I would blush with embarrassment. We were a team and what hurt him hurt me.

Such remarks were always accompanied by a smile and a little tap on the arm, but James didn't like the criticism and I don't blame him.

One of the things that hurt James the most, and me to a lesser extent, was the assumption that we fell out with Ed. The series had finished with a petty argument between James and Ed, and left many with the impression that we were no longer friends. Nothing could have been further from the truth and Ed remains a dear friend to both of us. James and I both went to his wedding earlier this year – the same wedding that Ed had talked about during our trek across Antarctica.

One aspect of this that upset people was the fact that Ed didn't collaborate in the writing of the book, *Race to the Pole*, that James and I wrote together about our adventure. But James and I had been commissioned to write a book about the race long before Ed was chosen as a third teammate – indeed, long before we were even sure we needed a third teammate. Writing the book was our means of income and therefore the justification to our wives for abandoning them for several months, and the decision was the publisher's, not ours. James and I toiled over that book for many months while Ed returned to his hospital – he went back to his work while we got on with ours. I think we wrote about Ed warmly and I hope that he found the book a great memento of our time together. What people forget is that we invited Ed to join us on the journey of a lifetime, not to change careers.

We returned to the UK elated that not only had we finished the race and made it to the South Pole, but that we had come second. Not bad for a team of novices. My elation was rather shortlived, however, as just a few days after we returned, so too did my leishmaniasis. It was a huge blow. I had been looking forward to celebrating, but instead I found myself back in hospital with the prospect of another month of treatment.

In many ways the second round of treatment was worse than the first and I found myself drifting into a depression. I convinced myself that the treatment would never work and became despondent about where my life was heading. I cheered myself up in that bleak hospital room by taking myself back to the wilds of Antarctica and dreaming about what challenges still lay ahead. If nothing else, I thought, we would do one more adventure together.

James and I both wanted another challenge to complete the

trilogy. We knew our time together had almost run its course – James's family was continuing to grow with the arrival of a daughter, Kiki, to whom I am godfather – but we wanted one final challenge to test ourselves and our friendship, another discipline to learn and environment to work with.

We had heard about a relatively new race called the Tour Divide, which was slowly becoming more and more popular. It was a three-thousand-mile mountain-bike race across the Rocky Mountains of North America from Canada to Mexico. The record, set by Matthew Lee, was seventeen days in 2009. That was more than two hundred off-road miles of cycling per day. It was hugely ambitious and sounded like the perfect way to round off our challenges.

The route would be tough. We would have to carry all our own supplies, as the rules stipulate that the race is unsupported. We would have to deal with bears and snakes and an ascent the equivalent of climbing Everest eight times. It was an enormous task, but first we would have to learn to mountain bike.

Of course I can ride a bike, as I proved by cycling to Monaco with my friends Cass and Leo when I was eighteen, but road-cycling on a hybrid with huge panniers is very different from mountain-bike racing with clipped-in shoes. I spent several days cycling around London on my road bicycle to get used to clipping my shoes in and out of the pedals. I arrived at a red light on Bond Street where I simply couldn't get my foot out of the clip in time. The bicycle stopped and then collapsed on top of me, in the middle of the road, in front of all the traffic. I was like an upturned tortoise unable to get my legs out and it took a kindly taxi driver to extricate me from the bike.

To get used to speed-cycling, James organized for us to take part in a road race up in Scotland called the Etape Caledonia, a 130-kilometre (80-mile) road race. In retrospect it was a pretty huge undertaking for my first big cycle in nearly twenty years, but we had to start somewhere and James loves a race. It finished with me in an ambulance some twenty miles from the finish after a miscalculated bend. I ended up with two broken fingers and a black eye.

Next we took to the mountains of Wales. Most people might learn to mountain bike as they might learn to ski, on, say, a nursery slope. Not us. We took to a black run with the UK's top mountain biker, Oli Beckingsale. It was one of the most painful and frustrating days of my life. I was black-and-blue with bruises. I re-broke my little finger and added another black eye to my injury list. What I discovered was that I was actually quite scared of mountain biking. With my feet clipped into the pedals, I felt I had no control. It was like being on a wild beast.

For six long months we pedalled and cycled in every corner of the UK. I began taking my bike away with me during filming assignments, including my two-week trip to Botswana and Kenya with Prince William. It was strange cycling around a wildlife conservancy past elephants and giraffes. James and I also travelled out to Arizona to get a feel for the route and the sort of terrain we would be travelling on. We met the current world champion, Matthew Lee, and made last-minute changes to our bikes, including fitting slightly larger wheels (29-inch rather than 26-inch) to roll better on the rough terrain.

A month before the race, I headed to Austria on holiday with Marina and spent my summer in a *Sound of Music* time warp. Meanwhile James had been asked by the Discovery Channel to take part in a series of challenges for a new series. He had already run the Marathon des Sables for them, coming twelfth, which made him the fastest Brit of all time in the race; but now they wanted him to take part in a multi-race across America. He would cycle from Los Angeles to Death Valley, where he would then run 120 miles non-stop before taking to his bike again up to the Great Lakes. There he would join Matthew Pinsent for a two-hundred-mile row, before cycling on to New York and swimming to the Statue of Liberty. It was the kind of challenge that only someone like James could complete. It was a great opportunity for him, although I did have my reservations about him doing it the month before our race across the Rockies. But he assured me it would be the best training for the race and I trusted his judgement.

Our friendship has always been based on mutual trust and respect. We have both relied on one another in ways that go beyond a normal friendship. In many respects our lives have been in one another's hands, and I would still trust James with my life. We have experienced and been through things that no one else will ever really truly understand.

After my parents, James was the first person I called when Ludo, our son, was born. James is Ludo's godfather, he was my best man, he is my best friend, but we have quite a fiery friendship. I still get nervous around him, and I don't know why.

I have described it as the 'gold effect'. As a gold-winning Olympian, you are the *best* in the whole world at what you do. There is no one better. You have proved that among the three billion people on earth you are the quickest, or the strongest or the fittest. When I look at it like that – and I do – I can't help but feel enthralled by and in awe of James. It brings out an inferiority complex in me. I have admitted it to James before, which is probably strange, but is also an example of how mixed-up I am. You may well ask why someone with self-esteem issues about their sporting and physical abilities would end up with an Olympic athlete – and not just any Olympic champion, but James Cracknell, famous for being one of the hardest athletes on both himself and his teammates.

In many ways, that is the essence of this book. It was an accident. It was never planned. It wasn't some lifelong ambition to team up with a professional sportsman. It just happened.

The result is sporting prowess by proxy. A rather misguided assumption has grown that I am some sort of sporting king. I turn up to events and races where I am introduced as 'Sporting Legend Ben', or 'Sporting Fanatic Ben'. I have even been on *A Question of Sport*, which is the unofficial seal of approval in the sporting hall of fame.

A sportsman I am quite obviously not. I weigh eighty-five kilos and I am essentially lazy. If it's a choice between a lie-in or a run, I would always go with the former (not that either is possible with two young children).

The irony, of course, is that my friendship with James has increased the pressure when it comes to challenges. Not only do I need to put in enough training to reach his lofty heights, but the public have a much higher expectation of my abilities than they once had. In some ways I suppose it is a good thing. James has always brought out more in me and he has encouraged me to push myself harder than anyone else. As I was cycling up those vertiginous mountains in Austria I would often think about how disappointed he would be if I turned up at the start line under-prepared or unfit. That thought was always enough to keep me pedalling, however much I was hurting.

It was 8 a.m. Austrian time on 21 July 2010 when I noticed a missed call from James's wife Bev. My mind raced. I knew she was out in the US and I struggled to work out the time difference. It would be nearly midnight on the West Coast. My stomach lurched. I *knew* something was wrong. We had known the Cracknells for long enough to know that they never called late at night, wherever they were. I tried ringing back, but it went straight to answerphone.

Something had happened to James. I was certain of it. I felt sick, but I would have to wait until morning US time to find out.

The rest of the day was painful as my mind created all sorts of terrible scenarios. None of them was as bad as the reality.

James had been on his bicycle in Arizona when he was hit by a petrol tanker at 70 m.p.h. He was unconscious and on a life-support machine in hospital.

An hour later I was on a train from Salzburg to Munich to catch a flight to London and on to Phoenix. I sat on the train as the German forests scudded past. I thought of all the adventures we had shared. I was numb with shock. It was the longest journey of my life and I was only grateful that Bev hadn't had to do the same thing as she was already in the States.

I was picked up at the airport by an ashen-faced Bev and Bernie Shrosbree, an old friend of James's, who had helped us with our preparations for the South Pole Race. More recently I had been training with him on my mountain bike in Poole. He had been part of James's support crew and was the first on the scene when James had been knocked off. He looked as if he was in shock as we drove to the hospital.

No one had been with James when the accident happened. A support vehicle carrying his trainer and physiotherapist was a couple of miles ahead of him on the road. (Arizona's minimum speed limit prevented the use of an escort; instead they would drive past him, wait for him to catch up at a junction, then go on ahead of him again.) Turning back when he didn't arrive as expected, the support vehicle arrived at the scene of the accident to find police lights flashing, blood on the road, James's helmet cracked in two, and his cycling shirt, which had had to be cut off, lying on the ground. The truck driver had stopped and called for an ambulance. James had been conscious at the scene, but drifting in and out. The paramedics had sedated him and taken him to the local hospital, from where he was flown by helicopter to the neuro-trauma unit in Phoenix.

The blow to the back of his head had caused two skull fractures, as well as bleeding, bruising and swelling of the frontal lobes where his brain had hit the inside of his skull. He had been transferred to intensive care, where he remained heavily sedated while doctors assessed the extent of the injury and whether an operation was needed to remove fluid from his brain. Every seventy-two hours they would reduce the sedation to try to elicit a response.

This is my story, not James's, so it is probably neither fair nor appropriate for me to describe the next couple of days, but it was a shock to see my best friend in that state, and worse to see the suffering of his family. I spent my time shuttling between a little motel and the hospital, where he remained semi-conscious. To me James had always been an impenetrable, bullet-proof being. In my mind he was invincible. Nothing could harm him.

Even after James was out of danger, the spectre of frontal-lobe injury, with its associated long-term problems – memory loss, erratic decision-making, difficulties with language, planning and complex thought – loomed large. He was told that he may never fully recover, but that he would see a big improvement in the first six months, further improvement between six and twelve months, and a final, smaller improvement between twelve months and two years.

After four weeks in Arizona, James was flown back to Britain and transferred to a private clinic in north London, where he spent three further weeks.

In hospital he was on anti-seizure medication, sleeping pills and mood stabilizers, but at home his treatment consisted of regular visits from an occupational therapist and a trip to a neuro-psychologist every week to ten days. He had to see a neurologist every couple of months.

We had of course ditched our planned race across the Rocky Mountains. We had already spent a great deal of time and money on the adventure and the BBC had even cut the first hour of the documentary, but James was in no fit state for the race.

The accident and its aftermath must have knocked his

self-confidence. I think he also felt some unwarranted guilt towards me. He admitted that he felt he had let me down. I struggled to pick up work after the cancellation of the trip, but I certainly didn't hold it against him. It was an accident, and accidents can happen to anyone anywhere.

The irony here, of course, was that in the past we had both been subject to criticism for our selfish adventures. People had accused us of reckless danger and taking uncalculated risks. We were the first to admit that there was an element of selfishness in our adventuring, but it had become our drug, and in many ways our careers.

Sportsmen and women often struggle with the transition from sports star to civilian, in the same way that military personnel struggle when they leave the services. There is an element of institutionalization in sport, in that athletes are told what to eat, when to eat, how long to sleep, etc. They are also used to being lauded and applauded. They are *different* from everyone else – then suddenly one day they are back to our level.

This is one of the reasons that depression is so high in sport.

James had found a new drug in adventuring. It was his way of remaining different. He was still able to compete on a national platform, but in a different way. He could still push himself to the limits. This was the man who could run a marathon in less than three hours, or win a triathlon. Indeed, he told me that his old coach had approached him before the accident and asked him if he would consider competing once again in the rowing for the London Olympics in 2012. It must have been a tempting offer, but also a deeply flattering one for a thirty-eight-year-old, who had been out of competition for so many years. In some ways I wish he had accepted the offer, then maybe the accident in the US would never have happened.

I'd be lying if I didn't admit to disappointment that we were unable to carry on with our challenge, but James's health was far more important. Not only would it have been dangerous, but also deeply unfair on our two pregnant wives.

James once admitted that one of the darkest periods in his life (until this) had been the Atlanta Olympic Games, which he trained for but never competed in, as he had fallen ill with tonsillitis just two days before the event. I remember him telling me how he could hear from his quarantined hospital bed the roar of the crowd watching the race. Now, for the first time, I had a small inkling of what that must have been like. We had spent just a year planning and training – a fraction of the four years undertaken by an Olympic athlete – but it was a tiny peek into the world of James Cracknell and in many ways it helped me to get to know him on another level.

Only two months after his accident, James had to be dissuaded from taking part in Britain's biggest road race, the Great North Run, when his physical state would have meant doing it in a wheelchair. A few months later, in January 2011, however, he did take part in the Yukon Arctic Ultra, a series of races on foot, skis or mountain bike up the freezing trail of the Yukon river in north-west Canada, over distances that range from marathon length to 430 miles. James elected to race the full 430 miles by mountain bike.

He never told me about the race. In fact, the first I saw of it was when it was on TV. It was a deeply moving film. It wasn't the James I knew. It's a sad reflection on the reality of head injury.

Our friendship has changed since the accident. The crash put untold pressures on his family life and marriage, so I don't want to sound too sorry for myself here, but in many ways I also lost a part of my best friend to that accident. Nothing has been quite the same since, although I hope that one day it will.

I walk down the street and everyone wants to know how James is. There has been a huge outpouring of emotion around him and

I hope it has proved to him how much this country cares about and respects him. As an Olympian, he has become a national treasure and people's sympathy towards him is genuine.

Our lives collided accidentally nearly six years ago and we have shared an incredible journey, during which we have travelled the world together, I have got married and we have had a clutch of children between us. I hope that one day we will complete our trilogy. I like the thought of us setting off in years to come, reminiscing about all the adventures we have shared.

12

Extreme Dreams

I had returned from so many trips a changed man that I wanted to give others the opportunity to change their lives through expedition too. I find challenges a cathartic way of cleansing the body and the mind, so the idea of taking ordinary people on extraordinary challenges had always appealed to me and the BBC eventually commissioned the series *Extreme Dreams with Ben Fogle*.

The premise was simple: we would select worthy volunteers who had suffered a setback in their lives through injury, illness, bereavement or perhaps redundancy. I would then attempt to rebuild their confidence and self-esteem through a series of challenges with an end goal.

It was a big project, but I was passionate about it and felt sure it would work. The first series, broadcast in the autumn of 2006, took us to Peru, Guyana, the Svalbard archipelago in the Arctic, and to climb Mount Kilimanjaro in Tanzania. It was during that Kilimanjaro expedition that I discovered that *Extreme Dreams* was as much an emotional journey as it was a physical one. From the group I took with me, it was trainee teacher Ben Thwaites who really moved me. Ben had been caught up in the Edgware Road tube bombing on 7/7. He had been deeply affected by what he saw and was one of the many victims who had suffered psychological effects from the atrocity. We would be trekking along, immersed in the Tanzanian environment, when the colour would suddenly drain from his face as he was catapulted back to that dark tunnel. It was hard to know how to deal with it.

Over the three series, I shared adventures with a diverse collection of individuals, but it was people like Ben who really stood out. We are so conditioned to look for physical injury that we, as a society, easily forget that the often invisible psychological damage can be just as debilitating as a lost limb. I wasn't a trained psychologist and frequently found myself out of my depth with the burden of emotional baggage that accompanied us on each trek. But over the years I shared some incredible journeys, and I feel blessed to have been a part of so many lives.

Guyana was my first proper experience of the jungle. By comparison, my three-thousand-mile Amazon boat trip when I was eighteen seemed like a luxury holiday.

We arrived in one of the rainiest sessions on record. The forest floor had flooded and within hours of arriving, my team, the film crew and I were wading up to our armpits in anaconda-infested floodwater.

Our leader was an ex-army officer called Ed, who was a complete legend. He was cool as a cucumber while all around was chaos. It was the second of our *Extreme Dreams* expeditions and one of the most challenging, technically, to film.

Having trekked for hours through the swampy rainforest, we crossed a river and found a place to build our camp. We'd all spent a couple of days at a field-training camp where Ed had taught us how to survive in 'the trees', as he called the jungle. Each evening my team and I would build one camp, while the film crew and porters would set another about a kilometre away from us. The idea was to make the filming as unobtrusive as possible so that the experience was as real as it could be.

Using our machetes, we hacked away at the thick, virgin rainforest. We chopped at the leaves and branches in search of trees far enough apart to sling our hammocks, mosquito nets and waterproof shelters, or bashas. Ed had taught us to look out for the hazards of the jungle. Surprisingly, the biggest killer is deadfall that tumbles unexpectedly from high above as trees rot and decay in the heat and humidity. Then there is the flora and fauna for which the jungle is best known and, in some cases, loathed. It's fair to say that in the rainforest everything wants to bite, sting or cut you. He warned us which poisonous plants to avoid and instructed us never to bend down and put our hands into the leaf litter – 'always swipe at it with your machete first', in case one of the many poisonous snakes, spiders or scorpions is in it.

Full of fear and trepidation, we set our camp with surprising ease. You'd be amazed how cosy, safe and comfortable you feel in a flimsy silk hammock. With the mosquito net tucked under the buttocks it creates a veritable fortress against all the biting, stinging creepy-crawlies outside.

I lay in my hammock as the jungle came alive. I can't begin to explain the noises that echo around the rainforest at night. The descriptions sound too wild to be true, like figments of a drug-induced dream. But nothing can prepare you for the sounds that leap out of the darkness. I heard a chainsaw, then a car revving its engine, crying children and screaming babies. I heard manic laughter and coffee beans being ground, the whistle of a boiling kettle on the stove and a crowd chanting. A pneumatic drill rang out, and then it sounded like Take That singing inside a bottle.

It was a little like cloud-watching: I found myself matching all the noises, building images in my mind. It was totally bewildering. I drifted off to the sound of a sweet lullaby only to be woken several hours later by a completely different sound altogether.

The problem with the jungle is that it's easy to lose your sense of reality and your ability to distinguish between the imaginary and the real. This was one of those moments.

I woke with a start. I wasn't sure why, but I lay in my hammock wide awake. I strained my ears for whatever it was that had woken me. Silence.

My heart was pounding and I could hear the blood echoing in my ears. I began to sweat.

Snap, snap.

There it was, the snapping of branches.

Snap.

Something was out there. How big were those snaps? Were they twigs? Or was that the sound of something bigger? I lay there frozen.

'*Prrrrrrrrrrrprrrrrrrrrrrrrprrrrrrrrrrrrrrrrrrrprrrrrrrrrrrrr.*'

My stomach lurched. What the hell was purring? I pinched myself, hoping to pull myself from some awful dream.

'*Prrrrrrrprrrrrrrrrrrprrrrrrrrrrrrrprrrrrrrrrrrprrrrrrrrr.*'

There it was again – a deep, bass purring. It sounded almost like panting. My brain couldn't keep up. What is it, Ben? Come on, think. What purrs in the jungle?

Until now, all my worries and fears had been focused on the small, stingy, poisonous things. My biggest concern was the size of the spiders. I had been totally unprepared for this. Something large . . . that purrs.

And then it hit me. OMG. It's a bloody jaguar.

I lay frozen in silence. I could tell that I wasn't the only one awake. Even though the others were silent, I knew they were listening too.

Snap, snap.

What did we have here? The purring had come from my right and now there was the sound of snapping branches on my left.

My eyes bulged as I realized it was another jaguar. It was our first night in the rainforest and already we were surrounded by the jungle's top predator.

My ears strained to follow the animals in the darkness as they moved around our camp. Silence. They had gone.

In the morning we recounted the tale to the film crew when they arrived. Crew members Kirsty and Katie both looked as if they had stuck their fingers in an electrical socket. They had big rings around their eyes and they looked as though they had seen a ghost . . . or a jaguar.

It transpired that, after prowling our camp, the beasts had turned up in the crew's area to eat dinner. Katie and Kirsty had woken to the sound of crunching bones as the two animals ate. At one point, one of the jaguars had crept under Katie's hammock, its long back rubbing against the low-slung canvas. No one had got any sleep in the crew's camp.

The jungle jaguars were one thing, but it was an encounter with something a little smaller, but far more fearsome, that brought the realities of the jungle home, literally.

A thick, musky aroma enveloped the cabin. People peered around, wrinkling their noses in disgust. My face was black with dirt, my hair matted, my clothes steeped in a cocktail of dirty river water and sweat. My boots were still laden with mud. I repelled even myself with my pungency. I shudder to think what the rest of the business-class passengers made of me.

After two weeks' trekking in Guyana, we had stepped from the trees on to a small Cessna plane into Georgetown, where we had transferred straight to a flight to Barbados and thence on to London.

Coated in jungle grime, I took the Heathrow Express to

Paddington and then home to Notting Hill. It was probably a blessing that Marina wasn't home. Not because of my repugnant appearance, but because of what happened next.

I hauled my rucksack through the front door and, still wearing my military-issue jungle boots and the clothes I had been in for more than two weeks, I did the only logical thing. I made myself a cup of tea.

I decided to unpack my rucksack outside in the weak sunlight, where my rain- and river-soaked kit would have a chance to dry out. It was mid-March and the first signs of early spring were beginning to appear, but I still shuddered as my body attempted to readjust from the 100 per cent tropical humidity of the South American jungle.

I unclipped the rucksack buckles and began to pull sodden socks from its various pockets. I reached for the main section of the pack and, as I pulled the draw cord to open it, there was an unusual movement. Before I had time to think, something the size of my hand leapt from my bag. I recoiled in shock, falling flat on my back. My heart was beating nineteen to the dozen with shock and surprise. In all my years of travel, nothing like this had ever happened before.

'Shit, shit, shit!' I began to panic.

Somehow, a tarantula had managed to stow away in my rucksack. Unbelievably, it had survived the long-haul flight and now here it was, *free*, in my Notting Hill garden. Strangely, I wasn't as worried about a potentially poisonous spider loose in Notting Hill as I was about my missus's likely response to a 'probably deadly' spider on the loose in her garden.

But before I could move on to worrying about things like the neighbours' reactions, I had a more pressing concern. Where the hell was it?

It had ejected itself from my bag with such speed and agility that, although I had caught a fleeting glimpse of it, it had now managed to disappear into the undergrowth. In the words of Chris Tarrant, it was 'time to phone a friend'.

'Hello, Darren,' I whispered down the phone. Darren Beasley was the head keeper of Pets' Corner down at Longleat Safari Park in Wiltshire, where I had spent the best part of ten years being terrified by his assortment of creepy-crawlies: scorpions, giant millipedes, snakes, biting ants and a multitude of arachnids. To be fair to Darren, he had done a great job in desensitizing me to them all. I hadn't exactly become a Steve Irwin, but after a decade of handling I had become relatively competent in coping with various beasties. However hairy, scaly, slimy or poisonous they were, Darren loved all his creatures. But I also knew he had a particular soft spot for Rosie, the Chilean rose tarantula, so if there was anyone who would know what to do, it was him.

'What kind of spider is it?' he asked.

'Dunno,' I replied helpfully.

'What did it look like?'

'Effing huge and hairy.'

'What colour was it?'

'A hideous colour,' I replied even more helpfully.

'And where is it now?'

'Dunno. Somewhere in west London.'

He told me I needed to recapture it, but, given that all we knew was that it was big, fast and hairy, I needed to get some professional help.

'Like the police?' I suggested. I'm sure it would have been a first for Notting Hill Police Station (although I did once call them to report finding a lost tortoise, so maybe they were expecting it!).

He suggested I call London Zoo and get a keeper round to help me in my search for our lost friend. Six hours later and two keepers had come and gone. We had scoured the garden. We had lifted every leaf and turned every branch. We had found dozens of missing mouldy tennis balls, but no South American arachnids.

As far as Marina is concerned, the spider is currently living at London Zoo; but it's more likely propping up a bar in Notting Hill Gate.

While the object of the *Extreme Dreams* experiences was to take the team members out of themselves in order to help them rebuild their lives, occasionally they came as a timely distraction for me too.

'That's it from Crufts 2008 here at the NEC. Goodnight.' I signed off after presenting another year at Crufts dog show and in just twenty-four hours I would be in the middle of the Libyan Sahara in North Africa, filming for the second series of *Extreme Dreams*.

The next morning I met my teammates at Gatwick airport. It had been a long few days in Birmingham. There is an intensity to live TV that can be energy-sapping and I was looking forward to some time in the desert.

I sat in the departures lounge next to one of my teammates who was reading the *Sun* newspaper. 'Ben's Presenting Is a Dog's Dinner' screamed a headline on page three, next to Lizzi from Cornwall. The article went on to detail how the BBC had been inundated with complaints about me and described me as a 'rubbish presenter'.

I am the first to admit that I'm not everyone's cup of tea as a presenter. While I'd like to consider myself professional, I'd also describe myself as erratic. I sometimes say things that surprise even me, but I also think it's what makes me an individual.

I've worked in the business for long enough to accept that you can never appeal to all of the people all of the time. Terry Wogan once confided to me that he works on a 50:50 ratio of love:loathe – 'although some people carve a perfectly good career out of

30:70,' he told me, adding, 'The more some people like you, the more the other group will loathe you.'

Although I'd like to say I have a thick skin, I am in fact extremely thin-skinned. I hate criticism and I'm easily hurt and offended. If presenters were part of the evolutionary chain, I'd have died out long ago. And today, in Gatwick airport, I was deeply offended.

'Never read your own press,' my mother once said to me. 'After all, today's news is tomorrow's chip paper.' Unfortunately that is no longer the case. Today's news is around the world within a couple of seconds and online for all eternity.

The most dangerous place for someone in the public eye is the internet. It's a minefield for the easily offended.

'Never, ever, Google your name,' warned Clare Balding when we started presenting Crufts together. But the reality is that curiosity usually gets the better of you. Like a moth to a light, you know you shouldn't but you can't help yourself.

Ratings for Crufts were up a million on the previous year. I'd been lavished with praise by other papers, but this one criticism really stung. Luckily for me, I was escaping the UK to seek solace in the Sahara.

Back in 2008 Libya was firmly under Colonel Gaddafi's control. His image stared out from every billboard. His propaganda was scrawled on every wall. Police patrolled every corner. We arrived by night because of the country's strict rule of no daytime flights, either international or domestic, in case passengers saw things about which the government thought they shouldn't know. The airport shops were doing a roaring trade in Gaddafi's trademark Ray-Ban sunglasses. They were fakes, of course, with an image of the colonel instead of the Ray-Ban logo. There were watches and cigarette lighters of the Libyan leader, and even children's dolls.

Tripoli, the capital, is a pretty city, a mix of Italian art deco and

North African Moorish architecture. It's a vibrant, exciting place, but for us it was just a stopping point on our journey south into the desert and Berber country.

The expedition was simple: we would cover a couple of hundred miles across the Sahara to the ancient settlement of Ghat, close to the border with Algeria. We would take camels to help us carry our kit and collect water from various gelters, or water holes, along the way. We would navigate with compasses and rudimentary maps, but, as with every trip in the series, the television crew would follow us even if we went wrong.

My team of five had already been depleted, as one of its members, an English Nigerian, was refused permission to enter the country.

We set off with our laden camels into the heat of the desert. It was the first time I'd been back into the Sahara since I had run the Marathon des Sables four years before. The race may have physically destroyed me, but I really liked the environment. I love deserts, provided I don't have to run across them. They are my favourite type of climate with their dry heat and cool nights. We spent a day trekking, then set camp in a wadi, next to a fire and under a ceiling of stars.

Next morning I was rather alarmed to find myself completely surrounded by animal trails. No area of sand had been left unmarked. Everywhere I looked there were footprints or drag marks of varying sizes. I was perturbed to see a series of dog-sized prints around my sleeping bag. It looked as if there had been an animal party while I was asleep.

As I was pulling on my desert boots and applying sunscreen for the day ahead, we heard a blood-curdling scream. I froze to the spot, trying to work out from whom and from where it had come.

There was a moment of chaos as the film crew raced towards the remains of the fire. There, clutching his arm, was a local

Berber, the colour drained from his cheeks. He looked terrified. What was wrong?

He lay back on the sand, his eyes wide and dilated; he was shaking violently. The locals were talking animatedly, but it was impossible for us to work out what was going on.

'What is it?' I asked repeatedly. 'What's happened to him?'

One of the guides made the shape of a small creature with his hand. The man had been stung by a scorpion. That suddenly explained all the tracks around our sleeping bags.

The following few days passed in a haze of heat. We got lost, ran out of water and struggled to bond with our camels. On the second night I tied my camel to my ankle in an effort to stop it wandering off in the middle of the night, only to wake in the early hours being dragged across the sand in my sleeping bag.

One of my team, Ashley, a fanatical Sunderland supporter, had been complaining of chest pains. Although we were dehydrated and tired, there seemed to be no logical explanation for the type of pains she was experiencing. On the third day, shortly after reaching the top of a steep valley, she complained of yet more chest pains. Alex, our medic, got out his stethoscope and listened carefully.

She had angina, and we became worried about the pressures of the environment on her weak heart. We had to evacuate her to hospital as soon as we could. The insurers organized for a vehicle to transfer her to the nearest airport, where a private jet flew her to Liverpool hospital. Less than twelve hours after Alex's diagnosis, she was in the cardiac ward.

On the penultimate day of the trip we were caught in the middle of a sandstorm. I had experienced one before during the Marathon des Sables, but this was on a different scale. Huge storm clouds gathered in the sky as we marched across the barren landscape. The wind began to pick up and within a matter of minutes we couldn't see our hands in front of our faces. We pulled our buffs high over our noses and bent our heads low. The sand stung at our legs as we sought shelter, but out here there was nothing.

Richard Farrish, our cameraman, appeared in one of the Toyota Landcruisers, pulling up behind us.

'It's too dangerous,' he hollered above the din of the wind. 'We're going to make a storm shelter with the vehicles.'

The three 4×4s were parked in a line, one in front of the other, to create a windbreak. We then used kitbags and film equipment to fill in the gaps underneath the cars and dragged tarpaulins between the vehicles and up the sides. It was a sort of scrapheap-challenge windbreak. We lay on the ground with our backs to the cars while the wind and sand roared all around us. The vehicles had created a small vacuum from the storm.

The sky turned yellow, then blood-red as the sun began to set. The storm raged on all night. I slept in my ski goggles with my buff pulled up over my nose and ears. In the morning, however, we were able to carry on and made it to Ghat, though not before two other team members, Lindsay and Angela, had collapsed with heat exhaustion.

It had been quite a trip. I returned to the UK having put the Crufts criticism behind me. With this trip we had pushed our group further than we'd ever done before, but things were about to get even tougher.

Just two days after returning from Libya, I was off again with another team. This time we were heading for East Africa.

The last time I was in Uganda, I had been invited there by a charity called Hives Save Lives, which was being supported by Sugar Puffs, the breakfast cereal. They wanted me to make a short film about the charity's work in the country. They had also invited Liz McClarnon from the girl band Atomic Kitten. We would be spending a week together following the project.

'You'll also be going with the Honey Monster,' said my agent over the phone.

'What do you mean, with the honey monster?' I replied, a little confused.

'As in "Tell them about the honey, Mummy".' She put on the deep monster voice from the famous television ads.

'What – *the* Honey Monster?' I said, sounding almost star-struck.

Hives Save Lives was a charity that helped finance local people to build beehives, which were then given to schools and orphanages as a means of micro-financing. Traditionally, Ugandans had harvested honey by destroying the nest each time, but this was a much more efficient way of working. It was a simple idea that had big potential in teaching new skills and helping those most financially vulnerable.

Apparently there is only one Honey Monster costume and we were warned it was incredibly fragile and very valuable. I wondered whether it was the same one I had grown up watching in all those commercials. I also wondered who the actor would be. I half-expected to find Jude Law or Kenneth Branagh moonlighting. You can imagine my surprise when I discovered it was Ahmed, our driver.

It was one of the funniest sights to watch him dressing up in the enormous ginger costume. It was nearly 38°C by the time he put the head on. We were on the outskirts of a small village that had benefited from some of the hives and we were to walk in together, hand in hand.

'The kids are going to love this,' squealed Liz with excitement, as we strode into the village centre, leading Ahmed, who was melting in the heat.

The next few moments can only be described as pandemonium as the children fled for their lives. They screamed in horror as the Honey Monster approached – at least I hope it was about the Honey Monster and not Liz and myself.

It took an hour to get the terrified children back, and even then they hid behind legs and in doorways. Whenever Ahmed moved, they shot away again. In retrospect, it must be pretty terrifying when a giant ginger monster wearing football kit walks into your village.

In the hope of reassuring them, I used the international language of football and suggested a game. It is amazing the power soccer has throughout the world. Several dozen children converged on the dusty pitch and I pulled a football from my bag. Liz and I split the kids into two teams and we proceeded to race around under the burning African sun, the children shrieking in delight.

A young lad passed the ball across the field to me and I started to run, dribbling the ball around tiny legs. I had covered half the field when I heard a chorus of laughter as a giant ginger foot tackled me. The Honey Monster raced up the field, pursued by a dozen giggling children, and proceeded to score.

That had been a memorable trip. This time, for *Extreme Dreams*, there were no Honey Monsters or Atomic Kittens. We were heading to the Rwenzori Mountains on the border with the Congo. For many years the area had been controlled by guerrillas, who had used the remote mountain range as a hiding place from government authorities.

Our goal was to climb to the summit of Mount Baker, which at almost 5,000 metres (16,400 feet) is one of the highest peaks in Africa. To access the remote mountain we would first have to traverse the infamous Bigo Bog.

The Rwenzori Mountains in Uganda are also known as the Mountains of the Moon, a name thought to derive from second-century writings by Ptolemy, who claimed that the source of the Nile lay in a range of African snow-capped mountains, which he described as the Mountains of the Moon. While the Nile cannot in fact be found here, the name is still fitting due to the year-round snow on the mountain tops, a feature of only three African mountain ranges.

The Rwenzori Mountains are home to both the Upper and Lower Bigo Bogs. The mountain range has one of the highest rates of rainfall in the world, creating very boggy conditions, of which the Bigo Bogs are the most extensive example. They are so watery it is thought that they were once lakes that have since filled with sediment and vegetation. This forbidden terrain is home to striking flora, including lobelias and giant groundsels – species that can adapt to the startling changes in temperature at high altitudes, which have been described as 'summer by day, winter by night'.

My team this time included a middle-aged man, who was technically blind. He still had a small amount of vision left, but the doctors had given him only another few months of sight. This was his last chance to see the world, in a very literal sense.

The difficulty with this trip was that everything would have to be carried on foot. There was no access for land vehicles, planes or even helicopters. Not even horses and mules could be used in the boggy terrain. While it provided a great challenge for my team, it was a logistical nightmare for the film crew, who needed nearly a ton of filming equipment.

Most people have no idea how much equipment it takes to make a programme. There are boxes and boxes of it. Spares and parts, generators and fuel for charging, and spare generators in case one fails. And that doesn't even include the kit and crew tents, as well as all their personal equipment. Although the film team was relatively small – fifteen, including medics and guides – they had more than a hundred boxes and bags of kit. We needed a small army of porters to help us – sixty to be precise. Sixty is the point at which porters require porters for their food and equipment, and so on. And so we set off like some Victorian expedition. I half-expected to see a porter with a grand piano or a sedan chair strapped to his back.

For days we pushed on through the relentless bog. It was unlike anything I had ever experienced before. It sapped our energy as we negotiated roots and tussocks of grass surrounded by thick mud. We sank up to the thigh with each step, leaving a thick, smelly tide-mark on our trousers. Occasionally someone would misjudge a step and be up to their waist in fetid bog.

The first couple of days brought only slow progress. The environment certainly slowed us down, but also some of the team were having difficulties. The days had been long and we'd often been trekking into the darkness, which had been tough enough for those with full vision but almost impossible for someone with failing sight. Another of the group was also struggling with the conditions. The doctor became worried about her and warned me that she might well need to be evacuated if she continued to deteriorate. The problem was that our location was simply beyond the capabilities of a helicopter, so any evacuation would have to be manual, on a stretcher carried by us.

It led to one of the toughest decisions I have ever had to make. It was clear to all that our progress was being hampered. If we picked up our pace now, I calculated that we could just about catch up on lost time; if we didn't, we would simply run out of time and food and be forced to return early. Did we carry on with the very real likelihood that none of us would make it? Or did we send those team members who were struggling back with a medic and some porters?

The whole point of *Extreme Dreams* was to give ordinary people the chance to achieve extraordinary things. It was about giving them all the opportunity to defy their doubters and achieve something great. The decision I faced threatened the very principle of the series. If I turned any of them back, I was merely doing exactly what others had always done. I had given them this incredible opportunity and now I had to decide whether to revoke it.

I looked at the others in the team, equally worthy men and women, desperate to reach their goal and achieve something for themselves.

I hate responsibility – I always have done. In some ways I have spent my life shirking it. I much prefer to pass it to others and I'll be the first to step back if I'm given the opportunity. But here, in the middle of Uganda, I was leader and I had to make a call. Reluctantly, I told those two team members that it would be safest for everyone if they returned. I hate myself for doing that; it still makes me feel sick when I think of the devastated looks on their faces. Here was a man with just a few months of sight. But I stand by the decision. I genuinely think it was the right thing to do.

We soon picked up speed and within a couple of days we had left the hot, steamy, tropical lowlands and begun to ascend the Rwenzori Mountains. One night we found a small mountain cabin on the side of a beautiful lake. The last people to have stayed in the hut had been rebel soldiers. The graffiti on the walls and the spent bullets on the ground were slightly unnerving.

The crew decamped into the cabin, while my team and I set up camp on the shore.

'Coming for a swim?' I asked Darren, a rather large London cabbie, who had come on the trip to lose weight and get his life back together.

We hadn't washed for days and were still covered in a thick layer of bog mud. Despite the cold, the clear water of the lake looked enticing. We waded in wearing our underwear while Rob the cameraman filmed us from the shore. The water was just a couple of inches deep but with each step my feet sank into the mud. We continued to wade out in search of deeper water, but the further we walked, the deeper the mud. Darren was by now up to his waist in thick, stinking mud. In fear of disappearing deeper down, he proceeded to belly-flop forward as a way of distributing his body weight a little more. He floundered in the shallow water like a beached whale, covered from head to toe in mud. I could see Rob bent double with laughter. I shrugged my shoulders and followed him. We were muddier than we'd started, but at least we'd had fun.

Soon we crossed the snow line as we ascended the boulder-strewn mountain. A thick, rolling fog enveloped us as we trudged on through the thin air until eventually we reached the summit. Then, at that moment, the cloud cover parted to reveal the entire snow-covered mountain range beyond. It was incredibly moving to watch Darren and our fourth team member, Katie, in tears at their achievement. We had certainly pushed them, but they had done it. They were truly blown away by their success, and so was I. I felt like a proud teacher.

Of course, what goes up must come down. The cameras may have stopped rolling, but we still had the not insignificant task of walking out – in this case a four-day trek. As is so often the case, much of the drama happens on the return journey. From experience, people put all their efforts and energy into the summit and forget about the descent.

On the second day of the return journey Katie slipped down the mountain, breaking her arm. Without the use of both arms, it was almost impossible to edge her way down the mountainside and we had to take turns supporting her for the next three days.

As ever, it had been an eventful journey, but I was beginning to worry that we were pushing our volunteers too far. If we weren't careful, we were going to lose someone and I would be held accountable.

I have long been obsessed by an often forgotten corner of the world: Papua New Guinea. My fascination is mainly due to an extraordinary human phenomenon known as 'cargo cults'.

Papua New Guinea, in Melanesia, has been populated for over sixty thousand years. Trading between the island and South-East Asian communities may have begun more than five thousand years ago; however, interactions between its inhabitants and European explorers did not begin until the sixteenth century. In 1828 the western half of the island was claimed by the Dutch empire, becoming Netherlands New Guinea, a region, post-decolonization, that is now part of Indonesia. In 1884 the north-eastern quarter of the island was annexed by the German empire, becoming German New Guinea, while the remaining south-eastern corner became a British protectorate and by 1888 was formally annexed by Britain. In 1902 British-controlled Papua was placed under the authority of Australia. During the First World War, German New Guinea was invaded by Australian troops and, after a very small conflict, it too fell under Australian administration.

During the Second World War, Papua was a central site of the Pacific war, as it was invaded by Japanese troops in 1941. Australian civil administration was suspended and instead an Australian military administration was put in place. Extensive fighting, largely initiated by the Japanese attack on Rabaul, continued until the end of the war in 1945. Nearby Vanuatu, though not a site of conflict, was also a strategic site for the Solomon Islands campaign and was home to two American military bases. One Japanese bomb did fall upon Vanuatu, but reportedly its only victim was a cow.

The far greater impact of the Second World War upon the peoples of both New Guinea and Vanuatu can be seen in the development of emergent religious practices and beliefs. Papua New Guinea is famous for its linguistic and religious diversity, as it is home to over 850 languages and manifold belief systems, while Vanuatu has the highest number of languages per capita in the world, with its nine million inhabitants speaking a total of 1,300 languages. In both nations millenarian cults and practices known as 'cargo cults' existed prior to the Second World War, yet were dramatically affected by the military presence and use of previously unseen equipment and products.

The first recognized cargo cult emerged on the Mandang coast of Papua New Guinea during the eighteenth century, after the arrival of a Russian explorer who bestowed gifts of steel axes and cloth upon the populace. The term 'cargo' is a broad category referring to high-value goods, ranging from jewels to washing machines, and the theme underlining all cargo cults is the emphasis upon a messianic figure who will emerge (often in a Doomsday context) bearing great gifts of wealth rightly owed to the Melanesian people. Many cargo cults synthesize elements of Christian theology with traditional Melanesian practices of gift exchange and the role of Melanesian 'big men' – individuals who achieve high status in Melanesian society and give gifts in order to consolidate strong social bonds. The idea that the European cargo had been stolen or taken from the native people by Europeans was common, leading to outbreaks of animosity between the islanders and colonial forces. Often attempts were made to usher in the new messianic leader and age of cargo by the mass destruction of livestock and property.

The events of the Second World War led to significant changes in the cults, most famously on the island of Tanna, Vanuatu (then the New Hebrides). With the arrival of American troops, many islanders were drafted into building military hospitals, roads and runways. The presence of the American forces exposed the local people to a range of previously unimagined goods and technologies, including canned foods, Coca-Cola, cigarettes and refrigerators – all items encompassed within the category of cargo.

At the end of the war American troops and their possessions were quickly recalled, leading many inhabitants of Tanna to try to invoke the return of cargo. Prior to the war, a cargo cult dedicated to a prophetic figure named John Frum had emerged on the island, encouraging the people to renounce Christian and European ways in favour of Melanesian customary practices or 'kastom'. In the light of wartime developments, new emphasis was placed upon American servicemen and their role in the coming of cargo, and some began to envision John Frum as a black GI: 'John From America'. In addition to practising kastom, adherents of the John Frum cult began to imitate the rituals of the American forces by constructing mock aircraft and runways, building radios and service towers out of card and rope. In the late 1950s the Tanna army emerged, part of the John Frum Movement that advocated the non-violent replication of American military practice through performing military drills with bamboo rifles.

In 2007 the John Frum Movement celebrated its fiftieth anniversary. It is still an established religious belief system, celebrated in Tanna every year on 15 February, John Frum Day, with dancing, feasting and military-style parades. The John Frum Movement is also now an official political party which holds seats in the Vanuatu parliament.

While John Frum is the most famous of the cargo cults, others have also emerged in Melanesia since the Second World War. The Yaohnanen people advocate that it is not John Frum but his brother who will lead the devout to the land of cargo. His brother is thought to have travelled many seas and married a very powerful woman, and in the 1970s was identified as HRH Prince Philip. A number of gifts were subsequently exchanged between the Prince and the worshippers, culminating in Prince Philip sending a photograph of himself smiling and holding a ceremonial staff.

Meanwhile, back in Papua New Guinea in 1968 a cult emerged with the belief that the only man who knew the secret of cargo was President Lyndon B. Johnson. The cult's adherents rebelled against the Australian authorities, refused to pay their taxes and managed to raise $75,000, which they offered to President Johnson, sending him a letter inviting him to become king of New Hanover. The president reportedly did not reply.

Finally, with *Extreme Dreams*, I got the opportunity to visit this faraway land.

Papua New Guinea is the best place I have ever visited. I say that with some certainty. Partly because it is the question I am most commonly asked, and partly because it's true.

There can be few places in the world as surreal, beautiful and incredible as Papua New Guinea, or PNG as it is known. It is the only country to which I have ever been where I genuinely felt I had stepped back in time. It is one of the hidden gems of the Pacific Ocean, and getting there takes for ever.

My team and I flew to Sydney, where we took another flight to Cairns in the north of the country, before finally catching our Air Niugini flight to Port Moresby, the capital of PNG. We were on our way towards the Sepik River in the north of the country, from where we would be embarking on an expedition along an old Second World War route, the Black Cat Trail, which begins in the township of Wau in Morobe province and ends in the fishing village of Salamuana on the coast of the Huon Gulf.

The track started out in the 1920s as a trail for gold prospectors, who would navigate along the leech- and crocodile-infested trail in search of riches and wealth, but the area gained infamy when on 8 March 1942 the village of Salamuana was captured by the Japanese. They had tried to take Port Moresby by sea, but were defeated in the Battle of the Coral Sea, so they attempted it by land from the Owen Stanley mountain range, along the famous Kokoda Trail, basing their operation in Salamuana. Following a series of battles, they made it to within thirty miles of the capital. After this, Salamuana became a major

Japanese supply base and a few months later they made one last attempt to reach Port Moresby, this time along the Black Cat Trail.

A number of bloody clashes ensued between the Japanese and the Australian 17th Brigade. The Japanese entrenched themselves along the trail, surviving mortar attacks and aircraft strafing. The attacks and counter-attacks continued until 15 May, when the Japanese launched a full-scale attack, supported by a hundred Japanese planes, forcing the Allies to retreat.

The Black Cat Trail is rarely remembered today except as a tough trek which is, according to one local expatriate, 'suitable only for masochists and Israeli paratroopers'.

Port Moresby – or Pot Mosbi in Tok Pisin, the local dialect – is on the steamy shores of the Gulf of Papua. It's a strange city, with high unemployment and a rather volatile society. We were met at the airport by an armoured bus and an armed security guard and we drove through the peaceful streets with the riot shields pulled down over the windows. I peered through the narrow slats as we crossed the city centre. In many respects it looked like any other financial and government centre, until we passed a bank. There guarding it stood a Papua New Guinean, his torso bare, a bow and arrow slung over his shoulder. You certainly don't get security guards like that outside Barclays or HSBC.

Our guard explained that the security measures were due to the high incidence of rioting. According to him, riots start un-expectedly and often for no apparent reason. Whether that was true or not, we saw no evidence, as we were quickly transferred to a small airfield for our onward journey to Wau.

A short flight later, after landing on an impossibly steep hill, we took a final open jeep ride into the forest to a research station, where we would acclimatize and prepare for one of the toughest jungle trails in the world.

My team was an interesting bunch, but there was one

outstanding character, a pretty young girl called Sarah. She had stood out at the Welsh selection camp where she had revealed her story, which would dominate my life for the next couple of months.

Sarah had fallen in love with her childhood sweetheart when she was just seventeen. She wasn't close to her own family and Simon filled the void. She had been incredibly happy and content, and they finally married. Life was great until Sarah got the call we all dread. Simon had died in a car crash. It had torn her apart. She hadn't come to terms with her loss. She was grieving deeply and, almost six months later, she still hadn't held a memorial or a funeral for her husband.

Sarah was fragile and hurting, and I hoped the trip would help rather than hinder. I have seen so many instances of people trying to escape their demons by going overseas. The truth of the matter is that you can never escape yourself. It's like burying your head in the sand or closing your eyes and pretending no one can see you. Just because you are in a new environment doesn't solve the issue; it merely travels with you. You might be able to block out your problems temporarily, but at some stage you have to face reality.

I have always been a firm believer in talking things through. A problem shared is a problem halved and all that. Bereavement is, of course, a very different thing and (I'm touching wood as I write this) I have been very lucky with my limited encounters.

My biggest fear is leaving others grieving. To see Sarah used to break my heart. I wanted to hug her and tell her it was all going to be OK, but it wasn't. Nothing would ever bring her husband back, but what I could do was offer her the chance to get her life back and address her bereavement.

Now whether a TV show was the right place for this to happen is another issue. If I'm honest, I don't think it was. But she was here now. She was here of her own volition and I was going to help her however I could.

We spent a couple of days learning jungle craft – how to put up our hammocks, mosquito nets and jungle bashas to protect us from the rain.

Our guide was a tiny Papua New Guinean called Sandy with the biggest feet I have ever seen on a human being. They weren't so much long as wide, splayed out like pads. They were incredible. It was the first time I had ever been envious of someone else's body parts.

For several days we trekked through the leech-infested forest. I hate leeches. I don't feel I have to justify that statement. I'm sure if you are a doctor you could wax lyrical about their medicinal virtues, but when you're picking them from your eyes and your balls, there really isn't much going for them.

They sit on branches waiting for the vibrations of falling feet. Then they estimate the optimum time and make a Russian-roulette leap into the abyss, hoping to land on a juicy arm or neck, from where they can effortlessly navigate to just about any part of the body. They do it without feeling, and I mean that in every sense of the word. I have lost track of the number of times I've been woken to a dawn chorus of 'F**k!' as people discover bloated leeches all over their bodies.

I used to stare in wonder at Sandy's feet as he walked the trail barefoot over roots and sharp spines. He would flick the leeches from his feet using the point of his machete. My feet would have been shredded after half an hour on that jungle floor, but Sandy's were toughened to it.

The trail was littered with grim reminders of the Second World War. We walked past crashed fighter jets embedded in the ground and anti-aircraft guns that had been suffocated by the jungle. Each evening we would string our hammocks in old Japanese and Australian camps. They were littered with dog tags, tunics and old leather boots. The floor was covered with spent bullet cases, and occasionally we saw skeletons sticking out of the ground. It was eerie camping in the middle of this. I would lie in my hammock each night and imagine what it was like here in 1942. It must have been a terrible place. War of any kind is a dreadful thing, but jungle warfare is particularly awful. It was shocking to think how many lives must have been lost here. For me, it tinged the trek with sadness.

About four days into the trip I overheard a conversation between Sarah and another of the team. I knew that Sarah hadn't told anyone else on the team about her loss.

'What's the first thing you're going to do when you get home?' Liz asked Sarah.

'I don't know – what about you?' she replied, spinning the question to avoid answering.

'Hug my husband,' Liz replied. 'Are you married, Sarah?'

'Yes.'

'What's his name?'

And so the questioning continued. I don't think it's appropriate to report the full conversation, but Sarah carried on about Simon in the present tense, as if he were still alive. It broke my heart. It still breaks my heart to think about it now.

But it created a problem. Sarah's story was part of the film. The whole production team knew and the viewers would also know, but she hadn't told her teammates. It wasn't an issue for me; after all, she needed to grieve in her own time and talking about it had to be a natural process, not one hurried up by television. But London wasn't happy. They wanted her to open up and they wanted me to confront her about it.

I have my principles and I can be stubborn. I tried to reason with the producers, but I was told that if I didn't talk to her, then the director would. If someone had to do it, it was going to be me.

I'm not going to divulge the conversation we had on that hillside, but we both cried, and Sarah, quietly and discreetly, revealed her secret to her teammates away from the cameras. I was so proud of her that day. She had overcome an enormous hurdle and was beginning to confront reality, but I hated London for making me do it.

Once again we were racing against the clock. We needed to reach the river in time to build a couple of bamboo rafts for the final journey to Salamuana, and we were up against it.

Early one morning, as we reached a clearing, three young Papuan children appeared. We hadn't seen anyone for days.

'Come!' They gestured away from the path.

Sandy translated that they had been waiting for three days for our arrival and that the village had prepared a celebration. We had to go, so we trekked through the jungle until we reached an enormous pair of gates, probably more than four metres high, made from leaves and vines. We were told to wait there.

Slowly the gates swung open to reveal a pretty little village with half a dozen longhouses. A dozen men appeared in headdresses and loincloths, holding spears and with bows slung over their shoulders. They stamped their feet on the ground, chanting, then raised their spears aloft and began to move towards us. We stood frozen to the spot as they circled us menacingly. Having formed a ring around us, they escorted us into the village, all the time stamping their feet, chanting and singing.

As we entered the village, another group appeared from behind one of the longhouses, and then another. The village was festooned with flowers, and vines had been strung from house to house. I noticed an old wartime bomb hanging upside down as a bell, and the wing of a crashed plane had been used as a roof.

Singing echoed from the jungle beyond as a group of more than a hundred women and children danced into the village. We stood gripped with amazement as more and more people flooded around us. Smiles radiated from every face as they sang and danced with pure joy and happiness. It was one of the most un-affected scenes I have ever witnessed. I have been lucky enough to see ceremonies all over the world, from Africa to Latin America, but, wonderful as they are to watch, I have always found that commercialism affects their sincerity. But here, now, in the middle of the jungle of Papua New Guinea, it was different. There was no motive for this great show. No money exchanged hands. We didn't even film it. It was simply done as a part of their culture.

By now, hundreds had joined in the highly choreographed dance. One group of men would sing and stamp their feet, and just as they finished another group would begin. It was like a dialogue of song and dance.

For an hour the ceremony continued as we all watched, open-mouthed at the spectacle. Cirque du Soleil had nothing on this. I looked around me to see the cameramen wiping their eyes. Sarah had tears streaming down her face. It was undoubtedly one of the most moving experiences of my life.

At the end, each and every man, woman and child filed past us and shook our hands, placed garlands around our necks and paint on our faces. They then invited us to share in a great feast.

It was totally baffling – but then maybe that was the purpose, because it was also unforgettable. Occasionally I'll be up a mountain or stuck on a ship and I'll find myself travelling back to that happy place. It always puts a smile on my face. When I was younger, I used to cheer myself up by watching the film *Dumb and Dumber*; it was guaranteed to lift me out of a mood or minor depression. Now I just take myself back to that joyous scene in the Papua jungle.

In the end we had to tear ourselves away. I shall never forget the sight of a thousand men, women and children, dressed in full ceremonial wear, waving us off down the trail. We all walked in silence for the rest of the day, lost in our thoughts and the magic of that encounter, until we reached the river, where we built a bamboo raft for the completion of our journey down the estuary and out into open water.

I'll also never forget the look on Sarah's face when we reached the end. It was the first time I had seen her looking genuinely happy. The experience had been good for her, but she still had a long way to go and that's why I invited her to join me on the final expedition I was going to make for that series, to Mount Roraima in Venezuela.

Sandy, our guide, held my hand tightly before we left and stared at me hard. I was taken aback to see tears in his eyes.

'Don't forget me, Mr Ben,' he said. 'Please don't forget us. We will never forget all of you.'

I was overcome. I had never met such warm people, big-hearted people.

'I won't, Sandy, I promise,' I said as I hugged him. 'Let me leave you something of mine,' I added. 'How about my machete?'

He shook his head.

'My knife? Watch? Shirt? Hammock?' I went through my whole bag, but he shook his head to everything.

'Is there anything you want?' I asked.

He smiled and nodded his head.

'It's yours, Sandy. What is it?'

He pointed to my feet.

'My boots? You want my *boots*?' I asked, surprised that, of all my kit, he wanted my £10 ex-army jungle boots. I hated those boots.

'But, Sandy, your feet will be too big,' I said, pointing to his magnificent splayed feet.

He pointed to the boots again and held his hands together.

I would have handed them over happily, but I couldn't bear the thought of the damage they would do to his feet, which were at least twice as wide as the leather army boots.

He continued to stare at me and then at my boots, so reluctantly I unlaced them and handed them to him. He looked like a child at Christmas.

'I have never owned a pair of shoes,' he smiled. He pushed and shoved, grunted and groaned as he squeezed his mighty feet into those old boots. I could see the sides of his feet straining against the leather as he tied the laces into neat bows.

'There!' he said, standing proudly, before walking in a little circle. 'They're perfect, Mr Ben, just perfect.'

The last time I had been in Venezuela I had been nineteen and desperate to explore the world. I had spent the best part of a year travelling around Latin America and had ended up in Manaus in Brazil, which I had first passed through on my journey up the Amazon. I took a bus up the first trans-Amazonian road that headed north through the rainforest, up over the border to Ciudad Bolívar and eventually to Caracas, the Venezuelan capital. I had somehow managed to contract amoebic dysentery on the journey and ended up with my bottom in a bin in the middle of a busy bus station. I've tried to avoid that station ever since.

Venezuela has become a bit of a laughing stock in recent years on account of its president, Hugo Chavez. In 2007, having already redesignated Venezuela a 'Bolivarian Republic', redesigned the flag and created a new currency, President Chavez announced that the country's clocks would be turned back by half an hour so that it stood apart from its neighbours.

There is, however, a region of the country where time seems to stand still: the vast area of land known as the Gran Sabana. These fifteen thousand square miles of rainforest – nearly twice the size of Wales – were virtually inaccessible until three decades ago, and the area is commonly known as the Lost World.

This was the destination for my final expedition of series two of *Extreme Dreams*. It's a place that has captivated me since childhood. I distinctly remember reading a *National Geographic* magazine at school about an expedition into this fabled region on the borders of Venezuela, Brazil and Guyana.

It is dominated by about a hundred vast, flat-topped mountains, called *tepuis* in the language of the indigenous Pemon people. No one is really sure quite how many there are, because it is simply too difficult and too dangerous to explore them all. These table-top, cliff-edged giants soar up to a mile above the jungle, and the sandstone that forms them is more than two billion years old. This means that the tops of the mountains have been isolated for millions of years.

Mount Roraima, 2,810 metres (9,219 feet) high, is arguably the most famous of the *tepuis*, because it was the first to be explored. In 1877, while the debate over Darwin's theory of evolution was raging in England, the *Spectator* magazine asked, 'Will no one explore Roraima and bring us back the tidings which it has been waiting these thousands of years to give us?' But it was another seven years before two British explorers, Everard Im Thurn and Harry Perkins, would make the first successful summit of a mountain deemed unclimbable by Sir Walter Raleigh. Even today, only a handful of the *tepuis* have ever been explored.

It was after listening to a Royal Geographical Society lecture about Thurn and Perkins' daring expedition that Sir Arthur Conan Doyle wrote *The Lost World*, his tale of a land still inhabited by dinosaurs. Life imitated art, and the area soon adopted the name of the book. Today, the region is best known as the home of the tallest waterfall in the world, the Angel Falls, which cascades off another of the table mountains, Auyantepui. The legend of its discovery would have provided a perfect case for Conan Doyle's best-known literary creation, Sherlock Holmes.

The story goes that in 1921 Jimmy Angel, an accomplished pilot, met an old Alaskan prospector named J. R. McCracken in a Panamanian bar. McCracken regaled him with a tale of a mountain of gold in southern Venezuela, previously documented by Portuguese explorers and also by Colonel Percy Fawcett, the British explorer who later went missing for ever in the uncharted jungles of Brazil. The following year, the two men headed south from Caracas, flying over hundreds of miles of rainforest. The old man sat in the co-pilot's seat directing Jimmy and soon they had reached the Gran Sabana. McCracken used an old compass and map, picking out a flat spot on which Angel was able to land the plane.

Wading into a river that snaked its way across the flat mountain top, McCracken proceeded to fish out vast nuggets of gold. The pair worked fast and loaded more than seventy-five pounds of ore, but daylight was fading, so they had to leave with just a fraction of what was available.

McCracken sold his haul for hundreds of thousands of dollars, but fell ill and died a few days later, leaving a distraught Angel to spend the rest of his life trying to relocate that mountain. On one ill-fated return expedition he crashed into the jungle and spent eleven days hacking his way back to civilization. It was in 1935 that he discovered the 979-metre (3,212-foot) falls that would later bear his name. He eventually lost his life in 1956 when his plane flipped over. His ashes were scattered over the Gran Sabana in the hope that they might rest with the gold that had eluded him for thirty-five years.

As a child, I was as smitten with Angel's story as I was with Conan Doyle's mysterious Jurassic world, teeming with pre-historic beasts. It seemed astonishing that mankind had explored the deepest oceans and even set foot on the moon, and yet this vast area of the planet's surface remained largely unknown. I vowed that one day I would visit the Lost World for myself, be it to discover gold, dinosaurs or something else altogether.

I was even more excited by the fact that many of these table mountains remained unexplored. Locals talked of mountain dinosaurs and great lions that had lived in isolation for millions of years on these vast islands in the sky, and for decades there had been speculation about the great wealth of minerals hidden on the summits. Mount Roraima had remained the focus of much attention from scientists and explorers over the years. Seventy per cent of the flora and fauna on the summit is found nowhere else on earth, and much of it has yet to be documented by scientists.

Now, more than twenty years after first reading this incredible story, I was finally heading into the Lost World to climb Mount Roraima. And so I set off, clutching a battered copy of Conan Doyle's book.

I had chosen one member from each of my trips to join me on this final expedition, but for me it was all about Sarah. I had found myself inextricably entangled in her life. Whether she realized it or not, I couldn't stop thinking about her. Were I my wife, I would probably have been a little suspicious, but Marina understood. I have always worn my heart on my sleeve and find myself emotionally involved in subjects all the time. For me, the hardest part of *Extreme Dreams* had been the people. I had found myself caught in the complex spiders' webs of their lives.

Unsurprisingly, getting to the Lost World is not easy. A flight via Amsterdam and Aruba in the Caribbean eventually deposited me in muggy Caracas, whereupon I transferred for the two-hour flight to Ciudad Bolívar in the east of Venezuela, on the edge of the Gran Sabana. We flew, as Jimmy would have done, over an endless sea of jungle. Every so often, the green was broken by a single red tree towering over the rest of the forest. Then came another three-hour flight by Cessna to Santa Elena de Uarien, which included a layover in Canaima because of exceptionally heavy rain.

We followed the course of a river for several miles. This is one of the world's gold hotspots and we flew over vast gold-mining camps deep in the rainforest. The water was brown with silt stirred up by the dredging.

'I need to have a wee,' called out one of my team members, who shall remain nameless.

'You'll have to go in a bag,' I shouted over the buzz of the engine.

'I can't go in a bag!' She sounded shocked.

'Then you'll have to hang on,' I hollered.

'I can't. We'll have to pull over,' she yelled back.

Pull over! Had she totally lost her marbles? We weren't in a car on a family day out – we were in a Cessna flying over the Amazon rainforest.

'Please, please stop the plane!' she pleaded.

Incredibly, the pilot called one of the mining camps.

'This is Alpha Delta Yankee Three. Can we land for a pee?' I heard him say over the radio.

And so it was I experienced my first emergency landing in a light aircraft in the middle of the jungle so that someone could take a comfort break. You couldn't make it up.

Mission completed, we carried on and eventually landed in a small jungle clearing. Then, after one final bone-crunching, off-road car journey, we reached Peraitepuy, a Pemon village and the most popular starting point for those on their way to Roraima. The trek would take us ten days across open savannah and the rivers that criss-crossed it. It soon became apparent that two things were going to dominate our adventure: water and puri-puris.

Water is a key feature of the Gran Sabana, with each *tepui* generating its own weather system. It rains a lot, and we had to make plenty of river crossings. But while rain and water can generally be managed with the right equipment, puri-puris are seemingly unstoppable. They're the Houdinis of the insect world: tiny gnats, able to get in and out of any material and known locally known as *plagas*, meaning plagues. Imagine a Scottish midge crossed with a Scandinavian mosquito and you'll get some idea of how unpleasant they are. They are also seemingly immune to all repellents and clothing. They drink 100 per cent

Deet as if it were orange juice, and bite through midge-proof clothing like butter. On my first day, I counted 150 bites on my ears and arms alone, and my left eye had swollen closed as a result of their attacks. All our faces became pockmarked with tiny red bites, and our heads were painfully itchy. We pressed on through these biting clouds until our bodies could itch no more, sometimes resorting to smearing mud on our skin in order to create another barrier. It was pretty miserable lying in our hammocks at night, burning with itchy bites.

It was five days before we caught a glimpse of the fabled *tepuis*, rising from their surroundings like huge land-islands. Thick spools of cloud blanketed their summits, cascading off the sides in long tongues of smoke. The nearer, Kukenan Tepui, has been closed to trekkers and scientists alike for several years since an adventurer and his guide went missing on the summit. The other was the mighty Roraima, looming in the distance like an impenetrable fortress.

I found myself almost mesmerized by their scale and beauty. I had never seen anything quite like them. It seemed extraordinary for such isolated pinnacles of rock to dominate an otherwise flat savannah. We're used to seeing mountains in ranges, creating a rolling or jagged horizon. The *tepuis*, however, look more like objects forgotten by giants. (Indeed, local lore has it that they are tree stumps left when a greedy giant tried to cut down two vast trees to get at their fruit. The trees fell into Brazil, creating the country's rich rainforest, leaving just the stumps in Venezuela for the gluttonous giant.) Staring at the vertical walls of Roraima, I wondered how we were ever going to climb it. It looked impossible.

We trekked for up to ten miles a day as the weather alternated between steamingly hot tropical and steamingly wet tropical. The rivers were swollen by the heavy rainfall and brown with run-off from the hills above; we often needed to use ropes to cross them.

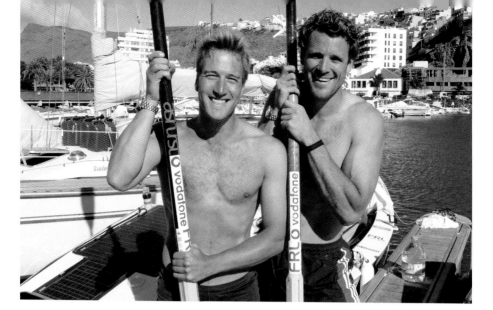

Above: Early innocence. This was taken a few days before James and I set off across the Atlantic. We were at the start line in La Gomera and were still excited about the challenge ahead.

Left: Aboard our little rowing boat, a week out of Antigua. We rowed much of the ocean naked to avoid chafing. It took us forty-nine days and changed our lives. We still have the boat.

Just a few weeks later we would be fighting for our lives after our boat capsized in rough seas. James took this photograph shortly after the boat had righted itself and I had clambered back on board. It's an image that still haunts me. We lost almost everything except for what you can see here.

Above: Training with James for the Tour Divide, a 3,000-mile bike race along the Rocky Mountains from Canada to Mexico. We'd just spent all night cycling the length of the South Downs.

Below: Skiing into the sun at the bottom of the world. For weeks on end we man-hauled into the stark white landscape. Sometimes it felt as if we were in our own little snow globe, but when the sun shone the landscape became ethereal, sculpted by the wind.

In Antarctica, halfway through
our 1,000-kilometre trek to the
South Pole. It was minus 40°C.

Extreme Dreams often turned into extreme nightmares but the adventures helped change lives. With my team in Chile, crossing the salt flats, which felt like walking on coral.

Mount Roraima in Venezuela soars behind me. It had been a childhood dream to visit it since reading Arthur Conan Doyle's *The Lost World* and it is one of the most dramatic places I have ever seen. The locals believe that dinosaurs live here. You can see why.

With friendly Papua New Guineans. One of the happiest sights of my life.

Above: Rashid and his family in their remote village. Like so many people suffering from noma, Rashid wore a towel over his head to disguise his disfigurement.

Right and below: The reality of noma. Mestikima before her surgery.

Above: Visiting Scott's hut felt like a pilgrimage. I had longed to come to this lonely place ever since I was a child, and there was a magical feel about it. Walking around, you can practically sense the ghosts of Captain Scott and his team.

Below: It was incredibly moving inside that little hut at the bottom of the world. It is steeped in history and the smells alone transport you back in time. The kitchen galley is still fully stocked with foods from the original expedition.

The Angel of Antarctica. Well, it looks like it at least. The wind and the currents of the ocean create fantastic pressure ridges along the shore that jut out like works of modern art. I never seriously thought I'd get to visit Antarctica and now I've been there twice. I'm the luckiest person in the world.

They are like highways through the vast savannah, and we paddled down some of them in dug-out canoes; it was a welcome relief to take to the water and enjoy the change of scenery. We often found ourselves accompanied by a flotilla of tree trunks and jungle detritus. This whole area is a national park and fishing is permitted only with a government licence. Even with one, it felt pretty strange fishing for piranha with primitive bamboo rods and crude lines.

After ten days' trekking from Peraitepuy, we at last reached Roraima's base camp, which is set at an altitude of almost two thousand metres above sea level, but is still only at the foot of the *tepui*. As we pitched our tents, the camp was bathed in tropical sunlight. This was soon superseded by an enormous thunderstorm, which sent a torrent of water through the middle of the camp and flooded my tent.

By now, our bodies had been baked, bitten and soaked in equal measure. As we shared a large spaghetti bolognese for supper, I began to see why this Lost World had remained lost for so long.

We set off early for the ascent. The track passes through a number of climate zones, including a thick cloud forest. The jungle here is also home to an army of venomous snakes, including the bushmaster, the fer-de-lance and the rattlesnake, but it is the mapepire – also referred to as the bothrop – that has the most fearsome reputation and is responsible for more fatalities than any other American reptile. These terrifying snakes infest the forest, often hanging from trees and striking unsuspecting passers-by. So afraid of them are the locals that a number of our porters refused to continue from base camp. As we pressed on with our experienced guides, I thought that the snakes made a fittingly Indiana Jones-type threat.

Dense cloud clung to the side of the mountain, dousing us in freezing rain and turning the trail to mud. Everything was covered in a thick blanket of moss and lichen, and dangling vines looked worryingly like snakes, creating a forestscape that was reminiscent of something from a tale by the Brothers Grimm. We edged our way along a rough trail, which by now had turned into a cascading stream. Mud clung to our boots as we waded through rivers and clambered up the steep path.

Onwards we slipped and splashed until we reached a huge waterfall cascading off the summit, which itself was hidden in cloud. Eventually the vegetation thinned and we reached 'the Wall' – a five-hundred-metre cliff of quartzite, which dwarfed us like ants below. Many early explorers had turned back here, defeated by the sheer face. Luckily, we knew we wouldn't have to climb it as – in the manner of a good Conan Doyle novel – there is a secret gateway called 'the Ramp', discovered by Everard Im Thurn and Harry Perkins in 1884.

One of the few vegetated parts of the mountainside, the Ramp bypasses the wall and leads to a fissure in the side of the mountain, from which a steep scramble takes you to the top. The narrow plume of a waterfall cascading off the summit creates a sort of portal on to the Ramp. In really heavy rain, it is sometimes impassable due to the power of the falls under which you have to walk, like a giant shower. Slowly we wended our way along the narrow trail, then zigzagged up the final path and onwards, above the cloud.

As I clambered on to the summit, what I saw was astonishing. The scenery at the top of the mountain is like a moonscape from a B-list sci-fi film: impressive blackened rocks of every shape and size interspersed with tiny, colourful gardens. The anarchic landscape is fissured and eroded, scattered with deep gorges and chasms, babbling red rivers, glistening white crystals and pink sandy beaches. It is at once surreal, eccentric, beautiful and dreadful, like some crazy, drug-induced Dali painting.

Roraima's summit covers thirteen square miles. In the past, adventurers and explorers have been lost for days in its rocky maze; some, less fortunate, have been lost for ever. Rescue helicopters are rarely able to land due to the extreme conditions.

The rock formations create the illusion of preposterous shapes. Everard Im Thurn depicted the summit as an 'apparent caricature of umbrellas, tortoises, churches, cannons and innumerable other incongruous and unexpected objects'. I saw profiles of my friend Charley, one of Fidel Castro, and even one of my wife's Christian Louboutin shoes.

The rolling mist added to the eerie, otherworldly scene as it funnelled up the sheer rockface like smoke. Pterodactyls wouldn't have been out of place here; indeed, some say that the *tepuis* were among the pterodactyls' final nesting places before they died out. Local lore insists that dinosaurs still inhabit these high-altitude 'islands'. It's certainly the case that plants have adapted to the surroundings in an evolutionary trend that reflects the nutrient-poor soil. Up here, a carnivorous bromeliad has evolved tube-shaped leaves that form water-filled death-traps for unwary insects.

Up and down, over the rocky surface, our guide escorted us carefully through the maze of sand-blasted sculptures. For three hours we trekked in silence, stunned by our surroundings, until we reached the ironically named 'El Hotel', a cave system used by climbers to shelter in overnight.

I pitched my tent on the soft, sandy floor of the cave as heavy rain once again enveloped the mountain, producing a watery curtain at the cavern's entrance. The puri-puris had left us at the base of the mountain, and the thick, tropical air of the savannah had now been replaced by the chilly mountain temperatures as the cloud rolled in and out like waves. The cave certainly provided a warm shelter as we sat around the camp stove (open fires aren't permitted; neither is the removal of anything from the summit), eating rice and beans and discussing the trek. We were alone on that mountain top and, for just one night, we felt like pioneering explorers visiting a new, unchartered land.

I had completed another lifelong dream.

'Can I ask you a favour?' said Sarah the next morning. 'I'd like to hold a service for Simon.'

I was stunned. Although I had hoped the trip would help with her healing, I had never dreamt the experience would have such a profound effect on her.

'I don't think I'm strong enough to read it myself,' she continued. 'Would you do it?' I can honestly say, with my hand on my heart, it was probably one of the biggest honours of my life. I was blown away that she would ask me to do something so personal.

She wanted us all as the congregation, so the film crew, the director, the assistant producers, the team, the porters and I converged on a flat rock near to the edge of the *tepui*, overlooking the savannah below.

Cloud scudded across the pale-blue sky. I could hear the squawk of macaws from the valley beneath, and a gentle wind snapped at our jackets as we stood in silence. The mountain had become nature's church.

I held the paper with Sarah's handwritten message and began to read the words, but I was overcome with involuntary bursts of sobbing. 'Come on, Ben,' I berated myself, 'hold it together.'

I carried on, still breaking into sobs more often than not. I was aware of tears streaming down everyone else's cheeks too. I have rarely been so moved as I was by those few words put together over the course of our time in Papua New Guinea and Venezuela. Sarah stood there silently. That she had chosen to share this intensely private moment with us spoke of what the trips had done for her.

Shortly after we returned to the UK, I received a letter from Sarah in which she spoke honestly and openly about how much the experience had helped her, and a few years later I got another letter to tell me she had finally met someone and they had decided to get married.

If anyone deserved a happy ending it was Sarah. Every so often, when something bad happens or I find myself in a difficult situation, I think about Sarah and what she went through, and suddenly things don't seem so awful.

As was so often the case in *Extreme Dreams*, it was as much a life-changing experience for me as it was for my team. I had fulfilled my childhood dream. I may not have seen a *Tyrannosaurus rex*, but I had caught sight of the rare *grillo de agua* – a water cricket that can inflict a painful bite – and even glimpsed the *Oreophrynella quelchii*, a tiny black toad so primitive that it neither swims nor hops, but just crawls.

Conan Doyle's characters left their Lost World through a secret cave. I would be taking the more conventional hike down. But for now, the Lost World had finally become a reality. As I closed my eyes I'm sure I saw a herd of *Diplodocus* drinking from a river of gold. The real world once again became the stuff of dreams.

13

Pushed to the Limit

Extreme Dreams was pushing me and my teammates closer and closer to the edge, and I was beginning to worry about safety, but it was an expedition across Nepal, the third expedition of series two, that nearly ended in disaster.

We flew from London via Qatar to Kathmandu. The last time I had been here was eight years earlier, when I had gone in my role as travel editor for *Hello!* I had become an ambassador for the World Wide Fund for Nature (WWF) and we had spent an incredible couple of weeks in the lowlands, towards the border with India, where we had helped with a rhino-relocation programme between Chitwan and Bardia National Parks. To this day it remains one of the most extraordinary experiences of my life.

The idea of the relocation was to ensure there was an even balance between national parks to avoid overpopulation, but also in case of disease. We rode on elephants into the forest in search of Asian rhino, which are bizarre-looking creatures, like a cross between an African rhino, with a long nose and one horn, and a dinosaur, with an armour-plated body. It took a convoy of twenty elephants, each with four people riding on their backs, to track through the thick undergrowth. Scientists, vets and anaesthetists were all part of the expedition. We left in the early hours and trekked as the sun rose. It was breathtakingly beautiful as we swayed our way across rivers and lakes.

Eventually we isolated a female rhino and her calf, both of which were suitable for relocation. Silence descended as we slowly circled the two beasts. Occasionally the female would snort as a branch snapped underfoot, her ears twitching.

Once we had them surrounded, we began to close in on the two magnificent creatures, until they were enclosed by a wall of wrinkled grey skin. The female snorted again and backed a few steps. She realized they had been cut off.

And this is where something amazing happened. She looked for the weakest elephant. She actually sought out the youngster who was most likely to buckle. As she circled, the elephants stood their ground, though mine was twitching nervously. The rhino could sense her nervousness and made a mock charge. My elephant reared up, trumpeting in fear, and tried to run. The mahout attempted to reassure her, but she continued to trumpet. She was a youngster who was yet to develop her arrogance and, although she might have been bigger than the rhino, she knew the damage that horn could do and she wasn't happy.

You could taste the tension as the vets raised their tranquillizer guns. Once darted, the animals would certainly take flight. We would open our elephant barricade to let them through, but it was crucial that we kept up with them. Asleep, a rhino can physically crush its lungs under its own weight; if they escaped us before they fell to the ground, they would certainly die. We had to load them into a crate and bring them round as quickly as we could.

The two darts hit the fleshy rears of mother and calf. Chaos ensued as both animals bolted. Elephants trumpeted and reared, and the forest echoed to the noise of animal calls. The race was on.

Riding on the back of a running elephant is a strange experience. It's a little like sitting on a slow-moving bucking bronco at a party. The movements are slow but dramatic. Lose your grip and you'll be an elephant pancake.

Eventually the drugs began to take effect and it wasn't long before the rhino collapsed on to the forest floor. A cascade of humans tumbled from the elephants, including a rather over-enthusiastic German TV presenter. He made a small crater with his not inconsiderable girth and raced to the rhino. There was a gabble of excited German as he thrust his hands on to the female's thick hide.

'*NO!*' screamed a Nepalese vet.

More chaos ensued as he explained that one drop of the drug was enough to kill a human, and that it had been absorbed into the blood and therefore through the rhino's skin on to the German's hands. He was spirited away by a doctor, while twenty men heaved and hauled to get the mighty beasts on to an enormous land-sledge and into their crates.

It was like a scene from *King Kong*, with the elephants dragging the sledge like a team of giant husky dogs. We reached the huge wooden crates and hauled the ten-ton beasts inside. One side was closed while a vet entered with the reverse drug. I watched as he ran from the crate and the mighty wooden door was dropped closed. It must have taken five seconds for the rhino to come around – and she wasn't happy. The crate rocked and rolled with anger. Hell hath no fury like a caged rhino.

The two crates were eventually loaded on to lorries and so began their long journey to a new park and their place in environmental science.

I hadn't been back to Nepal since, but I'd always dreamed of trekking in the Himalayas. Again, we had an interesting mix of people. The teams were often chosen as much for their suitability to television as for their physical and mental ability, but, given that, the premise of the series was still to give everyone the opportunity to achieve.

We had been trekking for a couple of days. The going had been tough, but it had been manageable. Most of my team were doing well, although one, Nicole, had been struggling with the heat and the altitude. She had been overcome with waves of nausea and faintness and we were keeping a close eye on her.

We carried on and made camp that night. The next day we packed up and continued deeper into the mountains towards our goal of Pokhara. Nicole continued to be a worry. She had become quiet and withdrawn. She was off her food and she had been falling back behind the group. I had seen the signs before, so I got the medic to give her the once-over. He couldn't find anything wrong, but she was light-headed and unsteady on her feet.

I decided to tag her, marking her every step. I watched her like a hawk as we walked along the wall of a drainage canal. I kept up a monologue, but she remained silent, lost in her own world.

We were in the middle of the group, which had strung out along the canal. The camera crew and Mark, the director, were up at the front of the line, setting up the cameras on a steep scree climb. It was a five-hundred-metre wall of loose rock, with a thin animal trail zigzagging up the face. In places, it dropped vertically. One missed step or clumsy slip and you would tumble down the cliff to certain death. It was certainly dangerous, but our safety team and local guides decided it didn't require ropes. In retrospect, I should have roped myself to Nicole, but that's easy to say now.

We were halfway up when Nicole stopped. I was just a few inches behind her. Something was wrong. She swayed slightly and then began to topple towards me. She had fainted.

I hope Nicole won't mind me describing her as a not in-considerable girl, and with her heavy rucksack she formed a formidable ballast as gravity took hold. I grabbed at her arm to stop her tumbling off the precipitous trail, but she had already gained momentum. I had all her weight, but my legs struggled to hold against the loose gravel, and before I knew it I had begun to slip too.

I can honestly say that this was one of those moments when I thought I'd meet my maker. The only other experience I had had in my life that was like it was when James Cracknell and I were capsized while rowing the Atlantic. I had thought then that that was it, but it wasn't; I had lived to tell the tale.

Now, as one foot slipped away from me, I grappled at the ground with my free arm, desperate to clutch at something, anything, to stop us falling to our deaths. Not on my watch. We had urged people on, but I wasn't going to let anything bad happen to any of my team.

My weight cantilevered towards the edge and gravity took hold. Here we go, I thought. Make it quick. My arm flailed, and just as I lost control it made contact . . . with Paula, another team member. She had wedged herself with a rock and I was able to steady myself on her arm.

Paula had saved our lives – but, more significantly, we'd nearly lost Nicole's. We got her to flat ground, by which time she had come round, but she was disoriented and confused. She was talking incoherently and vomiting violently. She may have survived the mountain, but now we had to save her from what-ever had caused the near fatal fall.

After a medical check, our doctor insisted we had to get her to a hospital as fast as possible. The only answer was to carry her to the nearest village, an hour's hike away uphill, and then call in a helicopter to take her to Kathmandu.

The helicopter would have to fly in high over the foothills to this tiny village perched on the side of a steep slope. Terraces had been cut into the side of the mountain and we raced from tier to tier, trying to find one large enough and clear enough on which to land a chopper. An hour later and we had decided on one that we felt would do. Next we needed to create a large, colourful visual target for the helicopter to identify from the air, so we tied our jackets together to create a marker.

A few hours later we heard the distant thud of the chopper. It went straight over our heads before making another pass. They couldn't see us.

I stripped my yellow shirt off my back and, half-naked, ran around furiously waving it. Why couldn't they see? It took more than six passes before finally they spotted us.

The helicopter was able to land on the narrow plateau, its rotor blade just a few feet from the mountainside, and before we knew what was happening, it had disappeared off into the horizon with Nicole.

We sat around the campfire that night in silence, mulling over the day's experience. It had been a reality check for the team and we still had a long way to go. My worries had almost been realized. It had been a near miss, far too close for comfort.

The final few days of the trek were a bit of a let-down. We had all been shaken by the experience and it took the shine off the climax to the trip. It was another reminder not only of my own mortality, but also of my responsibility to others.

A third series of *Extreme Dreams* was commissioned and we continued to push the boundaries of our participants' abilities. The challenges became tougher, but it is a little story about a road trip in Peru of which I am rather ashamed.

We were four weeks into the shoot and I was due to meet my next crew in Arequipa in three days' time. We had spent the last few weeks in the hot, steamy bowels of the deepest canyon on earth, the 3,354-metre (11,000-foot) Cotahuasi Canyon. I was already tired and weary from weeks and weeks of trekking and filming and had been struck by some unknown lurgy for the previous few days. All I knew was that it was vital that I rested during this short break, before travelling onwards with the crew to Santiago in Chile and out into the Atacama Desert.

It had been a tough trek for all of us, but we were elated to have reached the lost city of Marpa and it was the first expedition of series three in which we had *all* got to the end. We were still in a state of euphoria when we finally boarded the bus for the ten-hour journey back to Arequipa.

We had been driving for a couple of hours when we hit a roadblock. Dozens of people milled around on the roadside and the tail of traffic disappeared into the distance.

'*Huelga, huelga*,' shouted someone. 'Strike, strike.'

We stepped from the bus and wandered along beside the stationary traffic. Ten, twenty, thirty minutes later and we were still walking past buses, cars and trucks, all spilling their human content on to the roadside. It was like a refugee camp. Families had created temporary shelters beside the road. Babies screamed while some drivers honked their horns fruitlessly. There must have been hundreds of vehicles snaking their way to the edge of the river in the middle of the village.

Eventually we reached the head of the block – the bridge. It had been barricaded by huge boulders and buses. A group of Peruvians held banners and boards aloft and chanted in unison. We could make out similar scenes on the other side. The bridge was impassable.

'Is there any other way of crossing the river?' we asked a harassed-looking official.

'*No, es cerrado* – it's closed too,' he explained. It transpired that locals had barricaded every bridge within a hundred miles and there was no alternative means of crossing the river.

'How long have they been striking?' we asked.

'A week.'

We were at an impasse. If we stayed, we would merely be joining the longest traffic jam in the world. They had already been there for a week; who was to say it wasn't going to last for another?

We began the long walk back to our bus to break the news.

Apart from the inconvenience, I had twenty people awaiting my arrival in Chile. They couldn't begin filming without me and we were firmly locked into our dates. We had to do something.

For an hour we sat on the bus as more and more traffic built up behind us. Food and water were already becoming scarce, and there were rumours that the army would be drafted in to keep the peace.

From what little we could understand, the locals were striking against a recent hike in bus fares. The rise was above inflation in a region already suffering economically. While I sympathized with their cause, I wished they could have done it somewhere else. Still, I suppose that is the point of a strike – to make life difficult for everyone. They were certainly doing that. There must have been five thousand people on our side of the river alone.

We needed a plan. My eyes scoured the bus and settled on an enormous box marked with a red cross. Our medical supplies.

'What if we have a medical emergency?' I thought to myself. 'What if we *have* to cross that bridge?'

We made our plan. We would simply dress a 'volunteer' as a casualty, explain that we needed to get to hospital and negotiate our way through the blockade. It was slightly insensitive, but it sounded faultless.

One of my team members, Ann, a charity worker, volunteered to be our guinea pig. We giggled as we wrapped her in bandages doused with our leftover Heinz ketchup and iodine. Alex, the medic, carefully inserted a drip beneath her bandaged arm, the needle pressed firmly against her skin. We sprinkled some talcum powder on her face to give her a slight pallor and we added a patch over her eye for good measure.

She looked pretty convincing with her bandaged head and arm, but the drip gave added gravitas.

We were too busy admiring our work to explore any deeper moral issues, and before we knew it we had sent the bus driver to the head of the queue to explain our situation to the locals. The idea was to tell them that she had taken a tumble and hit her head, so we needed to get her to hospital as quickly as we could. We were sure that, being Catholics, they would be seduced by human compassion and allow us through.

It's amazing how quickly you can lose control of a situation.

'*Muerte.*' I only had to catch the tail-end of our driver's plea to know that we might have taken things a little far. 'She will die,' he had said.

Chaos ensued as the thousands of drivers and passengers, many of whom had been stuck there for more than a week, were tasked with rebuilding the bridge. Timbers were hauled into place, while women and children ferried rocks from the piles of rubble that had been placed in the road. It was a hive of activity, as boulders were pushed to the side and barbed wire was cut.

We raced back to the bus with the news. The lie might have escalated in scale, but it seemed to have worked.

There was a cacophonous splutter as cars, buses and trucks all cranked on their engines. Thick clouds of black diesel smoke clung to the road as each and every vehicle pulled to the side.

We looked on, stunned by the response. But nothing could have prepared us for what happened next.

'My children, I am so very sorry,' said an American voice as someone boarded the bus. It didn't take us long to realize that he was a man of the cloth. His dog collar rather gave it away.

'May the Lord be with you,' he said, as he walked up the aisle. 'I have come to read the last rites to your dying friend.' He crossed himself solemnly and looked to the sky above.

'We're all going to Hell,' I thought.

I looked at my feet. I couldn't bring myself to make eye contact with the priest and didn't dare look at anyone else.

'I am going to come with you to the hospital,' he reassured us.

I began to sweat.

The tide of cars continued to part, and before we knew it we were bouncing clumsily across the rough wooden bridge that had been reassembled by the strikers and their refugees, joined spiritually in their bid to help save a woman's life. We passed screaming children and their harassed-looking mothers. There were anxious men who were losing valuable income for every hour and day they were stuck behind that blockade. As if these people didn't already have enough hardships in their lives.

And there were we. Breezing through the blockade.

I looked at Ann, bandaged and attached to her fake drip. I could see her one eye flickering around the bus. She looked terrified and I could have sworn I saw a tear.

We sat in silence as the bus left the bridge. We watched as dozens of locals swarmed on to it and began to disassemble it once more. Boulders were heaved back into place and women and children began the laborious task of reconstructing the piles of rubble. On the side we had crossed to, once again the line of traffic began to part for us as we passed similar scenes of wretchedness.

The American priest stood at the front of the bus. His mouth moved but the words remained silent. He held his rosary beads and prayed for Ann.

'They have been striking for a week now, you know,' he said. 'I have been here for ten years and I've never seen anything like this.

This strike could change everything. It could finally make a difference to their lives. They are good people,' he continued. 'They deserve more in life.'

We were through the road-block, but now we were stuck with a fake casualty and a real priest. An American one! Call it divine providence, but as we reached the end of the line of traffic, a young boy rushed towards the bus and flagged us down.

His mother was dying and he needed the priest.

'Go, Father,' we insisted.

I'm sure God knew we were lying, and I have an awful lot of good to do to make up for it.

The final *Extreme Dreams* expedition was across the Atacama Desert in Chile. It sounded like a tough challenge, but it was even more significant because it was the end. The BBC had decided not to commission any more, so this would be the last adventure.

We would begin in San Pedro de Atacama, close to the point where the following year the thirty-three miners were rescued from their underground incarceration.

I had already been away from home and Marina for more than a month and I was feeling jaded and homesick. I had been looking forward to this final trip partly because it would be in my favourite conditions, desert, but also because it marked the end of two long months away. I was ready to get home – well, to Austria at least, where my sister-in-law was getting married in just a couple of weeks' time.

The production company had left the toughest bunch of participants for last. As usual, they were a mixed bag: a paralympic swimmer; a world-record-holding free diver, who had been maimed in the bombing of Sharm El Sheikh in Egypt; an army doctor; and a medal-winning air ambulance paramedic.

The challenge was to trek across two hundred miles of the Atacama and summit a previously unclimbed peak in the south of the desert. The varied landscape of the desert had all sorts of challenges to throw at us.

It was our teammate Haydn, an air ambulance paramedic, who first complained of a headache. We were sitting in our little mess tent when he described light-headedness and breathlessness. My altimeter showed that we were at about four thousand metres, just about into the height where altitude sickness can occur.

Altitude sickness, or acute mountain sickness as it is more commonly known, can be a silent killer in the mountains. There are two types: high altitude pulmonary oedema and high altitude cerebral oedema, known as HAPO and HACO.

At altitude the body begins to produce more fluid (it's the reason feet and hands sometimes swell in planes), and that fluid needs to go somewhere. In the case of HAPO, it floods into the lungs and can lead to a dry drowning. It can be diagnosed by listening to the lungs with a stethoscope – you can hear a crackling with each breath.

HACO is equally dangerous, but much harder to diagnose. In this case the fluid goes into the head, where it begins to place pressure on the brain. The symptoms usually include a sort of drunkenness and confusion. It too can lead to death if left untreated.

The only way to treat altitude sickness is by descending to sea level. It is incredible how quickly the symptoms can disappear, but it all depends on the haste of the descent. I have seen guides literally pick up casualties and run them down the mountain – we had to do this with Tom in a wheelbarrow on Mount Kilimanjaro in the first series of *Extreme Dreams*.

One indicator of mountain sickness is the amount of oxygen in the blood, and this can be tested easily using a non-invasive device that fits over the finger and registers the oxygen-saturation levels (SATS). At sea level, most people should have between ninety-eight and a hundred percentiles, and this gradually reduces the higher one goes. Anything below ninety-eight and you'll probably be hospitalized.

We slipped the little machine on to Haydn's finger and waited for the LED to flash.

Sixty-nine, it read. Alex and I looked at each other and shook our heads. It couldn't be sixty-nine. We were too low. That was the sort of measure you'd get at the South Col on Everest, not at 4,000 metres in the Atacama Desert, where whole communities live unaffected.

We put the machine on to another finger and waited again.

Sixty-seven.

I could hear alarm bells ringing in Alex's head as he registered what was happening. Haydn was slurring his words and he had difficulty walking. These were all the symptoms of HACO. We had to do something and do it fast.

We were high on a plateau and miles from the nearest community. There was nowhere for a quick descent. We would have to use the survival bag. We had carried this cylindrical tent on all the high-altitude expeditions, but had never had to use it.

We tore open the bag and unravelled the plastic contraption. About the size of a large man, it looks like a giant tube of Smarties. The top has a pressure-proof seal, into which the person clambers before the tent is pumped up. I say tent, but it is more like a capsule. There is a small see-through plastic panel near the face, but apart from that it makes me claustrophobic just thinking about it.

We bundled Haydn inside and zipped it closed. By now he was nearly unconscious. We hooked up the little foot pump and began pumping air inside. The unit works by building a pressure around the victim as you pump air in; the more air you pump, the greater the pressure and the lower the artificial altitude.

Within minutes we had brought him down to 3,250 metres and then to 3,000. Already he had become much more alert.

'Guys, I'm fine,' I could hear him protesting from within the plastic capsule. 'Honestly, guys, I'm fine now. You can let me out.'

Alex looked at me and shook his head. 'This is very common,' he explained. Once pressurized, victims think they are completely fine, but once depressurized they relapse and it's often fatal. Alex insisted that we had to keep him inside.

Haydn's protestations had become more panicked. Claustrophobia was setting in and he was desperate to get out. I peered through the little window. It was steamed with condensation.

'Haydn, wipe the window!' I had to cup my hands between my mouth and the capsule so that he could hear me through the thick plastic. We were taking turns on the foot pump. Even the film crew had downed their cameras to help.

We took turns chatting to Haydn, trying to take his mind off things and reasoning with him whenever he got agitated, which was becoming more and more frequent. We had left the SAT machine in there with him and he kept holding it up.

'Look,' he would say. 'Ninety-seven. I'm fine. *Let me out!*'

There was minor panic when he revealed that he had his knife in there with him and was going to pierce the capsule.

In the meantime, we had called the emergency services, who were coordinating a rescue. There were no helicopters in the region, but a four-wheel-drive ambulance had been scrambled and would be with us in about four hours.

Four hours is a very, very long time, especially when you have someone threatening to cut themselves out of a life-saving capsule, without which he would almost certainly have died.

We each spent five minutes pumping to keep up the pressure and a stream of fresh air inside. Just as we had reassured Haydn, then the director began to complain of similar symptoms. He was becoming disoriented and confused; he had a headache and he was breathless. Incredibly, he too had come down with HACO.

When the ambulance finally arrived, they were both loaded into it, Haydn still in his life-saving bag, and driven at high speed to San Pedro de Atacama.

We were just three days from the end of the expedition and decided to carry on director-less.

It was surprisingly emotional reaching our goal. It was the day of my first wedding anniversary and I called Marina on our satellite phone from the summit. I had been away for well over a month and it was time to go home. I was emotionally and physically exhausted, and I also had to get back to Austria for my sister-in-law's wedding.

'Nobody move!' hollered Matt, our safety officer.

We were standing outside our bus. What on earth had happened now? Someone must have dropped a contact lens or something, I thought, as I froze to the spot.

'I've just found a landmine,' he said, looking understandably worried. Somehow we'd stumbled into a minefield. We had reached the end of the challenge. I had completed more than a dozen expeditions all across the world in some of the hardest and most dangerous environments on earth, and now here we were at the end of the final journey, standing in the middle of a minefield in the Atacama Desert. I couldn't believe this was really happening. The law of sod works in interesting ways.

During our trek we had passed some minefields marked with the familiar skull and crossbones, and we had carefully avoided them, but here we were, suddenly slap bang in the middle of one. It was terrifying. We didn't know if this was just a rogue mine or if they were everywhere. I held my breath as we all scoured the ground with our eyes for any evidence of more devices. We could see nothing but rocks and dust. Gingerly, we stepped towards the bus. I scrunched my eyes with each step. My heart was racing, but exhaustion had got the better of me. It's amazing how fatigue can cancel fear.

Alex continued to look, and carefully marked out a few visible mines, noting their GPS coordinates. Somehow we made it out of the minefield intact, but the adventure wasn't yet over.

We spent a couple of days in San Pedro de Atacama, in the middle of the desert, before flying to Santiago for our onward journey home. It was a significant milestone in my life – I had just had my wedding anniversary, and here I was on the other side of the world. Another chapter in my life was closing. *Extreme Dreams* had been an extraordinary adventure. I had found myself inextricably bound up in the fabric of people's lives. What had started as a TV show had once again crossed the threshold into real life, like so many projects before it, and I had once more found myself emotionally exhausted. It had happened during the *Castaway* experiment and again while rowing the Atlantic.

I don't think anyone ever really understood what *Extreme Dreams* meant to me, nor how profoundly it affected me. To be honest, I never thought the programmes did justice to the experiences. Repetitive, fast-paced and littered with false jeopardy, I sometimes watched them from behind a pillow. They were sensationalized and one-dimensional, whereas most of the journeys had been emotional and multi-faceted. I always thought the films tried too hard to make tough expeditions look tough. The effect was that the two often cancelled each other out. Marina used to laugh out loud as she watched. I never minded, though; I had had the most incredible three years, travelled the world and made friends for life. And now it was time to move on. But first I had to get to Salzburg.

I watched as the desert swept by, thousands of feet below our plane. A smile broke across my face as I reflected on the lives that had been changed. I had come a long way from those early schooldays.

'This is your captain,' announced the Tannoy. 'Is there a doctor on the flight?'

Jenny, the army doctor, had also been suffering from altitude sickness, though she had very much been in denial. She, like so many of my teammates on *Extreme Dreams*, had been blinded by 'summit fever' and her desperation to reach the end. We had been monitoring her closely, but she had taken a turn for the worse and was having difficulty breathing. She was in a mask attached to a portable oxygen cylinder. She had already finished two cylinders and this was the last.

The pilot decided to make an emergency landing, but we were simply too heavy with fuel to do so, so he had to dump the tanks. I watched as £100,000-worth of aviation fuel evaporated into thin air before we could begin our descent into São Paulo airport in Brazil. Medics, an ambulance and a fire engine were waiting on the runway with their blue lights flashing.

Jenny was evacuated off the plane along with one of the assistant producers who had volunteered to look after her, and they spent the next couple of weeks in a Brazilian hospital. It certainly wasn't the ending I'd hoped for *Extreme Dreams*, but then again I shouldn't have been surprised: we'd had more than our fair share of mishaps and misadventures.

I arrived at the wedding with hours to spare. Thinner, browner, hairier, but also just a little wiser. The transformation of Ben Fogle had reached another stage and I was ready for a new challenge.

I was living a Jekyll and Hyde existence, moving between different worlds. I would be in a Papua New Guinean tree house one day and handing out a BAFTA in black tie on another. Although I have always enjoyed this dichotomy, I think it confuses some people. I used to struggle with the rapid change of lifestyle from week to week, but I have learned to love it. In many ways it has made me the person that I am. The only time it affects me is when there is a rapid, blatant, unfair inequality in wealth.

I remember asking my father once why he gave up travelling to developing countries and his answer surprised me: 'It was when I realized I couldn't make a difference.'

As an optimistic nineteen-year-old, I couldn't understand his sentiments. Surely if we all felt like that then of course we wouldn't make a difference?

As a teenager I wanted to save the world and end poverty. I'm often asked who I respect most in the world and arguably it would have to be Bill and Melinda Gates. They want to make a difference, and they *will* make a difference through their crusade to rid the world of malaria. I always wanted to have the ability to make such a profound change and I still hope I can. I don't know how, or when or where, but it is my lasting wish to do something.

Part Four

14

The Face of Poverty

In many ways I would describe myself as a 'Live Aid child'. Of course, Bob Geldof had no idea of the long-lasting effect he was going to have on the world and Generation X. Like many, those images of starving children scarred me for ever. Geldof empowered a generation to believe that we could all make a difference.

I can still remember Michael Buerk's desperate reports from the Ethiopian famine and I was there at the old Wembley Stadium for the marathon concert in 1985 with my parents and my aunt, Alex, who was working for Elton John at the time. Even then we knew we were part of something special.

When I bumped into Bob Geldof recently at a party, I told him how much he had helped shape my life. 'I didn't do it for you,' he replied in his familiar Irish twang. He had a point.

The worldwide reaction to the famine was unprecedented. For Ethiopia, however, it created a long-term image disaster and even today the African country is synonymous with hunger and drought. Ask someone on the street what Ethiopia means to them and I bet you they'll say 'Famine.' The country's government has tried to shake off the manacles of Live Aid ever since, but while the awful famine may be in the past, the legacy of hunger and malnutrition lives on in the guise of a hideous disease called noma.

I first heard of noma when I ran the Marathon des Sables. We were all given a leaflet about the flesh-eating disease, which affects children across the world with an extreme facial disfiguration. I had been appalled at some of the photographs and had been happy that a percentage of money raised by the MDS had gone to a small charity called Facing Africa based in Wiltshire.

A few years later I was reminded of the disease by a doctor treating me for leishmaniasis. Noma is a bacteria produced by the body and triggered by malnutrition. It was first recorded during the Second World War in fascist concentration camps across Europe, where scientists used prisoners as human guinea pigs. The prisoners were starved and contracted noma, which the scientists then studied. Since then it has been recognized across the world, from India to Latin America. The young Peruvian boy whose story was told by Desmond Wilcox, Esther Rantzen's late husband, in the memorable 1983 documentary *The Boy David*, was suffering from the disease.

Most scientists and doctors agree that in the twenty-first century this disease should be consigned to the history books. Alas, it still affects children across the world, but for some reason it is particularly common in Sub-Saharan Africa.

It was noma that would bring me to Ethiopia, as I followed the work of Facing Africa and a team of surgeons from Great Ormond Street hospital. The BBC had been approached by a production company who wanted to make a film about the charity's work in Ethiopia and my name came up. It was a match made in heaven.

Ethiopia is a surprisingly green country. I probably say that because I was half-expecting to find the land of those childhood memories; however, the reality couldn't have been more different as we flew over the lush green countryside.

Addis Ababa, the capital, is a vibrant, bustling city, with arguably the best coffee in the world. I love coffee. It is my one luxury in life. I can honestly say that I can't live without it. It is my fuel and my drug. Even the most remote Ethiopian homes can brew a macchiato to make Italians weep. Ethiopia was the birth-place of coffee and when Starbucks tried to bring its franchise here, it was on the condition that the US coffee chain used Ethiopian arabica beans. When Starbucks refused, Ethiopia's own chain of coffee shops was opened, called Kaldi's, a direct rip-off of Starbucks right down to the familiar green emblem, font and the dodgy cakes. In fact, the only difference is that Kaldi's tastes infinitely better.

Although I had found a small amount of literature about noma, I had been shocked by how little I could learn on the internet about the disease; in fact, type 'noma' and you'll get hundreds of reviews about the Michelin-starred restaurant in Denmark. The two nomas couldn't be more different – one of them about the finest food in the world, the second brought about by starvation and malnutrition. Excess versus scarcity.

In Addis I met up with Dawit, who was to be my guide and translator. With his shaven head and stylish dress sense, he was the coolest Ethiopian I had ever met. He wouldn't have looked out of place in London. He had a good sense of humour and an easy manner. Highly intelligent, he had found work as a fixer for TV and film crews working in Ethiopia. His last job had been with Damon Albarn on one of his Gorillaz videos. For a man who had never been to England, he was pretty anglicized.

It was while working as a fixer that he had come across Facing Africa and their work with noma victims. What began as a job working with a film crew making a news story about the disease had ended as a job working for the charity.

Dawit's role was to find the patients. You might have thought this would be simple, but in a country where the victims are at best kept hidden in the shadows – they are often described as 'Children of the Shadows' – and, worse, are sometimes abandoned, finding the young victims is far from easy. Often whole villages will deny any knowledge for fear of attracting bad luck.

So several times a year Dawit would set out in his vehicle on mini-expeditions to find patients. Sometimes other NGOs like Médecins Sans Frontières, Save the Children or the UNHCR would come across young victims in refugee camps or in orphanages and hand them over to Dawit, but more often than not he had to become a detective, asking around and simply following his nose.

The first patient we were off to visit was an eleven-year-old girl called Mestikima, who had contracted the disease as a baby. Her family had been embarrassed by her disfigurement and, like so many, had at first hidden her from view to cover their shame. Later, regarded as a bad omen by her family, she was given away. Just like that. How could someone do that to their child, their own flesh and blood?

Becoming a father has changed my whole attitude to children. I always felt a compassion for vulnerable kids, but becoming a father produces a hormone that makes you want to protect them. It isn't until you hold your first child in your arms that you fully appreciate the beauty and fragility of life. That little child trusts you implicitly, and your animal instinct is to protect your own. The day that Ludo came into my life was the day I started living for somebody else. I would give my life for my children; it is part of the deal of becoming a father, a parent.

If Mestikima's family had looked for someone to take care of her because they couldn't afford to feed her, then that is one thing, but to abandon a child because of her appearance is another. I hadn't yet met Mestikima, but, a little like Sarah in Papua New Guinea, my emotions had already become entangled with her.

An Addis family had offered to foster her, so we drove to a neighbourhood on the edge of town, where she now lived. A couple of stray dogs scavenged on the dusty street, where a young boy herded a little flock of goats. As I knocked on the large metal door, I heard the rush of small feet and the door creaked open. A face appeared in the gap.

'Hello,' said a young boy in English. 'Come in.' He had an enormous smile on his face and as soon as we had come through the gate he went tearing off into the house, shouting 'Mestikima, Mestikima!'

A woman with a friendly, warm face appeared from the house, wiping her hands on her apron. She ushered us inside and offered us fresh coffee. We sat in silence next to a net-curtained window that cast a gentle white glow across the room. I could hear chickens and a cockerel in the yard.

'Mestikima!' called the woman as we sat there awkwardly.

There was a pause, then the soft patter of sandals on the hard floor. A young girl wearing jeans and a T-shirt peered round the corner. She wore a scarf over her face.

'Come,' urged her foster-mother in Amharic.

She came into the room and sat next to the woman, her feet dangling from the edge of the sofa. I could tell her head was bowed.

'Mestikima,' said the woman.

The girl looked up and pulled the shawl to one side of her face. She had a beautiful complexion and delicate features. From what I could see, she had a pretty little face, but her eyes, or the eye that I could see, looked sad. That eye told of the burden and sorrow that had plagued her life. She clenched the bottom of the scarf in her teeth, ensuring it was kept close to her face, constantly adjusting it so that it cut her face in two. Her right side was hidden beneath the colourful swirls of fabric.

I asked Dawit to translate and went to sit next to Mestikima. She looked so vulnerable sitting there. I wanted to scoop her up and embrace her. I fished my camera out of my bag and started scrolling through photographs of Marina and Ludo.

'She is very pretty,' she said looking at a picture of Marina. Her words were slightly muffled by the scarf.

I showed her pictures of the ocean and of double-decker buses. I found a small map and showed her how far I had travelled. I hate talking through interpreters. You lose the spontaneity and also half the meaning. You also lose the minutiae of intonation. It is difficult to express sensitivity and emotion, which are usually gobbled up in the pause between question and translation. Dawit was doing a good job, but I couldn't help but think his translated questions sounded gruffer than mine. The poor girl looked terrified.

'Can you say to her that I have never seen noma?' I asked Dawit. 'I completely understand if she doesn't want to, but would she let me see?' I felt I sounded mawkish and voyeuristic, but, I reasoned, if I was going to understand the disease and its effects, I had to know what it looked like.

Dawit translated and I saw Mestikima nod gently. Dawit gestured for her to remove her headscarf.

Slowly, she drew the scarf to one side to reveal the reality of noma. The right-hand side of her face was missing. A large hole enveloped her cheek, her eye had dropped from its socket, and half her nose, her lips and her cheekbone were missing. I could see her skeleton. There were two faces here: one angelic, young and innocent, the other hideous and ugly, monstrous even. I am sorry to sound so sensationalistic, but that is the reality of noma.

It truly is a terrible disease and I was shocked. I had seen photographs of children with the condition, but nothing had prepared me for its severity. Even Dawit was shocked. It is certainly an image I'll never forget.

I couldn't begin to fathom how anyone could treat her. Where would they begin? How do you build eye sockets and cheekbones? And what about the gaping hole with no skin? The revelation of the extent of her noma had merely created more questions for me than it had answered. Mestikima was relying on the team of plastic surgeons who were flying out from London on a mercy mission. Her future was in their hands, but were her injuries simply too substantial? She would have to wait to find out.

Dawit invited me to join him on one of his searches for noma victims, and we set off for a week of looking in a region where he had been told there may be some sufferers.

Our first stop was Jimma, a market town surrounded by agricultural land, where noma is rife. We pulled up at the market and I followed Dawit, who was wearing a white T-shirt printed with a large photograph of a young girl with noma. It was a pretty shocking photograph, but that was the point. People stopped and stared open-mouthed as we walked around the busy market, and a huge crowd gathered as we handed out brochures with more photographs and information about the work of Facing Africa.

There was what sounded like a heated exchange of words before Dawit turned to me and said, 'They say there is a man, a market trader, who looks like this.'

A woman had agreed to lead us to where he worked. By now there was a significant crowd behind us.

Dawit spotted someone wearing a grubby surgical mask and we followed him into his home. Away from the crowd, he removed his mask to reveal a face ravaged by noma. It is rare to find adults with the disease, because most victims die before they reach adulthood. The man explained to us that he had suffered from it all his life. Without lips, he slurred his words and used a handkerchief to blot the dribble that ran from his mouth.

'I am just a simple market trader,' he said as Dawit translated, 'but who wants to buy from someone with a face like this? I am a human being like you. What have I done to deserve this?' He had questions that we could never answer.

'I just want to be normal,' he said.

I was moved by our encounter. He told us how children taunted him and customers often bypassed him for fear of catching the disease from his wares. It was a wretched situation.

Next we headed a couple of hours south of Jimma and into the hills. We abandoned the car and trekked to a small rural village where Dawit had been told we would find a young man with noma. Under the baking African sun we passed fields being ploughed at impossibly steep angles by oxen. In Ethiopia, much of the most fertile, flat land is used for export coffee, leaving the vertiginous slopes and hillsides for small-scale subsistence farming.

In each village we passed through we showed photographs, provoking the same open-mouthed horror we'd experienced in the market. A few people said they had heard of a young man with no face in the village to which we were heading.

A couple of hours later we reached our goal. It was more a family settlement than a village. The large family welcomed us with excitement and soon a young man appeared with a grubby towel draped over his head.

'This is Rashid,' said Dawit.

I shook his hand, and as the towel dropped from his face I could see the by now familiar markings of noma. I listened as Dawit chatted with his family. Rashid's noma had left him with no jaw or gums and talking was almost impossible. I struggled to hear him as he nodded or shook his head to Dawit's questions. It seemed that only an uncle could understand his speech impediment.

Dawit took some photographs, but once again it would be up to the surgeons to decide whether he could be operated on or not. These plastic surgeons were becoming gods.

In the UK, plastic surgery has become synonymous with aesthetics rather than need. Where twenty years ago it was something to be carried out in privacy, it is now common to read about and even see photographs of celebrities undergoing it and, worryingly, it has become the aspiration of a terrifyingly high percentage of young girls to have breast-enhancement procedures, or 'boob jobs' as we know them. What we forget is that the value of 'cosmetic' surgery depends on circumstances. A woman who has lost a breast to cancer arguably has a different need from a woman who simply wants bigger breasts. Plastic surgery isn't all noses, bums and tits, and in the case of those young Ethiopians, it was the key to a new life.

Before my trip to Ethiopia I had visited a charity called Changing Faces, based off the Euston Road, near University College Hospital where I received my treatment for leishmaniasis. I walked past their offices each day and hoped that some time I would have an excuse to go in.

James Partridge, the executive director, founded the charity after rolling his Land Rover as a young lad. He received severe burns to his face which left him disfigured. He set up the charity as a way of improving his own confidence by changing people's attitudes to facial differences like his. Basically, he got fed up with people either staring at him or trying to avoid him.

James had taken part in a Channel 5 project several years ago which involved catapulting him into prime time as their news presenter for a week. It was the first time anyone with a facial disfigurement had appeared reading the news on national television. Ratings went up. End of story.

James is a charming man, eloquent, thoughtful and measured. I wanted to know what could be done to improve these young children's lives.

'It's about educating people,' he explained, 'about letting people know that appearance is only skin deep and that it's what's underneath that really counts. It's hard enough to get that message out here in the UK. In the developing world, which is bound in social and cultural mores that are hard to shake, it's even harder.'

I returned to Ethiopia a couple of weeks later. It felt good to be back. By now, Dawit had become a familiar friend. He drove me to the Cheshire Home in Addis Ababa, where all the prospective patients had spent the past fortnight waiting for the surgeons to arrive. Part-funded by Facing Africa, the home was used to give the patients time to get ready. They were treated for fleas, given courses of antibiotics to clear infections and bacteria, and fed calorie-rich food to build them up. I joined in games of football and volleyball and helped hand out bananas and peanut-butter crackers to the kids, before overseeing a group teeth-brushing and mouth-washing. It was a funny sight.

The number of patients had increased since my last visit, and now more than a hundred were waiting eagerly. Mestikima rushed up in her familiar scarf and hugged my leg.

Four surgeons had volunteered on this mission: Larry Fourie, a private plastic surgeon from Liverpool; David Dunaway, a craniofacial surgeon; Tim Lloyd, a maxillofacial surgeon; and Neil Bulstrode, another plastic surgeon. When they arrived, the clock started ticking. They had a huge amount to do before the operations could even begin, and their first task was selecting the patients.

It was one of the most saddening sights to see those people lined up along the veranda of the home. Even more patients had arrived in the last few days, many having walked for days in the hope of treatment. Patients weren't just suffering from noma, but all sorts of facially disfiguring ailments. There were women with engorged tumours and growths, and children with birth defects. One little girl, who couldn't have been more than three years old, had a lip the size of my fist.

The most common afflictions were burns. Given that most Ethiopians have fires with cauldrons of boiling water in the middle of their dark adobe homes, there is a high incidence of children and adults tripping into the flames or, worse, into the boiling water. Left untreated, the burn scars begin to tighten, pulling fingers into claws and heads into necks. I was shocked by the strength of burn scar tissue. In many cases it simply needed to be cut to relieve the pressure.

I was equally horrified to see the number of victims of hyena bites. Having worked with hyena over the years on various wildlife shows, I knew that they were feared for their ferocious instinct to render their prey defenceless by attacking the face, before leaving them to die slowly, but here was my first real evidence of this – and in humans.

I saw a number of people with teeth marks across their faces, and one young woman had had her nose bitten off. I've never been particularly fond of hyena, and seeing what they were capable of only cemented that feeling. We may know them as laughing hyenas, but there is nothing funny about a hyena bite to the face.

It was heartbreaking looking up and down that wretched line. Each face was strained with hope and desperation. For many, this was their last chance.

I stood in the corner as each patient entered the room for their check. It must have been daunting for them as they were examined, prodded, poked and questioned by what looked like an army of white doctors. The anaesthetists had to be sure that the children could cope with the long hours under general anaesthetic, and the maxillofacial surgeon needed to check how much bone and skin could be salvaged from other parts of the body. On top of all of this, the doctors had to work out how to juggle the operations. There were only four surgeons and two operating theatres; what's more, they would have only a week to complete the surgery. Some of the larger procedures could take two surgeons up to ten hours, while some of the smaller ops might take an hour or two. Was one big procedure worth five smaller ones? These were the impossible questions they had to answer. They had to plan how they would operate on each case before working out a framework in which they could get through as many patients as they could, as effectively as possible. There was no point beginning an operation that they might not have time to complete.

For the first time in my life I was forced to confront the kind of questions we simply never have to address in Western society. Do we give priority to young or old? Men or women? And what about those who had had treatment before? There was one girl with noma who had already been operated on by an Ethiopian team. They had replaced her nose with a huge skin graft, leaving her with what could only be described as a trunk, or proboscis, as the doctors called it.

At last the decisions were made, and it was a huge relief to hear that they had decided to operate on both Rashid and Mestikima.

I have never been good with blood, so the idea of watching a ten-hour operation was a pretty daunting prospect. When I was a child I used to come home from school and sit in on my dad while he operated on dogs and cats. I found it fascinating and at that age had no phobia of blood, but as I grew up I became more and more squeamish. When I was eighteen I fainted while having my travel vaccinations and it has worsened ever since. I even close my eyes when television gets too gory.

The doctors were based at the Korean Hospital in the centre of Addis, where they had the use of two operating theatres for a week. They had brought a huge amount of equipment with them from England. Dressed in my scrubs, I walked into the hospital theatre, where Ciara, the surgeons' Irish assistant, was busy laying out all the sterilized instruments. The last time I had dressed in surgical scrubs had been for the birth of my son, Ludo. The doctors had taken a last-minute decision to operate and before I knew it Marina was in theatre, with me in my blue scrubs at her side. It was a pretty scary experience, only made bearable by the little pot of screaming gold at the end.

Rashid was wheeled into the room. He looked terrified. Noma's ravaging effect on the mouth and jaw makes anaesthetizing incredibly dangerous. Most patients can be put under general anaesthetic and then have a pipe inserted down their throat so that their breathing can be controlled by a machine, but Rashid's mouth was so disfigured that the anaesthetist had to ensure the pipe was in before the anaesthetic was administered.

Soon Rashid was under and the operation began. The surgeons worked around his mouth, removing rotten teeth and cutting away dead skin tissue and bone. He was unrecognizable. Noma causes bones to fuse together in a process called ankylosis; it was the fusing of Rashid's jaw that made speech almost impossible for him. Using a series of tools that could have come from my home DIY kit, the doctors wrenched and sawed to divide the bones. It was a deeply unpleasant process to watch, but this was only the beginning.

Once the jaw had been released, they had to go about creating a new jawbone. Another surgeon, David, entered the room and inspected Rashid's now shaven head, before cutting in with his scalpel. Then, using a small machine, he began sawing into his skull. He cut a large circle and removed half the skull, leaving the brain exposed. Are you feeling sick yet? Because, rather in-explicably, I wasn't. I was completely engrossed and captivated by what was happening. I was hooked.

The surgeon placed the piece of skull on a small table and proceeded to work at it with a hammer and chisel. Using a pair of magnifiers strapped to his face mask, he tapped away at the side of the bone in an attempt to splice it down the middle. Once that was done, he held one layer to Rashid's unrecognizable face and began to draw on it with what looked like a sharpie. He was marking out the cheekbone. Then, using a tiny knife, he began to cut the bone to size. He whittled away rather like a woodworker on a stick.

When he had finished, he reached for what looked like a tiny Meccano set of screws and metal plates, some just a millimetre across. Small holes were drilled into the new cheekbone and soon it had been screwed into place. The remaining skull was placed back on to Rashid's head to protect his brain and the skin was sewn back together.

Cheekbone complete, another surgeon began to work on Rashid's arm, using a scalpel to cut what can only be described as a 'steak' of skin from under the forearm. It was so thick I could see all the muscles, veins and bone. Carefully they separated one of the two main arteries from the arm, then tied both ends off. They then proceeded to remove the whole section of arm, complete with artery. It was an incredibly complex task: if they damaged the blood supply, the skin would be useless.

The hours ticked by. Before I knew it, I had been standing in the theatre for over six hours, and I was still transfixed. Everything seemed to be going well – and then we were plunged into darkness. There had been a power cut.

There was mild consternation as the doctors and surgeons struggled to find an alternative source of power. The anaesthetist was forced to breathe manually for Rashid, using a hand pump, while the surgeons strapped torches to their heads and to the magnifying glass above Rashid's head.

I raced around the hospital trying to find an alternative source. Eventually I discovered that the fridge in the staff kitchen still had power. It was at the other end of the hospital, so I rushed about collecting extension cables, stringing them together like a giant necklace along the corridors and up the stairs. I linked ten of them in order to bring a small trickle of power into the theatre, but it was enough to run the surgeons' light and Rashid's breathing. It was a pretty terrifying experience, but the doctors had remained cool as cucumbers.

The power cut was a reminder that this was first-world surgery in a developing country. Suddenly I began to notice the broken tiles, the large cracks in the walls and the bucket full of water in the corner catching drips from the ceiling.

The skin was removed and the doctors now set about working on Rashid's neck, where they found his carotid artery, which they pulled from his body and tied off. They then proceeded to 'plumb' the arm skin to his face. The two ends of the artery were reconnected into his neck and face.

'Watch this,' said David proudly. The new skin looked wrinkled and pale – to be honest it looked dead, which technically it was, as it was without a blood supply. David worked away with his tiny instruments.

'It should take a couple of seconds,' he whispered. And I watched as the blood surged through the skin, pulling it taught across Rashid's cheek and filling it with colour. A small amount of blood appeared around the corners of the skin. 'Lovely,' said David.

It was like watching a magician at work.

Now they began to work on his leg. His leg? What on earth did his leg have to do with it? I was genuinely perplexed. Was there no part of his body that would be left untouched?

'We're harvesting skin,' explained Tim. They used what looked like a cheese-grater to slice off a thin piece of skin from his thigh, which they then placed over the exposed bone on his arm. It was like reassembling a Mr Potato Head.

At last, ten long hours later, Rashid was wheeled from the theatre. It was nearly midnight and the doctors had worked without stopping. What I had witnessed was a miracle.

Over the next couple of days they proceeded to work through dozens of patients, including Mestikima. She was like a delicate flower walking into that theatre. My heart ached for this vulnerable child. I can't begin to imagine how terrifying that place must have looked to her. If there was ever a time when a daughter needed a mother and father, it was now. I held her hand and led her into the operating theatre where the transformation of her face and her life would begin.

It takes a long time to recover from such dramatic, intense and invasive surgery, and most of the patients spent the next week recuperating in the hospital ward. Mestikima was still heavily sedated, but before I returned to the UK I went to see Rashid, who was already sitting up in bed.

'Rashid!' I called as I walked through the ward. He was wearing a pair of pyjamas, playing with a jigsaw.

He looked up at me with his new face. It was still swollen and discoloured, but it was amazing. The skin across his cheek stretched neatly to his nose and down to his mouth, where he had a new pair of lips. His eyeball – the sight in which, sadly, could not be saved – had been elevated back into its socket by his new cheekbone. It wasn't a perfect face, but then again, what is?

'You have to remember what we started with,' explained David. 'We didn't begin with a blank canvas.' I didn't need reminding; the transformation was astonishing. To many his new face would still be an ugly tangle of skin and bone, but to Rashid and all of us it was beautiful.

Rashid still hadn't seen the transformation and the doctors had agreed to let me bring him a mirror so that he could see for himself. Dawit had spent a great deal of time explaining the reality of the surgery to the patients to ensure that their expectations were realistic.

I handed the mirror to Rashid. Slowly he lifted it to his face and stared into it. He moved his hand to his face and gently caressed his new cheek and his lips. He turned his face from side to side, up and down, then stared long and hard. What was he thinking? Was he disappointed? Shocked, maybe? Dawit had told me that many noma victims have never looked at themselves in a mirror. Perhaps this was the first time he had ever seen himself?

He glanced up at us briefly, then returned to staring at his face. He was transfixed. He ran his forefinger down his face and then along his arm. I wondered whether he was trying to work out why he had bandages on his arm and leg. He stared and stared, and then he turned to us and smiled.

I heard a stifled sob from David the cameraman. It was a tiny smile, restricted by his mouth movement and the stitches on his face, but it was a smile that spoke a thousand words. Rashid didn't need to say anything. He held the mirror to his face again and resumed his stare. It was one of the most special things I have ever seen. As the camera stopped rolling, David ran from the room. The moment had been too much for him. I too was struggling to hold back my tears, but it was too much. This single tender moment had affected me more than anything before. This was my adult Live Aid moment. It had put my whole life into perspective. Rashid had put a mirror to our society and our unhealthy obsession with looks and appearance.

A couple of weeks later I heard news that Mestikima had been having complications and I returned to Addis. She was still in hospital because her skin had become infected.

I felt terrible knowing she had been stuck in that place ever since her operation, but the doctors were hopeful that they had corrected the problem. I held her hand as they removed the bandages from her face.

It was like looking at a different person. The forearm skin fitted neatly across her face and, although it was still slightly discoloured, there was none of the swelling I had seen on Rashid's face. 'Remember the template,' I recalled David telling me. She looked beautiful, and despite the long time in hospital, there was a spark in her eyes. Like Rashid, she had been given back her life.

Before I left Ethiopia, I headed into the countryside again to see Rashid and another young patient called Asnake back in their villages. I wanted to know how they had reintegrated into society. Were they still deemed unlucky? Were they still seen as social pariahs?

Dawit and I walked across the hot countryside towards Rashid's village. As we turned a corner in the trail, a young lad strode towards us.

'Morning,' I nodded breathlessly. Then I noticed a broad smile across his face.

'Rashid? Is that you?'

He enveloped me in a huge hug. I could hardly recognize him. The skin had begun to heal over and he looked a different man. He looked younger, fitter and happier. He walked with a spring in his step.

He marched ahead of us, leading us back to his family. There were cheers as we walked into the village. Dawit beamed with pride.

Rashid's family invited us to join them for lunch. I sat cross-legged on the floor of their dark, smoky home while they prepared *injera*, the ubiquitous Ethiopian dish of flatbread. After lunch Rashid invited me to join him in the fields.

He rigged the oxen to the handmade wooden plough and we walked the field together, marching up and down the furrows as he drove the plough deep into the soil, turning it over in great waves. He gestured for me to take over and handed me the long whip. I held tightly as the two powerful beasts plodded forward, Rashid walking several steps behind, nodding his approval and smiling under the midday sun.

'I have a life,' he had said to Dawit.

As I reached the end of the field, I tried to pull the plough around on itself, but managed to spook the oxen, who took off into the neighbouring field, dragging me behind them.

'Rashid!' I hollered as I disappeared down the hill with the runaway plough. I could see him on the hill, bent double with laughter.

The surgery had changed these young lives for ever. When the film *Make Me a New Face* went out in spring 2010 there was an unprecedented reaction and the small charity Facing Africa was inundated with unsolicited donations and offers of help. It was the first time I fully realized the power of television to change lives.

15

Middle Earth

'How would you like to be Chief Scout?' asked Ffion Hague.

I didn't know what to say. The politician's wife was offering me the dream role, something I had been unconsciously building towards all my life.

Through all my adventures and travels there had been the underlying challenge of trying to overcome my early childhood shortcomings. I had battled my way across oceans and led teams through some of the most inhospitable terrain on earth, and now it seemed I was finally being rewarded for my efforts. I had never planned it, but suddenly I was being offered the role of a lifetime.

I was stunned, but also deeply humbled. Becoming Chief Scout would finally give me the chance to share everything I'd learned. I would be able to enthuse and encourage.

Public life should have prepared me for disappointment and rejection, but I will admit that I was gutted when, a few months later, in May 2009, the role was eventually awarded to Bear Grylls.

Coping with rejection is an important lesson in life. For a brief period when I was young I flirted with the idea of becoming an actor. I had been involved in drama at school and had even performed at the Fringe at the Edinburgh Festival. My mother had been an incredibly successful actress back in the 1970s and 1980s, so it was only natural that I too would entertain the idea.

I applied to every drama school and got rejected by the lot, all twelve of them. I can still remember my utter misery when I was turned down by the final one. I lay on my bed in floods of tears. My mother came into my room and sat on the corner of the bed.

'My darling boy,' she said, stroking my tear-stained hair, 'if you become an actor, you'll have to learn to face rejection like this every day of your life.'

They were poignant words. I still find it tough to cope with rejection. I still can't control my emotions. Also, I find that my imagination runs away with me before I have time to be realistic. In the case of the Scouts, I had already pictured myself in woggle and scarf and practised the 'Dib dib dib' in the mirror. It was an important lesson, though. Some things are worth waiting for in life, and what goes around comes around.

I consoled myself by heading off for a two-week work trip to New Zealand, one of my favourite places.

'Wooooo-haa!' I hollered as the aircraft swooped over the saddle of the mountain. The world dropped away, and the bleak rock and ice of the valleys was replaced by a panorama of snow-capped peaks, gleaming lakes, lush forests and cascading waterfalls, all illuminated by the late-summer sunshine. I'm sure angels sang. I am rarely lost for words, but the majesty and scale rendered me speechless. I wanted to swear and cry at the same time. I had never seen anywhere so beautiful.

I was in a helicopter, speeding at 150 m.p.h. down Milford Sound, a fjord in the south-west of South Island, New Zealand,

and I had just entered *Lord of the Rings* country. It may well be Frodo's Middle Earth to cinema audiences, but it is also the late Sir Edmund Hillary's upper earth, steeped in adventure and derring-do – just as he was.

Sir Edmund, who died in January 2008 at the age of eighty-eight, was arguably the greatest ever New Zealander. His ascent of Everest with Tenzing Norgay in 1953 was the twentieth century's defining moment in adventure. Not content with the world's highest mountain, he led the first overland trek to the South Pole since Amundsen's in 1911. He also walked to the North Pole and led a jet-boat expedition from the mouth of the Ganges to its source.

Sir Edmund used this diverse landscape, from Mount Cook to the Franz Josef Glacier, as a training ground for his great adventures. It is difficult to know whether he typified a nation, or whether the nation has taken its character from him. Whatever the answer, the hero has been embraced by his countrymen and women, and New Zealand has become a one-stop shop for adventurers, attracting adrenalin junkies and extreme sports-people from all over the world.

I sped over Middle Earth as miles of deserted magnificence slipped past, before we settled on a beach strewn with jade. A quick paddle and we were airborne again, swooping over forest and river, heading for the ice. Again our pilot took us down, this time on to the surface of a glacier. Otherworldly doesn't begin to describe it.

Queenstown is indisputably New Zealand's adventure capital. It was here that A. J. Hackett launched that first commercial bungee jump twenty years ago. In winter, people from throughout Australasia come here to ski and snowboard; in summer, there is no end of wackier options.

Next to Lake Wakatipu and dwarfed by mountains, Queenstown has a European flavour, with its boutique shops and coffee houses. (The 'flat white' coffee on offer throughout the country was better than anything I have tasted in London or New York.) The town's laid-back atmosphere belies its adrenalin-fuelled heart. It wasn't long before I found myself hurtling down the Shotover River at 70 m.p.h. in just a few inches of water on a jet boat, another Kiwi invention. Deft control and two turbo-engines make short work of shallow and white water, enabling 360-degree spins and lots of fun. A spot of rafting, some of New Zealand's excellent Sauvignon blanc and the sweetest crayfish I have ever eaten, and I was off once more.

From Queenstown I headed north to Kaiteriteri, the gateway to the Abel Tasman National Park, one of fourteen across the country. The park is at the northern end of a range of marble and limestone hills, and the area is honeycombed with caves and potholes.

Various tracks run through the park, of which the thirty-mile coastal trail is by far the most popular. It has some of the most scenic beaches, coves and bays in the country. The trail, which runs through the forest and along the many sandy beaches, takes most trampers (as hikers are called) between three and five days of walking and kayaking. I set off in my canary-yellow kayak along the calm turquoise waters of the Tasman Sea. At some points the water was so clear and the sand so white that I felt as though I was floating on air.

Between Bark Bay and Awaroa Head is the Tonga Island Marine Reserve, in which fish, dolphins and a seal colony have taken advantage of the fishing ban. A fleet of water taxis enables trampers to switch between paddling and walking, delivering kayaks to rendezvous points along the route. The area was teeming with life, and it was wonderful to paddle next to seals that have a habit of jumping on to passing kayaks.

I then headed south-east, along the coastal highway to Kaikoura, a pretty little town backed by the steeply rising foothills of the Seaward Kaikouras. What used to be a whaling town has now become a whale-watching town, attracting thousands to see the local 'big five': the sperm whale, the common Hector's dolphin, the dusky dolphin, the New Zealand fur seal and the killer whale.

I headed out on a whale-watching boat into the choppy waters in search of one of the majestic sperm whales that live in the area year-round. To help our search, the captain used a hydrophone to listen for whale song. Sperm whales have been recorded 'singing' at an ear-popping 163 decibels. For an hour we followed the song, until eventually the whale, an adult male, surfaced.

Whales are powerful symbols for the Maori; legend has it that a Maori elder, Paikea, travelled on a humpback (as told in the book and film *Whale Rider*). I watched mesmerized as the whale frolicked next to our boat, so close that I could smell the fishy spray from its blow-hole. For ten minutes I stood transfixed, until it took one final bow and, with a flick of its tail, disappeared back into the depths of the South Pacific.

For my final experience here I planned to ascend one of New Zealand's many peaks.

It was on Australasia's highest mountain, the 3,754-metre (12,316-foot) Mount Cook, that Hillary practised for his Everest assault. Mount Cook is one of the world's most dangerous peaks, having claimed more than two hundred lives. During my visit it was closed after the latest accident, so with some relief I returned to Queenstown to take on a slightly more accessible mountain, the 2,340-metre (7,677-foot) Double Cone of the Remarkables.

The Remarkables are an impressive range overlooking Queenstown, and they become a popular ski area in winter. In summer, Double Cone offers a semi-technical climb for which you need ropes and harnesses on the latter part of the ascent, and which takes the best part of a day. I teamed up with Independent Mountain Guides, a favourite company of the local film industry for its expertise and charm. Hugh Barnard, my guide, and I began our trek at 1,524 metres (5,280 feet), just below the chilly waters of Lake Alta, at the bottom of the three peaks of the Remarkables. The sun had long melted the snow and ice that entomb this area in winter, and the walking was reasonably easy.

Soon, though, the terrain steepened, with outcrops and tussocks hidden among the scree. There was no trail, but the occasional cairn led us to the South Wye Saddle, where we roped and harnessed up. Hugh gave me a quick lesson in how to set a fixed anchor point. Soon we were clambering our way up a sort of chimney on to the ridge of the mountain. Until now, my sights had been firmly set on hand- and footholds, testing the rock for stability before each step. As I clambered on to the saddle of the mountain, I looked up, and there before me the land opened out like a canvas. Was this, I wondered, how the Remarkables got their name?

A short break, then we carried on up the more technical part of the ascent. Hugh would climb while I waited below with his fixed anchor point to stop him tumbling from the mountain into the abyss; then he would anchor himself and I would clamber up to him. So in this way, stage by stage, we rose towards the summit. The vertical drop on either side gave me momentary vertigo, but up, up, we climbed. Cloud scudded past below, occasionally shrouding us in a chilly blanket of mist.

As we scrambled up the final sheer pinnacle, the cloud lifted and New Zealand revealed itself once again. Our peak was no Everest, but I felt exhilarated as I surveyed the view stretching before me. In the words of Edmund Hillary, I had 'knocked the bastard off'.

New Zealand may be an adventurist's playground, but it is also the stepping stone to one of the most unique environments on earth – Antarctica.

16

Great Scott

Beneath a smouldering volcano, next to a frozen ocean strewn with icebergs and penguins, is a small wooden hut often described as one of the most important buildings in the world. The simple structure embodies both the best of humanity and the heroic era of adventure and discovery, and I am one of the privileged few to have made the long pilgrimage to this remote place – Captain Scott's expedition hut in Antarctica.

I first visited Antarctica in 2009 when I took part in the footrace to the South Pole with James Cracknell and Ed Coats, but I have been fascinated by the great age of polar exploration since I was a child and first picked up a Ladybird book about Captain Scott. Like many boys, I was captivated by the heroic sacrifice of a man and his team willing to give their lives to science and discovery.

The story of Scott and his men has been a driving force in my life. It is a story once known by everyone, but now largely forgotten. To recap, on 17 January 1912 five men from the British

Antarctic Expedition commanded by Captain Robert Falcon Scott arrived at the spot they calculated to be the South Pole. To their dismay, they found not a continuation of the white expanse, but a tent flying the Norwegian flag. They had been beaten by the Norwegian expedition led by Roald Amundsen.

Scott wrote in his journal on arrival at the South Pole, 'Great God this is an awful place and terrible enough to have laboured to it without the reward of priority' – a sentiment with which I could wholeheartedly agree when James, Ed and I arrived to find we had also been beaten by the Norwegians we were racing; and we had it easy by comparison. We had to wait for seven days for a flight out, but a hundred years ago the five demoralized explorers faced an 850-mile return journey, hauling their sledges across the ice to their base camp at Cape Evans.

I am still haunted by the photograph of them at the South Pole. Their self-portrait should have been full of joy and happiness at reaching their goal, but instead their faces are filled with disappointment and humiliation. They look dejected and demoralized, weathered, worn and beaten.

Freezing temperatures and dwindling supplies sapped the team of energy and on 19 March 1912 the three surviving men pitched their tent with just 110 miles to go. They were just eleven miles from One Ton Camp, at which they would find food and fuel, but the weather turned in and sometime between 29 and 31 March they perished on the icy plains of the Ross ice shelf. Their bodies were found the following summer by a rescue party. Scott's journal was removed from his frozen body and their tent was buried beneath the snow.

The journal told their tale of misery and hardship. 'Had we lived,' wrote Scott, 'I should have had a tale to tell of the hardihood, endurance and courage of my companions which would have stirred the heart of every Englishman. These rough notes and our dead bodies must tell the tale.'

The story captured the imagination of a nation. When war engulfed Europe, Captain Scott's expedition was used by the Ministry of Information as a showcase of endurance and fortitude against all odds. His became the ultimate tale of heroism for a generation tired of war. His story gave some relief to those grieving; it gave meaning to sacrifice.

Captain Scott stood for heroism, endurance, spirit, endeavour, fortitude and stoicism. He personified the human spirit: a man and his team prepared to sacrifice their lives in the pursuit of exploration and discovery: 'To Strive. To Seek. To Find. And Not to Yield', as their memorial reads. Yield they did not. Almost a hundred years later and his story still has resonance.

What always surprised me most was the fact that Scott's death eclipsed Amundsen's success. News of the Antarctic disaster caused a sensation in Britain and newspaper circulation rocketed. Scott embodied the heroic fantasies of pre-war Britain.

It shouldn't be a surprise. We Brits have always loved a tale of heroic failure, a struggle against adversity, whether self-inflicted or not. You only have to look at the success of Danny Boyle's film *127 Hours*, the true story of Aron Ralston, who got trapped by a boulder and had to sever his own arm to save his life; or the popularity of Joe Simpson's *Touching the Void* or Jon Krakauer's *Into Thin Air*; or even *Into the Wild*, the tale of a young man who goes in search of the wilds of Alaska, only to succumb to a poisonous plant. All are tales of incompetence and disaster and tragedy. Heroic failures.

In some ways this is where I feel an affiliation with Scott. Not that I am a hero, but a failure who has a go. All my trips have been marked by failings. I've rarely won any of the challenges I've taken on, but it seems the public likes an underdog.

For me Scott's diaries are some of the greatest ever written, a testament to the power of words. I think it's safe to say that the discovery of his journal alongside his body, and the iconic photographs of Herbert Ponting and paintings by Edward Wilson, helped create the longevity of their story. Through the journal, Scott constructed his own hero. Now I was finally going to visit his hut and try to make sense of the complexities of the man and his mission.

The long journey to Scott's hut began in November 2010 in Christchurch, New Zealand. When I arrived the city was still recovering from the first in a series of major earthquakes. Whole blocks had been closed where buildings had collapsed or were deemed unfit for human habitation, but it had miraculously escaped this first earthquake with no casualties.

I was staying in the twenty-storey hotel next to the cathedral and, as I lay in bed in a deep sleep, I dreamt I was in an earthquake. I could feel the whole room shaking and vibrating, my bed jarring against the wall and a picture falling. My body hopped and skipped across the bed with the vibrations and I dreamt that it jolted me right from the bed and on to the floor. At which point I woke up.

Confused and disoriented, I clambered back into bed. It was still and silent. I could hear a couple of car alarms and dogs barking, but there were no sirens, so I went back to sleep assuming it had all been a dream.

It wasn't until breakfast the next morning that I realized I had just experienced my first proper earthquake. It had been 6 on the Richter scale – enough to send me tumbling from my bed. It was just another day in what New Zealanders have dubbed Quake City.

Christchurch is the international hub for Antarctica, with a number of nations, including the United States and Italy, all using it as their logistics base. My return to Antarctica was to follow the work of the Antarctic Heritage Trust for a BBC documentary celebrating Captain Scott's centenary at his small wooden hut.

I had heard stories about this famous 'hut' over the years, incredible tales of a place frozen in time, filled with more than ten thousand items of his original expedition gear. I had heard Lord Attenborough and Michael Palin both talk of this remote little building with such passion and excitement in their eyes that I vowed I would one day visit the most remote heritage site in the world, and now was my time.

Antarctica is a strange place, with even stranger politics. The continent has been split up and handed to a number of nations around the world: the UK, Norway, Japan, France, Italy, New Zealand and the USA all have a slice of the pie.

I can still remember my disappointment on reaching the South Pole after our long footrace and finding the American Amundsen–Scott South Pole Station. It wasn't just the size and clutter of the US base that disappointed me, but the fact that the American flag was the only one to fly from the Geographical South Pole. Why the American flag? Neither Scott nor Amundsen was American. Where were the Norwegian or British flags? I didn't understand it, and to be honest I still don't.

During our week-long incarceration at the South Pole awaiting rescue, we hatched a plan to 'borrow' the Stars and Stripes and replace it with the Union Jack. We never did, but for the sake of Scott I wish we had.

New Zealand Antarctica has its own training centre and kit store near Christchurch airport and here we were issued with our equipment for our three-week stay in the world's coldest and windiest place. Base socks, second-layer socks, snow socks, wool thermals, polyprop thermals, polyprop base trousers, polyprop base top, fleece jacket, windproof jacket, down jacket, salopettes, base gloves, second-layer gloves, mitts, goggles, balaclava, hat, buff, sunglasses, extreme-weather boots, Canadian boots; and then the extreme-weather gear (EWG) – extreme jacket, extreme boots, extreme gloves, extreme balaclava and extreme goggles.

Even for someone who had visited before, it was a daunting set of kit and equipment. Each piece had to be used correctly.

A huge American cargo plane flew us, and sixty international scientists, the eight hours from Christchurch to McMurdo, the US station on Ross Island. As we flew over the fearsome Southern Ocean I could make out white caps on the raging waves below. The rules of the flight stipulate that every passenger wears full extreme-weather kit, which is made for minus 50°C rather than the balmy 26°C of the plane, so I sat sweating in my seat and watched as enormous icebergs began to appear in the ocean below. Soon the rich blue was replaced by an endless horizon of white. We had reached Antarctica.

'Where's the runway?' I asked one of the researchers next to me.

'It's on the ocean.'

'What do you mean "on the ocean"?' I replied nervously.

'*On* the ocean. We land on the frozen sea,' he replied.

'And how thick is that?'

'About two metres.'

Two metres! We were going to land the biggest plane I have ever seen in my life on two metres of ice, above a deep ocean.

What was even more disconcerting was flying over the open ocean before touching down on the ice.

'Lucky,' smiled the researcher, uncrossing his fingers. 'They'll probably close this in a couple of days.' He went on to explain how the runway is moved each season and that the winter-operating runway, on which we had just landed, would soon be open water.

We boarded an enormous six-seater truck that rumbled across the ice.

'That's where the oil tankers come in,' said the driver, pointing to more ice.

'Planes?' I asked.

'No, ships. This is where they dock,' he explained. We had just landed on a harbour. 'The first ship's due in about ten days,' he added. 'You wouldn't want to land a plane here then.'

McMurdo is a strange place. This was where Werner Herzog based himself for his hit film *Encounters at the End of the World*. What I soon discovered is that reality here is even stranger than a Herzog film, and that's saying something.

This can only be described as a frontier town. It has a rough, transitory feel. It is practical rather than beautiful, with the feel of a mining town, full of workers on short-term contracts. Huge accommodation blocks tower above the frozen Ross Sea like student halls of residence. There is more than a whiff of former Soviet Union architecture. Tractors and caterpillar trucks rumble through the town, while scientists and researchers walk around in their red Canada Goose Antarctic-issue jackets.

McMurdo is black and grey, rather like an English city after a heavy snow has melted. Black slush and grime clings to the buildings. There are bars and bowling alleys and hairdressers and a supermarket that sells Oreos and Hershey's chocolate. There's even a dedicated police force to keep law and order in this remote outpost.

McMurdo's workers are ferried around by a bus known as 'Ivan the Terrible' – an American school bus with the biggest set of wheels I have ever seen; they must have been almost three metres high. My abiding memory is of the sound of reverse beeping. Given that most vehicles are tractors or trucks, they all beep in reverse, and there's a lot of reversing in McMurdo.

As we drove through the bleak streets and past a pretty little church, we passed a convoy of eight Massey Ferguson tractors. Once again they were oversized – probably four times bigger than a UK tractor – and they had huge wheels.

'For farming?' I asked, facetiously.

'No, they're driving to the South Pole,' said the driver.

That'll teach me.

Sir Edmund Hillary was the first to drive to the Pole – in a Massey Ferguson – and since then a number of vehicles have crossed the crevasse-riddled ice. Recently there has been much talk of creating a permanent road to the South Pole. Flying fuel and equipment to the Amundsen–Scott base on the bottom of the world is eye-wateringly expensive and a number of nations have been looking at the possibility of building an ice road across Antarctica.

McMurdo is not the kind of place you want to linger in, which was lucky for us, because we were staying at New Zealand's Scott Base, a short drive but a whole world away from McMurdo. Founded by Sir Edmund Hillary in the 1950s, there was a move to rename it after him, but he was always vehemently against it, arguing that Scott deserved the legacy more than he did. Since his death there has been another move to rename the base.

Scott Base was like an oasis by comparison with McMurdo. All the buildings had been painted an attractive green, giving it a warm, homely feel, and some were attached to each other by covered walkways. Everything was ordered and neat, the complete polar opposite of its US neighbour.

Our six-wheeled truck pulled up outside and was plugged into the electrics to prevent its engine freezing, while we were led inside to meet the base manager, a former British RAF officer.

We were each assigned a locker for our extreme-weather gear. One of the golden rules of the base was that no outdoor gear was to be worn indoors. As a result, people wander around in their thermal vests, essentially their underwear.

The walls of the main corridor were lined with photographs of the fabled 'over-winter' crews. Antarctica more or less shuts down for the long winter. As twenty-four-hour darkness and minus 55°C temperatures approach, there is a mass exodus. Just a skeleton staff stays to maintain the stations until summer returns, and these winter crews attain heroic status on the continent, lauded for their bravery. The photographs show a dozen heavily bearded faces, pasty white in various stages of evolutionary polar-jacket technology. The early photos from the 1950s show toughened men in sou'westers, clutching a couple of dogs. As the years go by the jackets become more sophisticated and the dogs disappear (they were banned from Antarctica in 1980), but, perhaps more tellingly, women replace the dogs, as they are finally integrated into the bases.

The base was a little like a land-ship; close your eyes and you could be at sea. Monitors around the base indicated the temperature, wind direction and speed outside. The sleeping accommodation included simple dorms and communal bathrooms.

There had been a great deal of anxiety at Scott Base several years ago when the Princess Royal arrived to reopen Discovery Hut, one of the historic huts on which the Antarctic Heritage Trust had been working. She had stayed at the New Zealand base, but there had been no facilities for her to have her own bathroom. Researchers at the base still marvel at what a good egg she was, even sharing her toothpaste.

We were shown the communal canteen, the library and the kit store, the mechanics workshop and the small post office. A little surprisingly, the biggest room in the base was used as a dressing-up room. It was filled with rails and rails of costumes. There were robot costumes, camel costumes and even a mermaid outfit. Dressing up, it seemed, is big in Antarctica. Even at McMurdo I had noticed a massive shipping container with the words 'Halloween Costumes' painted along the side.

One of the hidden dangers of Antarctica is static. Forget about frostbite or hypothermia – if you're living in one of the international stations (as we did for a few days), static is one of your biggest enemies.

Now we've all experienced static. I remember rubbing my shoes furiously on the carpet as a child in an attempt to give my sister a shock. Occasionally we all get a build-up that ends with an uncomfortable snap of static. But here in Antarctica it's different. This is static on steroids. This stuff could win wars, and it terrified us all.

'Just discharge yourself as often as you can on one of the metal plates,' explained the manager. 'Whatever you do, don't pick up a phone, computer, camera or anything electrical unless you've discharged yourself first.'

This was alarming, mainly because it was a totally new phenomenon. Dangerous static? How dangerous could this stuff really be? I would soon find out as we cleared the first corridor and entered the second. My hand brushed against Toby, the cameraman, and I thought I'd been Tasered. We both leapt into the air and screamed like girls.

If we weren't worried about static before, we were petrified now. I had never experienced a shock like it, and I had only gone for thirty seconds without discharging myself.

Now discharging is an ordeal in itself. The idea is to get rid of the static build-up before it gets too great, so in essence you still have to give yourself electric shocks. It's all about speed and haste. We soon discovered that if you whacked your hand as hard as possible against a metal item, you could avoid a shock – although I suspect you merely 'hid' it with the pain from the thwack. So for the following three days we walked around slapping and smacking every conceivable metal object. I forgot once for more than an hour . . . not something I would ever repeat.

'Check out the pressure ridges,' said Mike. 'They're putting on quite an ice show outside.' He pointed to the frozen sea beyond the base. I could make out a series of mounds and pinnacles jutting from the ice.

An ocean is a dynamic environment, constantly waxing and waning as the tide pulls and shifts the water beneath the crust of ice. This dynamism leads to vast 'pressure ridges', in which the ice has been forced upwards by the power of the tide, creating what can only be described as an icy wonderland.

It was like stepping into another world as we followed the marked trail through the yawing ice. You could hear it strain and sigh as we walked past towering stacks of ice with brilliant hues of blue. The ice had been forced into all sorts of weird and wonderful shapes. It was like walking through a frozen maze created by some surrealist sculptor.

Before we could head out to Scott's hut with the team of conservators, we all had to pass a field-training course, which would involve a couple of days' living out on the ice. We were taught to use the tents and stoves, how to escape from a sinking Haglund vehicle, how to build an emergency shelter, what would happen if one of us went missing in a blizzard, and how to avoid frostbite. It's amazing how quickly you forget basic skills. Despite my seven weeks here just a few years before, this was still an alien environment and I welcomed that retraining.

Soon we were ready to head out to Cape Evans and Scott's hut. The best way to travel around Antarctica is by Norwegian army Haglunds – tracked vehicles developed for use in the Arctic Circle. They look a little like Tonka toys, with their chunky doors and tracked wheels. Most importantly, they have an escape hatch on the roof in case they fall through the ice, which, according to our New Zealand hosts, 'only happens a couple of times a year'.

Our visit had already been soured by the news of a crashed French helicopter with the loss of all on board. The Scott Base has a memorial for the biggest aviation disaster in Antarctic history, when an Air New Zealand tourist flight crashed into Mount Elbrus on 28 November 1979, killing everyone on board. The disaster shocked New Zealand. In such a small country, everyone knew someone. This recent crash was a grim reminder.

We packed up the Haglund with two weeks' worth of provisions, tents and filming equipment, and began the long journey along the coastline to Cape Evans. It was uncanny to drive past the towering cliffs of icebergs trapped in the frozen ocean, and past islands that were no longer surrounded by water but by a thick crust of sea ice. The movement of the ocean had also created vast 'tide cracks' in the ice. The Haglunds were all equipped with portable army bridges that could be used to cross a crack up to two metres wide, but any wider than that and you'd be stuck. Every couple of hours we'd reach one of these gaping voids and the driver would get out with his ice screw to test the depth of the ice.

A few hours into our journey we came to a small Portakabin in the middle of the ice. As if this wasn't surreal enough, there was a frogman walking around outside in full scuba gear. He was diving where we were driving. Antarctica really is a world of the surreal.

We pulled up next to the Portakabin and asked if we could come in.

'Sure!' beamed a round American, snacking on a packet of Oreos.

Inside there was a small gas-burning stove in one corner and half a dozen diving bottles in the other. The middle, however, was occupied by a huge rectangular hole in the ice. It was like a window into another world. The bright midday sun penetrated the ice, creating a sort of blue grotto. It was without doubt one of the most beautiful things I have ever seen. The water was brimming with small crustaceans and a long line disappeared below. I could see the bottom.

'How deep is it here?' I asked.

'About three hundred feet,' he replied.

A series of bubbles appeared from the depths below and then

the distinct shape of another diver, Kathy, who surfaced into the Portakabin with a small bag in her hand.

'Looks like we've got visitors,' she said, removing her mask and clambering up the small swimming-pool ladder that had been set into the ice. She explained that they were marine biologists researching the sea life beneath the ice, and that she had collected some samples for measurements. She emptied her bag on to the ice to reveal some sea cucumbers.

'Cute, aren't they?' she cooed. I couldn't share her enthusiasm for their aesthetic beauty, but it was amazing that they could live in these conditions.

'Wanna see something neat?' she asked, as if watching a scuba diver emerge from a frozen ocean with a sea cucumber wasn't 'neat' enough.

'This is our ROV,' she explained, indicating the line that disappeared into the water, 'our Remote Operating Vehicle.' She explained that it was a remote submarine that had half a dozen cameras and claws, and could be used to collect deeper samples. If the hole in the ice were the window on to another world, this would be our eye.

The ROV was lowered into the water, while another researcher worked a small joystick linked to a little TV screen. The ROV began tracking beneath the ice and, just when we thought we'd seen it all, a huge black object appeared in front of the camera, blotting out the view.

The object soon appeared at the bottom of the hole and started to move towards the surface. What the hell was it? It was too big to be another diver. Soon it broke the surface of the water with a hiss of air. There was a waft of fish and then a long sniff.

It was an enormous seal. It sat there in the water looking around at the amazed faces staring down at it, sniffing and snorting while we stared in silence. The researchers had resigned smiles on their faces.

'He's OK as long as he doesn't leave the hole,' said Kathy, 'but they can do a lot of damage to our equipment.'

Apparently the seals often use the research holes for a 'breather', and the scientists and researchers have become used to their companions. 'It's annoying when they shit in here, though,' Kathy added.

The seal hung around for about thirty minutes before disappearing to surprise another lonely scientist.

We said goodbye to our American friends and continued across the frozen ocean. This was the same frozen ocean on which Scott and his men had lost their ponies to killer whales. They had been caught out by the thinning ice, which had drifted apart while they were crossing, trapping their ponies on the floating ice floes. A pod of killer whales had appeared, leaping on to the edge of the ice floes and creating tidal flows of water that washed many of the poor beasts into the sea and to a grizzly end. I could only hope we wouldn't have the same fate.

Soon Inaccessible Island came into view. Scott's men often described this island and one of their tents is still hidden somewhere on its summit.

We rounded the island and there in the distance was the famous wooden hut.

The shoreline was strewn with long, wide tide cracks. We pulled the Haglund up as far as we could and unloaded our heavy kit and equipment on to the ice, then we moved up towards the hut. Its sunbleached wood was worn and weathered, its windows hidden by the deep snow drifts that had built up during the winter. A couple of sledges stuck out of the drifts.

The wind had picked up. It whistled down the hill and along the side of the hut, snapping my jacket as I walked towards the door. It was bitterly cold. I wriggled my fingers to keep the circulation going.

For some reason I was nervous. I had built up this moment for so long. What if I was disappointed? It was one of the few moments in my life when I had no idea what I would find, or how I would react.

A small wooden padlock had been added to the outside of the hut by the Antarctic Heritage Trust to prevent unwanted visitors and the temptation of looting. I slid the key into the lock and twisted . . .

Nothing. I tried again. Still nothing.

'Ah, the bloody lock's frozen,' said Nigel, one of the conservators.

We spent the next hour holding a couple of handwarmers to the lock in an effort to thaw it, before finally the key turned.

I pushed the door open.

It was dark and musty. The first thing I noticed was the smell. It seems obvious, but in Antarctica there is no smell. Senses are numbed by the cold and smell is the first to disappear. During our race to the Pole, we lost the use of our noses for seven weeks. It wasn't until we boarded the aircraft home that it returned. Seven weeks of unwashed bodies isn't fragrant.

The interior smelt of old leather, pipe smoke, wood and horse. There was something else, a deep, powerful musty odour, which I would later discover was blubber. It was one of those smells that was almost nasty, but at the same time actually quite more-ish. I found myself breathing slowly and deliberately to sniff it all in.

Smell is such a powerful sense. It creates memories and acts as a catalyst to recall them. I can still remember the musty, dank smell of my grandfather's cottage in Canada. It smelt of old stuff, but I loved it. Just occasionally I smell it somewhere else and I find myself in a time warp. Suddenly I'm back in that cottage, counting worms while Grandma knits, and fishing with Grandpa.

I will never forget the smell of that hut. Some have described it as a museum, but the smell is what sets it apart. I have never been in a museum that smells of history. The smell of Scott's hut could tell a tale itself. The horse manure, the piles of blubber, Scott's great collection of pipes – it's all there in Ponting's images, in Scott's journal, and now, for me, in his hut.

The outer door led into the covered porch. Old wooden skis were propped up along the corridor that led to the stables where Lawrence Oates had tended the ponies. A large slab of seal blubber was piled in a corner. It had been used for their lamps and for food. I wondered whether the seal in the ice hole had relatives here?

As my eyes adjusted to the dark interior, I found the wooden door that would lead me to the inner sanctum and Captain Scott's world.

I tugged on the rope handle and the door creaked open to reveal a long wooden floor. Where the smell had stolen my senses in the porch, here it was the silence. Outside in Antarctica there is no such thing as silence. Wind is your constant companion. But in here it was silent.

Once again my eyes fought with the low light, but slowly I began to make out objects and furniture. The large dining table dominated the centre of the room, the bunk beds known as 'the Tenements', the laboratory, the photographic lab, the galley. Slowly, Ponting's photographs began to come alive. It was like time turning back a hundred years.

Jumpers, socks and jackets hung on bedposts and on hooks on the walls. Boots and slippers had been neatly arranged on the floor. Books, magazines and newspapers dated 1909 were strewn across tables. Above Oates' bed was a handmade collage of dogs. I knew he loved his animals, but here was first-hand evidence. It was mesmerizing. My eyes strained to take it all in.

I could see the packing crates used to divide the officers and the men. Most incredible of all were the thousands of items of food. Tins of sardines and ox tongue were stacked next to crates of Heinz baked beans and tins of Huntley and Palmer biscuits. It was a treasure trove of Edwardian items, a place frozen in time.

There was Ponting's developing lab, and next door, hidden behind another wall of crates, was Scott's cabin. I had seen the photograph of him sitting at his desk so many times, and here it was. A little more sparse, but undoubtedly his.

Sir Edmund Hillary, who did a great deal to preserve the hut, once said that he didn't believe in ghosts, but in this hut he felt the presence of Scott.

I am not particularly spiritual, but expeditions can have a strange effect on you and I often find myself talking to someone else. Here in the hut I was in the presence of others. I talked in a hushed whisper as I walked around this polar temple. It was an extraordinary feeling.

Over the next few days we followed the work of the conservators as they struggled against time and the elements to preserve all the items in the hut. A rise in temperatures in Antarctica has meant that the permafrost and ice around the hut now melts in summer, bringing moisture inside and destroying many of the items. It isn't uncommon for a conservator to spend two weeks working on preserving the label on a bottle of Lea & Perrin's Worcestershire sauce.

'Come and look at this,' said Nigel, leading me into the stable. Each stall was still marked with the name of the pony. Heaps of manure remained piled in the corner.

'Sniff that,' he said, holding out a canvas bag.

'Whooooa!' I recoiled quickly. It was without doubt the most disgusting thing I have ever smelt in my life. It made my nose wrinkle and almost gave me a headache. It was one of those smells that etch themselves into your nostrils. Smelling salts couldn't hide this.

'What is it?' I grimaced, holding the bag as far away from me as I could.

'We just dug it up from beneath the stable.' Nigel beamed with pride. 'It's hundred-year-old butter.'

Well, that would explain the smell.

A century on and they're still uncovering new things here. Hundred-year-old butter is one thing, but the previous year they had found a crate of whisky.

It took us nearly a week to clear the snow from the outside of the hut and each day we made more and more discoveries. The surrounding land was littered with crates, tins and fragments of the great Antarctic expedition. Seagulls pecked at century-old biscuits and flour that had been torn open by a hundred years of wind blasting.

'Look at this, Ben,' hollered Nigel, holding a chain that emerged from the ice. He passed it to me and I worked my way down it to a piece of leather, still partly buried. Gently I dug away at the snow to reveal a bone. What on earth was it? Half an hour later I had uncovered an entire dog, complete with skin and some fur, still wearing its collar, which was chained to the wall outside the hut. It sent a shudder up my spine. Everything about this place was tinged with misery and despair.

I wasn't sure if it was because I knew the story, or because sadness had crept into every corner of the remote peninsula, but there was more than a hint of the hardships endured by Scott, his men and their animals. Nevertheless, for Scott this little building became a home from home.

The hut looks out over the frozen Ross Sea and on to the Transantarctic mountain range beyond. Two islands in the distance, White Island and Black Island, mark the point due south. Observation Hill above the hut was where Scott's men looked out in hope for the return of their leader.

Also visible from the hut is the mighty Barn Glacier, sloping down from the sides of Mount Elbrus until it meets the Ross Sea. A sheer wall a hundred feet high marks the point where it reaches the ocean, or at this time of year, the ice. Occasionally we would hear enormous crashes, like thunder, as great chunks of ice collapsed from the glacier tongue, sending reverberations across the sea ice, creating more cracks. The thunder woke me a couple of times as it echoed around our camp.

One day I decided to leave the team and explore the glacier. I made my way across the slippery ice for an hour until I reached the mighty cliffs soaring high into the sky. Like the pressure ridges, they were a palette of blues and greys. I felt very small below that glacier.

I sat there for a couple of hours, staring back at the little wooden hut across the water. Scott's team would have done just this a hundred years ago. They too would have sought some solitude here.

I had just discovered that Marina was pregnant again, and here I was, as far away as you could get from home, on the bottom of the earth. Isn't it strange that the ultimate race to the South Pole came to involve two men from nations on the opposite side of the world? Where were the New Zealanders or the Australians or the Chileans or South Africans?

I had surprised myself with how much I was missing Marina and Ludo. Having a child changes a person in many ways. I'm not sure if it's a hormonal change, but the homesickness that I thought I'd overcome at boarding school had returned with a vengeance. Here, beneath the Barn Glacier, in the middle of Antarctica, I was longing for my wife and son. I would have done anything to hug them.

Just as I was disappearing down a teary line, a penguin appeared.

It was alone. It held its head high as it wandered past, its little flippers padding away at the ice. It waddled silently. Where was it going? Why was it alone? A huge smile broke across my face. I couldn't help myself. No matter how hard I tried, I couldn't stop smiling. I defy anyone to watch a penguin and not smile.

It was waddling at quite a speed, with its little flightless wings held close to its side, when suddenly it tripped and slid on its belly across the smooth ice, gliding across the frozen ocean.

I looked at the penguin and at my jacket. I had an idea. I walked back towards the glacier to give myself space, checked my jacket was fully buttoned and zipped to the neck, and began to run.

My feet slipped and slid occasionally, but I managed to build up a fair lick of speed. Just when I felt I had reached terminal ice-running velocity, I flung myself on to the hard surface with a thud and, sure enough, my jacket absorbed the friction and I glided on my belly across the ice.

'Yeeeee-haaaaaa!'

Halfway through our time, we had the opportunity to visit another of the historic huts, a little further up the coast at Cape Adare. This one belonged to another great polar explorer, Ernest Shackleton.

Scott and Shackleton once came to Antarctica together, but the latter's attempt to reach the Pole in 1906 drove his former teammate green with envy. Scott wanted to be the first to reach it, so it was probably an enormous relief to him when Shackleton failed. This failed attempt also highlights the greatest difference between their two styles of leadership. After leading his expedition to within a hundred miles of the South Pole, Shackleton turned back due to lack of provisions. Explaining his decision to return when he was so tantalizingly close to his goal, he told his wife, Emily, 'A live donkey is better than a dead lion, isn't it?'

Shackleton's hut is on the edge of a small peninsula, high on a hill overlooking a penguin colony and the frozen ocean beyond. Its location alone is brighter, lighter and more full of life than Scott's at Cape Evans.

The irony was that Shackleton built the hut here only because Scott, envious at the prospect of being beaten to the Pole by his former colleague, claimed rights on Cape Evans and McMurdo and made Shackleton promise he wouldn't land there.

Shackleton's was the polar opposite of Scott's. It reminded me of the sort of mountain huts you find in ski resorts. It was the kind of place I could live in (although I might have to persuade Marina on that one). It had an atmosphere that made me happy. I wanted to smile, to sit down and have a cup of tea, where Scott's made me want to weep. But was it the story that created the atmosphere? Was I merging my own feelings with the physical place? It's hard to tell, but being situated in front of a thriving penguin colony full of life and humour certainly helps.

Shackleton's legacy is one of the reasons for the downfall of Scott's reputation. By the 1970s there had been a shift in public opinion. Scott had become the object of a great deal of criticism as people questioned his methods, but it was Roland Huntford who put the final nail in his reputation in a biography that was effectively a character assassination, revealing Scott as an arrogant, mindless egotist. While many had criticized Scott in the past, no one had dared question his heroism.

Since then it has become something of a pastime to deconstruct Scott's legacy, to debunk the myth. We Brits have always been prone to the tall-poppy syndrome and Scott didn't escape the hatchet.

Meanwhile, Shackleton was adopted by many as a model of selfless leadership, of surviving through adversity, and Kenneth Branagh did for him in a television drama what John Mills had once done for Scott in his great film *Scott of the Antarctic.* Indeed, by 2005, when the BBC asked viewers to nominate the greatest

Britons of all time, Ernest Shackleton came eleventh, while Scott was fifty-fourth.

For me, there was one other player who did more for the legacy of Scott's great journey than anyone: Apsley Cherry-Garrard. He was assistant biologist to the expedition and his book *The Worst Journey in the World* is still described as the best travel book ever written. It was my bible before our South Pole race.

It includes the story of one of the smaller 'sub-expeditions', which many argue were the reason for Scott's failure to beat Amundsen to the South Pole: Scott and his men were there for science, while Amundsen was there to race. In this particular expedition, Henry Bowers, Scott's teammate, was keen to study one of the penguin colonies on the far side of Ross Island in a remote place called Cape Crozier. Cherry-Garrard, who accompanied him, tells the tale of their trip across the island to collect penguin eggs.

Cape Crozier had always seemed to me the closest thing to hell on earth, but a science team was heading out to that remote corner of the island and this was my chance to put an image to those descriptions.

It was bright and sunny and minus 40°C when we left Cape Evans by helicopter. The chopper was buffeted from side to side as we swept up mountainsides covered in thick glaciers. We watched as thousands of tons of snow and ice dropped away from vertical peaks. We passed over colonies of seals sprawled like slugs on the ice.

Soon the buffeting intensified.

'It's pretty windy,' said the pilot over the intercom.

From experience, when the pilot says 'pretty windy' it usually means a gale and that he is flying on the edge. My knuckles turned white as I gripped the seat and began to sweat, despite the minus 40°C.

The snowy slopes below gave way to the black crest of a hill overlooking the Ross ice shelf.

'There it is!' The pilot pointed at nothing in particular. He lowered the helicopter, which was still being buffeted by powerful gusts. From the safety of the cab, it was difficult to gauge how strong the wind was or how cold it was. It looked sunny and still. Only the jarring movements of the chopper gave a hint of what we were about to experience.

'I don't want to turn off the blades in case we can't start them again,' said the pilot as we landed on the scree.

As I opened the door, the strength of the wind ripped it from my hand and smashed it into the side of the chopper. We clambered out and it took two of us to close the door before the helicopter could take off again, leaving us alone on this stormy outcrop. I hoped it would return. The journey had taken Cherry-Garrard, Bowers and their companion Edward Wilson more than a week.

The wind howled across the scree and bit at my cheeks. It was the coldest we had experienced. You had to turn your back to the gale to get any reprieve. I could feel my hands losing their circulation as we stumbled along the saddle of the mountain towards a little flat area surrounded by rubble and boulders.

'There it is,' said Nigel, shivering. He hadn't been to Cape Crozier for more than five years. Officially, it is classified as one of Antarctica's historic sites, but there is very little here. More people have been to the South Pole and the huts combined than to this remote corner of Ross Island.

'Look closer,' he shouted over the wind.

My lips were turning blue and my words began to slur as the cold bit. I peered down at the ground. There was a little fabric pinned beneath a rock. My eyes followed it. There was another piece. The rocks began to appear more uniform in their arrangement. This was the stone house the explorers had built as a base from which to make excursions to study the penguins. They had used a tarpaulin as a roof, but one night a tremendous gale had ripped it from above their heads:

> I do not know what time it was when I woke up. It was calm, with that absolute silence which can be so soothing or so terrible as circumstances dictate. Then there came a sob of wind, and all was still again. Ten minutes and it was blowing as though the world was having a fit of hysterics. The earth was torn in pieces: the indescribable fury and roar of it all cannot be imagined ... The roof of our igloo was being wrenched upwards and then dropped back with great crashes: the drift was spouting in, not it seemed because it was blown in from outside, but because it was sucked in from within ... Already everything was six or eight inches under snow ... when the roof went I felt that this was the end. What else could I think? ... We had been out for four weeks under conditions in which no man had existed previously for more than a few days ... During this time we had seldom slept except from sheer physical exhaustion as men sleep on the rack; and every minute of it we had been fighting for the bed-rock necessaries of bare existence, and always in the dark ... When we were lucky and not too cold we could almost wring water from our clothes, and directly we got out of our sleeping-bags we were frozen into solid sheets of armoured ice.

There were a couple of tins and the bones of some penguins and fulmars that had sustained them after their food ran out, and there was a lamp. The team had been holed up inside their little house for several weeks. It was so cold that they got frostbite inside their sleeping bags, and all in the name of science.

Eventually they had made it back to Scott's hut, and the story was immortalized in Cherry-Garrard's account. This was the expedition which he described as 'the worst journey in the world' – a phrase that he subsequently used as the title for his book about the whole Scott expedition. Cherry-Garrard himself was not in the party that made the final assault on the Pole, but I think he was one of the key men in the Antarctic party. He leaps out from photographs and I can't help but imagine myself in his position.

Some argue that the Cape Crozier expedition led to the failure of the ultimate goal of a return journey to the South Pole itself. After all, this energy-sapping expedition had been undertaken just a month before their attempt on the Pole. Bowers surely wouldn't have had time to recover fully from such an ordeal? I find sanctioning it one of the strangest decisions Scott ever made. Some say that the Cape Crozier trip was used as a practice for the big one, and indeed they tested various rations to work out how much food they would need in their sledge bags in the race to the Pole; but to me it seems madness to send men on such an arduous journey just a few weeks before their polar assault.

Unlike Cherry-Garrard and his friends, we were able to make a rather quicker exit from the wind and cold of Cape Crozier . . . by the return of our helicopter. It was quite emotional pulling up above the ruins of that little stone igloo. I can't imagine what it must have been like for them back in 1912.

We spent the next few days watching the conservators painstakingly returning items that had been preserved. I watched balls of Edam cheese and bars of soap being put back in their original places, while new items were removed for future conservation.

'Look at these,' giggled Lizzy, one of the conservators, holding up a pair of expedition trousers.

They looked normal in most respects, except for the little tube of fabric protruding from the crotch area. Lizzy and the other girls were doubled up with laughter.

'It's a willy hole!' she said. 'For easy peeing.' She collapsed once again in uncontrollable fits of laughter.

On the final day of our shoot, Toby, the cameraman, brought his iPod and a set of speakers into the hut. He had downloaded some music from 1909, the kind of music Scott and his men would have listened to on their old HMV gramophone. It was 2 a.m., the sun was still high in the sky and the conservators were asleep. The music reverberated around the hut and the place seemed to come alive.

I walked around the hut one last time, tears welling in my eyes. I still can't imagine the kind of sacrifice those men made.

Much has been said and written about Scott. Over the last century he has been portrayed as a national hero and a heroic failure. I think both do him an injustice. I think it's time to see him as a man. A man of vision, a man of drive, a man of passion, a man with faults and a man with qualities that made other men want to follow him to the end of earth.

There is no doubt that Scott had many shortcomings, but to me his letters and diaries show a compassionate man who was constrained by his day. In the diary that was recovered from his tent were a number of letters to the wives and mothers of the friends and colleagues who died with him, as well as several letters to his wife, Kathleen. Scrawled in the front of his final journal are the words 'Please pass this to my wife.' The word wife has been crossed out and replaced with 'widow'. It still makes me shudder.

Scott, like me, was a family man. He loved his wife. In many of the Ponting photographs you can see pictures of her pinned to the wall. His letters to her are tender and moving. What I find hardest is the thought of him leaving his young son, Peter. My biggest fear is not of dying, but of leaving my wife and children without a husband and father. He must have felt that same fear, yet he remained lucid and resigned right up to his death.

'What lots and lots I could tell you of this journey,' he wrote. 'How much better has it been than lounging in too great comfort at home. What tales you would have for the boy. But what a price to pay . . . Make the boy interested in Natural History if you can; it is better than games; they encourage it in some schools. I know you'll keep him in the open air'.

Peter Scott went on to found the WWF and the Wildfowl & Wetlands Trust, important organizations that have arguably changed the world's attitude to the environment. As an ambassador for the WWF myself, I wish I could thank Captain Scott for those powerful sentiments.

In his final dying message to the British people, written meticulously in the back of his journal, Scott said: 'The causes of the disaster are not due to faulty organisation, but to misfortunes in all risks which had to be undertaken'.

Risk is something that resonates with me. The risks I have undertaken have been nothing in comparison with those of Scott, but they have been risks none the less.

When I was living on Taransay, one of my fellow castaways read me a poem by William Arthur Ward. It was the reason he came on the island, and I have believed in it ever since, as it says everything that I can't:

To laugh is to risk appearing the fool.
To weep is to risk appearing sentimental.
To reach for another is to risk involvement.
To expose your ideas, your dreams, before a crowd is to risk
    their loss.
To love is to risk not being loved in return.
To live is to risk dying.
To believe is to risk despair.
To try is to risk failure.

But risks must be taken, because the greatest hazard in life is to
risk nothing.
The people who risk nothing, do nothing, have nothing, are
nothing.
They may avoid suffering and sorrow, but they cannot learn,
feel, change, grow, love, live.
Chained by their attitudes they are slaves; they have forfeited
their freedom.
Only a person who risks is free.

Captain Scott died free.

The Antarctic Heritage Trust restoration project has cost
nearly £10 million, a great deal more than the original expedition. Some have disputed the justification in preserving a
building and its contents in an environment that will continue to
damage it.

'Isn't it strange working on an item for so long, only to return
it to the ravages of Antarctica?' I asked Lizzy.

'But this is where they belong,' she shrugged.

Some have argued that the hut should be dismantled and
rebuilt elsewhere, in New Zealand or perhaps somewhere in
England, where it could be preserved in a controlled environment, hermetically sealed in a dome like the *Mary Rose*.

It seems a lot of money to spend on what is sometimes
described as the remotest museum in the world, where only a
handful of lucky tourists, scientists or presenters will get to see it,
but it is the geographic location that makes this hut so special. It's
what makes it a living museum.

The hut is about the smells, the location, the journey, the
people, and the weather. Remove that and you'll lose its soul. Its
heart belongs here, a memorial to those brave men and their
sacrifice. A cathedral to exploration.

Before we left for home, the helicopter took us out to the

immense Ross ice shelf, the size of Wales. It was somewhere here that Scott, Bowers and Wilson perished in a polar blizzard. It is lonely out there, bleak and windswept.

For me, it was the final part of my pilgrimage. Somewhere beneath the ice are the entombed bodies of those three men. But the greatest tale of all is the fact that the ice is continually shifting. Slowly but surely migrating north. And one day the bodies will reach the edge of the ice, having completed their return journey from the South Pole. And Scott, the captain, will finally be buried at sea.

Epilogue

What next? This is the question I am asked more than any other. Every hour of every day, there is an expectation that there must be more.

And the answer is the most exciting of all: I don't know!

It was all an accident in the first place. I was never meant to become an adventurer. It just sort of happened. I fell into it. Or did I? Maybe subconsciously I have been forming and shaping it all along?

I never know what twist and turn my meandering river of life will take. It has already taken me way beyond anything I had ever dreamed or imagined.

Is life about destiny or luck? I'd argue that it's a little bit of both. After all, you make your own luck, and therefore direct your destiny.

'Add life to your days, not days to your life,' someone once told me. It may sound like a cliché, but I'd like to think I've embraced that idea.

One of my biggest fears in life is regret. I seize opportunities and run with them. Sometimes they work, sometimes they fail, but what I have learned is that failure only makes you stronger.

I have empowered myself in the pursuit of happiness. I'm not just saying this, but if I can do it, then *anyone* can. I sometimes worry that I'm going to wake up one day and discover that the last twenty years have all been a dream – but you know what? If I do, what a dream it's been.

If I am allowed one legacy in life, I want it to be that I have made a difference. I'm not there yet, but I've laid the foundations. I've travelled the world and explored my own physicality, and now it's time to stop doing things for me and start doing things for others.

I sometimes worry that I don't have enough time to dwell on the things I have done. I tend to live in the now rather than the then, so in many ways this book has been a cathartic process. I have scratched stories from the corners of my memory. I have certainly created a small compilation with which to bore my children in years to come!

This book has been written on a boat off the coast of Sri Lanka, in the wilds of Antarctica, in a New York hotel room, in a tent at the North Pole and in my little London hut. It's strange how my location affects my sentiments.

I am ridiculously nostalgic. I miss things before they have ended. I get teary after weekends away with my family because I don't want them to end, and, most surprisingly of all, I don't like change. I hate moving home or changing car or even mobile phones. For someone who has spent six months of every year for the last twenty years living under canvas or out of a travel bag, it seems a strange character trait, but maybe the constant travelling is the reason. I crave some forms of continuity in my life.

My family has changed all that. My wife, my son Ludo and my daughter Iona are my whole world. They are my light and my oxygen, and, as I have said before, my biggest fear is leaving them alone without me. I don't fear death, but I fear leaving my loved ones mourning. It wakes me up at night sometimes.

Having children has completed my circle of life. My own childhood complexes and insecurities have to be placed in a tiny little box and buried for ever, because it's now their time. They have a great adventure ahead of them.

'What's the hardest thing you've ever had to do?' is another question I frequently get asked when I'm buying a cup of coffee in the morning or waiting for the tube. Most people expect me to tell them tales of toil on the Atlantic or of nasty creatures in the jungle, so it usually comes as a surprise when I say it was the time I had to leave my little boy and my wife to spend a month in Antarctica.

As a child, the debilitating homesickness I suffered was so powerful, my whole body ached when I was separated from my family and it took a year at boarding school to finally rid myself of that ache. There were no tears when I jetted off on my gap year nor when I left home for my university years. A year on an Outer Hebridean island was a breeze and rowing the Atlantic was made a whole lot easier without the burden of homesickness. It took marriage and parenthood to cause a relapse. I've found myself stuck in deserts, jungles and mountains yearning for the comfort of home and the arms of my beautiful wife. It never stops breaking my heart to leave Marina, Ludo and Iona on the doorstep as I head off on another journey.

It still haunts me, the time that Marina came to meet me at Heathrow airport after I'd spent five weeks filming in Antarctica for *The Secrets of Scott's Hut*. We'd had dozens of reunions over the years but this time I would be met by Ludo too. The excitement was overwhelming. I couldn't sleep the night before. It was the kind of excitement I hadn't experienced since I was a child. I bought him toys and clothes in New Zealand and I dreamed of his embrace.

At Heathrow I could see them both in the crowd. Marina had a huge smile across her face but Ludo still hadn't seen me. As I got closer, he was still looking past me, and I suddenly realized he didn't have a clue who I was.

I may have the dream job but as with everything it comes at a price. Now I have two children, a handsome little boy and a beautiful little daughter, I also have the prospect of spending more time away. I have the most wonderful wife in the world who understands my turmoil and she is the most incredible mother to our children.

Compared to many I have it easy, just a few weeks away at any time. If I were in the army I might not seem them for nine months. If I were in the US army that could be two years. But I'm not in the army, I'm a broadcaster with a choice to make, and in some ways that makes it harder.

I sometimes think that people forget how hard it is for absentee fathers. We may seem callous, gallivanting around the world to exotic locations, but for weeks on end family life is reduced to staring at photographs of family moments frozen in time and fleeting phone calls home. Ludo's phrase for phones and mobiles is 'Hello Daddy'. At first it was incredibly sweet but now it makes me sad every time he says it.

As a modern father I would like to think of myself as hands on. When I am around, I get Ludo up in the morning and feed him breakfast. We walk to Portobello where I get my coffee and from there we go to playgroup or to baby swimming where I am invariably the only dad there. I put him down for his afternoon sleep and take him to the park with the dogs or to the zoo in the afternoon before dinner, bath, book and bed. I love doing it. We're like a little team. He has become one of my limbs and without him I can't operate properly, and now Iona has come along and done it all over again.

I try to be the best father I can be. I spend six months of each year doting on my family, relishing family life. But then I am gone and it starts all over again. The stifled tears on the doorstep as I leave, followed by the tears in the car as I pull away for some faraway land. My homesickness has returned with a vengeance.

I hope that one day Marina, Ludo and Iona will be able to travel with me and we can explore the world together. For now the children have a huge map in their room with a little me made out of Velcro by my wife, which they can move around the world together with an assortment of native people and animals.

I hope that one day they will read this book and get a small insight into what Daddy did and why he was away so much. I suppose like any father I want them to be proud of me and I hope they will understand a little about what drives me. I hope too that one day we will share adventures together.

I sometimes worry that life isn't long enough. There are so many things that I still want to do and achieve. I have been blessed in life and I hope I still have a great deal more to give. I think about everything I've got to look forward to and suddenly I feel excited again.

*

It was minus 40°C. Icicles had formed in my hair and on my thick stubble. My skis cut through the compacted snow as I worked my way across the valley.

We were high in the Arctic Circle in Svalbard, the archipelago between the Arctic Ocean, Barents Sea, Greenland Sea and Norwegian Sea. It is a remote, barren place. I had been here once before, during one of my first *Extreme Dreams*, when I had taken my team of adventurers (including the wife of one of the Chuckle Brothers!) on a trek across Spitzbergen, the main island. It was one of the few challenges in which we had failed to reach our goal due to poor weather.

Memories of my trips to Antarctica came flooding back – my momentous trek to the South Pole with James and Ed, and my pilgrimage to Captain Scott's hut on Ross Island.

Ahead of me, Rune and Stian, the Norwegians who had beaten us to the South Pole, were dragging a heavy sledge laden with equipment. Its weight strained their harness as they marched ahead of the group.

The sun was beginning to dip behind the mountains, and the temperature began to drop still further. It was as cold as I can remember and the chill began to bite at my previously frostbitten nose. Blood had stopped flowing to my fingers and toes. Finally we reached a small plateau, where we stopped and began to set up our equipment.

A gentle wind cut into the skin as we stared towards the horizon at two lone figures struggling through the cold. I could make out the familiar gait of Inge Solheim, who had also been part of the race to the South Pole. He had helped lead the blind polar explorer Mark Pollock.

A small herd of reindeer were foraging through the snow and ice. They are extraordinary creatures, perfectly adapted to this icy tundra. Their coats are extra thick for insulation, turning whiter in winter to protect them from their main predator, the polar bear.

The two figures trudged on towards us as we stamped our feet to ward off the cold which seeped into the bones.

Inge stopped, unclipped his skis and began to unpack his sledge, then the two of them began assembling their tent. It was one of the familiar red tents that we had used during our South Pole trek. I watched nostalgically as the two men shovelled snow on to the tent's skirt to keep the wind out. I used to look forward to snow-shovelling, if only as a means of warming myself up.

Once they had finished setting up camp, the two of them wandered towards us.

'Your Royal Highness, how are you getting on?' asked the BBC's security correspondent, Frank Gardner.

'It's cold, really cold,' came the reply.

My life has taken so many twists and turns, but this had to be one of my strangest incarnations.

His Royal Highness was the third in line to the throne, Prince Harry, who had joined the Walking With the Wounded team (which included two of the Battleback soldiers with whom I had run the Lewa Half Marathon, Jaco and Steve) for part of their charity trek to the North Pole in April 2011. Rune and Stian were here to help Frank Gardner, who had been left wheelchair-bound after being shot by Al-Qaeda in Saudi Arabia, and Inge was here to teach Prince Harry the art of polar travel.

And me? What was I doing back in the polar wastes of the Arctic Circle? Well, I was there as a news reporter for NBC News in America in my new role as a special correspondent for the biggest channel in the US. It was the beginning of a new chapter in my life.

As I filed my final live story to ten million viewers, my phone rang.

'How would you like to go and scuba dive with crocodiles in Africa?

It was a call back to wildlife and nature – my real passions in life, which I have barely touched on in this story. But that, as they say, is a whole other book – the story of how I became the accidental naturalist.

Picture Credits

All images courtesy of the author unless otherwise stated. PER = Pierre-Emmanuel Rastoin; AG = Alexis Girardet; TS = Toby Strong.

Section one
Page 7: BF and Marina courtesy Antoinette Eugster.

Section two
Pages 1–2: all images Ben Curtis/PA Archive/Press Association Images. Page 3: BF at Tin Bath Championships: Mike Wade/Isle of Man Newspapers; BF in East Timor courtesy Ken Lennox. Pages 4–5: all images courtesy PER. Page 6: BF with Sid Owen: Glenn Copus/Associated Newspapers/Rex Features.

Section three
Page 1: BF and James Cracknell before race and BF and James Cracknell overhead courtesy AG. Pages 2–3: all images courtesy AG. Page 6: all images courtesy Chris Lawrence/Facing Africa. Pages 7–8: all images courtesy TS.

Acknowledgements

Thanks to everyone who has helped and supported me over the years.

To Marina, the love of my life, the best mother to our children Ludo and Iona, and to our dogs Inca and Maggi for bringing us together.

To my inspirational best friend, James Cracknell, for all those incredible adventures and to his wife, Bev, for sharing him with me.

To Grandma Aileen and my late Grandpa Morris Fogle for all those incredible summers on Lake Chemong in Canada.

To my amazing family: Mum and Dad, Emily and Tamara.

To Monika, Jonathan, Chiara, Olivia and Rupert for being the most extraordinary family-in-law anyone could ever ask for.

To Hilary Murray, my agent and friend, without whom none of this would have been possible, and to all at Arlington for attempting to direct my meandering career.

To Alison Griffin, the best publicist in the world, for tracking me down in every corner of the world.

To Julian Alexander and the team at LAW.

To Jake Morland, Leonardo Anguiano, Ed Coats, Guy H, Guy E, Tamsin, Jo, the Salazars, my fellow MDS runners, Chris Lawrence and all at Facing Africa. To my friend, Alice Benkert, who left us too early.

To the BBC for all the incredible opportunities over the years. To Lion Television and all of those marooned on Taransay for the year. To Ricochet and all those who shared the mud, sweat and tears on *Extreme Dreams*, and to Teresa Bogan and the old team at *Countryfile*.

Thanks to Tim Green, Chris Kelly, Luned Tonderai, Alexis Giradet, Keith Schofield, Toby Strong, Richard Farrish, Lucy Bing, Lucy Wallace, Dee Koppang, Rob Hawthorne, Katie Crawford, Jay Taylor, Kirsty Mitchell, Tom Peppiat, Matt Smith, Mel Leach, Peter Willis, Alex Bohana, Will West, and all the film crews, directors and producers with whom I've shared journeys around the world. To all those, too numerous to mention, a huge thank you.

To Doug Young, Rebecca Jones, Alison Barrow and all Transworld for shaping and helping to bring my life story to the page, and to Hannah Fair for all your research.

And to everyone who has appeared in my accidental adventures, thank you!

Index

321